"Resilience is the final frontier in human psychology. Schiraldi has created a wonderful resource and valuable compendium of academic science and practical behavioral suggestions—a powerful foundation for the acquisition of resilience skills."

—**George S. Everly Jr., PhD**, Johns Hopkins University School of Medicine; executive director of Resiliency Science Institutes, International; and coauthor of *The Secrets of Resilient Leadership*

"With extensive experience in mental health, academic, international crisis, and military environments, Glenn Schiraldi is uniquely prepared to offer excellent and expert guidance in developing and maintaining resilience—clarifying the best principles and practices for optimizing our physical, mental, emotional, and spiritual health and fitness under challenging circumstances. As in his previous books, Schiraldi again offers wise, caring, comprehensive, and accessible guidance. We can rely on him with trust and confidence for negotiating life's challenges."

—**Edward Tick, PhD**, author of *War and the Soul*, director of Soldier's Heart (for successful warriors return), and clinical psychotherapist focusing on veterans issues

"This book is written for any person at any level of emotional health. The true beauty is that individuals—be they professionals looking to enhance their skills or people struggling with their own tragedies—can implement the strategies in their own life, and then use them to strengthen and help others. This guide will be a boon to every parent and homemaker. Nearly every chapter has something I'll use on a daily basis. As a mother and a counselor, I deeply appreciate Schiraldi's expertise and insight. An amazing book."

—**Janet Harkness**, homemaker, mother, and peer counselor

"*The Resilience Workbook* is clearly the authoritative work in the field. Schiraldi methodically takes the reader through the three critical steps of resilience training: gaining a basic understanding of the critical issues of resilience, helping the reader determine his or her own level of resilience, then guiding the reader through step-by-step exercises to build and maintain a resilient mind. Clearly a seminal work in the field of resilience."

—**Steve O. Steff, PhD**, president and CEO of Crisis Care International

"This is a great book! Comprehensive, authoritative, understandable, and practical. Schiraldi has pulled together the current research for mind and body, and produced a 'how-to' guide to inoculate you and those you care about against the inevitable trials of life. Even better, it is a guide to healthy, happy, fulfilling living in general. I'm getting a copy for every member of my family."

—**Thomas W. Garrett**, retired major general of the US Army

"Life's trials are inevitable. How we respond to them is a product of the resilience we consciously develop, and Schiraldi shows us how."

—**Greg Baer, MD**, author of *Real Love and Post-Childhood Stress Disorder*

"A remarkably comprehensive, yet accessible and practical, treatise on resilience. I really believe that everyone will benefit from reading and using it. While this book will certainly benefit high-risk groups, it is also a great how-to and must-read for business professionals, entrepreneurs, students, parents, and anyone else who experiences stress and adversity."

—**Alan D. Boss, PhD**, assistant professor of business at the University of Washington Bothell

"Schiraldi goes beyond preparing or finding a way back. This resilience guide leads us to higher ground. It is the very best I have seen for both pre-occurrence preparedness and post-exposure recovery—providing greatly encouraging, comprehensive growth and integration, especially in the core values of spirituality, meditation, religion, ethics, and morality."

—**Glenn Calkins, MDIV, LCSW, BCC**, firefighter, EMT, fire chaplain, and certified supervisor of the Association for Clinical Pastoral Education

"The importance of resilience in sports, the workplace, and life is far from a new concept. However, Schiraldi has provided one of the first truly comprehensive overviews of this critical human strength. Filled with practical advice, drills, skills, exercises, and real-life anecdotes, this guide offers us mental armor to fight the simple life challenges and daily frustrations that confront us all, in addition to the more serious and sobering anxiety, stress-provoking, and life-threatening challenges. The take-home message underscores the importance of building a mental and emotional structure that can weather a storm, and this book provides a well-researched and highly practical blueprint."

—**Spencer Wood, PhD**, member of the Association for Applied Sport Psychology, and president of Icebox Athlete Mental Skills & Toughness Training

The

RESILIENCE
WORKBOOK

Essential Skills to Recover from Stress,
Trauma, and Adversity

GLENN R. SCHIRALDI, PhD

New Harbinger Publications, Inc.

Publisher's Note

This publication is designed to provide accurate and authoritative information in regard to the subject matter covered. It is sold with the understanding that the publisher is not engaged in rendering psychological, financial, legal, or other professional services. If expert assistance or counseling is needed, the services of a competent professional should be sought.

Distributed in Canada by Raincoast Books

Copyright © 2017 by Glenn R. Schiraldi
        New Harbinger Publications, Inc.
        5674 Shattuck Avenue
        Oakland, CA 94609
        www.newharbinger.com

"Activity: Self-Compassion" in chapter 7 is adapted with permission from Kristin Neff's exercise "Self-Compassion Break," http://www.self-compassion.org.

Story of boy skipping in chapter 12 is reprinted with permission from *Teaching Children Joy* by Linda and Richard Eyre (1980), 152–154. © Deseret Book Company.

The "Pleasant Events Schedule" and the instructions for using it, in chapter 21, are adapted with permission from Lewinsohn, P., Munoz, R. Youngren, M., and Zeiss, A. 1986. *Control Your Depression*. New York: Prentice Hall. ©1986 by Peter M. Lewinsohn. Not to be reproduced without written permission from Dr. Lewinsohn. This modified version originally appeared in Schiraldi, G. R. (2001). *The Self-Esteem Workbook*, Oakland, CA: New Harbinger.

Figure 1.1, "The resilient brain," is copyright © 2004 Harderer & Müller Biomedical Art, LLC. Reprinted with permission.

Figure 1.2, "The effects of substances on brain function," is reprinted by permission of Dr. Daniel Amen, http://www.AmenClinics.com. Copyright © 2005 Daniel G. Amen.

Figures 2.1, "Optimal arousal zone," and 2.2, "Hyperarousal and hypoarousal," are adapted from figures from *Crash Course: A Self-Healing Guide to Auto Accident Trauma and Recovery* by Diane Poole Heller with Laurence S. Heller, published by North Atlantic Books, copyright © 2001 by Diane Poole Heller. Reprinted by permission of North Atlantic Books. See also Porges (2011), Miller-Karas (2015), and Ogden, Minton, and Pain (2006).

Figure 3.1, "Heart coherence versus heart incoherence," is adapted with permission from *Transforming Anger: The HeartMath Solution for Letting Go of Rage, Frustration, and Irritation* by Doc Childre and Deborah Rozman, copyright © 2003 Doc Childre and Deborah Rozman, p. 21.

Figure 4.1, "Emotional avoidance detour," was illustrated and conceptualized by Joseph Ciarrochi, Australian Catholic University, and David Mercer, University of Woolongong. Reprinted with permission.

Figure 10.1, "The happiness pie: Where does happiness come from?" is adapted from "Is it Possible to Be Happier?," from *The How of Happiness: A Scientific Approach to Getting the Life You Want* by Sonja Lyubomirsky. Copyright ©2007 by Sonja Lyubomirsky. Used by permission of Penguin Press, an imprint of Penguin Publishing Group, a division of Penguin Random House, LLC. All rights reserved. Any third party use of this material, outside of this publication, is prohibited. Interested parties must apply directly to Penguin Random House LLC for permission.

Figure 10.2, "Increasing happiness through intentional activity," is adapted courtesy of Dr. Melissa Hallmark Kerr, Co-founder, Brain Savvy, LLP.

Cover design by Amy Shoup; Acquired by Tesilya Hanauer; Edited by James Lainsbury

Library of Congress Cataloging-in-Publication Data on file

19   18   17

10   9   8   7   6   5   4   3   2   1   First Printing

Contents

Part 3   Thriving: Peak Functioning and Adaptive Coping

Introduction

Sarah had recently been widowed, leaving her to raise her six children alone. After an appropriate period of mourning, she became a respected employee at her new job and an even more effective leader of her family. Suffering a similar loss, a friend in Sarah's walking group became dispirited and depressed.

Cal is a Navy SEAL. His wife said he returned from each of his many deployments the same upbeat, communicative, and loving man he had been before he left. His SEAL teammate, however, became a heavy drinker and grew increasingly cynical.

Facing an imminent layoff, Wendy figured out a way to improve her performance and become indispensable to her boss. Her teammate at the office became paralyzed with anxiety and disengaged from her job.

There's an old African saying, "You know how well the roof has been built only when the rains come." Humans aren't much different. We all know people who have faced great challenges. Some cope well with their stress. Some stumble psychologically but then recover. People in a third group fall and never recover. What separates the first two groups from the third? Resilience! Resilience is the key to resisting stress, rebounding from it, and being your best. This workbook will show you how to increase your resilience.

What Is Resilience?

Most people already have a sense of what resilience is. In the course of my work, I've asked people in many settings what they think of when they think of "resilience." They've said:

- The ability to bounce back with new skills

- The strength to navigate tough situations, adapt, and function at a high level

- The property of resisting stress and shock and maintaining form (This was from an engineer!)

- The capacity to absorb stress and maintain *yourself*

- The ability to take a licking and keep on ticking (from an old Timex watch commercial)

- The ability to deal with the high, inside pitches and not fear taking a swing

- Great, no matter the forecast. Holds up better and longer in wet weather (from a Resilience Paint commercial; Stoltz 2014)

There are hundreds of definitions of "resilience" found in the psychological literature. We'll use this as our working definition:

Resilience comprises those inner strengths of mind and character—both inborn and developed—that enable one to respond well to adversity, including the capacities to

prevent stress-related conditions, such as depression or anxiety, or their recurrence;

recover faster and more completely from stress and stress-related conditions; and

optimize mental fitness and functioning in the various areas of life.

As this definition suggests, resilience is standard issue, meaning that we all already possess the strengths of mind and character in embryo—like seeds that can be grown. You wouldn't have survived this long if you completely lacked resilience. And you have the capacity to greatly expand your resilience.

Responding *well* to adversity suggests that we adapt calmly and capably to changing circumstances, drawing upon available strengths—be they mental, spiritual, emotional, physical, financial, or social (for example, mentors, family, or friends).

Resilience is a process and a staircase. You might be on step four of the staircase, and I might be on step one, but we can both keep moving up the staircase so that our resilience levels will hopefully exceed the rising tide of stress. You can enlarge your capacity for resilience by practicing resilience skills. As we build resilience, health and functioning typically improve.

Why Is Resilience So Important?

The benefits of building resilience are great and vital! First, resilience counters the *psychological* problems that trouble so many of us. Approximately 50 percent of American adults (Kessler et al. 1994, 2005) will experience a stress-related condition (see table 1), and prevalence rates for these conditions are increasing globally. Much of this suffering is needless. Resilience can largely prevent these conditions from developing or recurring. Should these conditions occur, resilience can reduce symptom severity and facilitate recovery.

Second, resilience counters many *medical* and *functional* problems. The emotional toll of stress-related conditions is bad enough. However, the mind and body are connected. So excessive, unresolved emotional stress makes us more vulnerable to a wide range of medical diseases, earlier death, and impaired functioning at work, home, and play.

Third, resilience is about mastery and growth. Resilience does more than fight problems; it promotes optimal well-being. Resilience helps us thrive mentally, emotionally, physically, socially, and spiritually—and function at our best, especially during difficult times. With resilience, we tend to be calmer, more productive, and enjoy life more. Conversely, those who lack resilience tend to have higher rates of absenteeism and of prematurely leaving their careers.

Table 1. Stress can play a role in initiating, maintaining, and worsening these psychological conditions, or stress-related conditions, and building resilience can help you deal with them.

Post-traumatic stress disorder	Excessive or chronic anger (for example, resulting in domestic violence, cynicism)
Depression	
Anxiety disorders	Sleep disturbance, exhaustion
Substance-use disorders	Eating disorders
Suicidal thoughts and behaviors	ADHD
Generalized stress or worry	Relationship difficulties

There are two important points about stress-related conditions worth noting. First, people show stress in different ways. For example, after being exposed to an overwhelming event or a series of stressful events, one person might develop PTSD. Another might develop depression or anxiety, or have suicidal thoughts. Some might experience two or more stress-related conditions at the same time or at different times. Still others might continue to function reasonably well despite being troubled by agitation or fatigue from troubled sleep—even in the absence of a psychological diagnosis. Second, these conditions share many common risk factors, such as unhealthy self-esteem, unresolved emotional upheavals, or excessive physical stress levels. Resilience building addresses these common risk factors, which can protect you against a wide range of challenges, including everyday stress.

Who Benefits from Building Resilience?

This workbook is for anyone, regardless of your present level of emotional health or functioning. You will likely benefit from this workbook if you:

- Simply want to improve your sense of well-being or your functioning at home, at work, in relationships, or in any other important area of life.

- Have experienced or are at risk for any of the stress-related conditions listed in table 1.

- Are recovering from a stress-related condition.

- Have survived or are likely to face potentially overwhelming stress, such as terrorism, abuse, war, other traumas, or divorce. Although survivors of such events may not develop psychological disorders, most will develop troubling symptoms afterward.

- Have experienced or are at risk for any of the many stress-related *medical* conditions. These include heart disease, hypertension, irritable bowel syndrome, chronic pain, fibromyalgia, rheumatoid arthritis, thyroid disease, psoriasis, obesity, metabolic syndrome, gynecological complaints, and cancer.

- Want to move beyond recovery and thrive.

- Are a military professional, police officer, firefighter, or other emergency responder. Individuals in these high-risk professions experience higher than average rates of the stress-related conditions listed in table 1, along with higher rates of divorce and prematurely leaving one's chosen profession. Although training for such professions typically prepares emergency responders extremely well *tactically*, many say that they were not prepared for the *emotional* aftermath of their experiences.

- Are a mental health professional, chaplain, trainer, parent, leader, or educator who wishes to optimize your well-being and that of others.

In short, building resilience can benefit all of us. Can you imagine anyone who would not benefit from growing resilience?

What Do We Know About Resilient People?

I wanted to truly understand what makes real people resilient, so I traveled the country over a five-year period and interviewed members of the "Greatest Generation." These were ordinary people who were called to endure extraordinary adversities—economic depression, hard work, war, and sometimes family upheaval. I interviewed forty-one survivors of WWII combat who returned well adjusted, built enduring marriages, and lived fruitful lives. Being eighty years of age on average when I interviewed them, they had much wisdom to share. While most of us will not experience combat, there is much we can learn about maintaining sanity and high-level functioning in everyday life from ordinary people who have. From this (Schiraldi 2007b) and other studies of resilient adults and children (such as Werner 1992), it's clear that some resilient people seem to capably sail through adversity, while others seem to falter for a time but rebound later in life. It appears that internal strengths and coping mechanisms better predict who will triumph over adversity than external circumstances. These strengths and coping mechanisms—the so-called protective factors—are what you will grow in this workbook:

- Sense of autonomy (having appropriate separation or independence from family dysfunction; being self-sufficient; being determined to be different—perhaps leaving an abusive home; being self-protecting; having goals to build a better life)

- Calm under pressure (equanimity, the ability to regulate stress levels)

- Rational thought process

- Self-esteem

- Optimism

- Happiness and emotional intelligence

- Meaning and purpose (believing your life matters)

- Humor

- Altruism (learned helpfulness), love, and compassion

- Character (integrity, moral strength)

- Curiosity (which is related to focus and interested engagement)

- Balance (engagement in a wide range of activities, such as hobbies, educational pursuits, jobs, social and cultural pastimes)

- Sociability and social competence (getting along, using bonding skills, being willing to seek out and commit to relationships, enjoying interdependence)

- Adaptability (having persistence, confidence, and flexibility; accepting what can't be controlled; using creative problem-solving skills and active coping strategies)

- Intrinsic religious faith

- A long view of suffering

- Good health habits (getting sufficient sleep, nutrition, and exercise; not using alcohol or other substances immoderately; not using tobacco at all; maintaining good personal appearance and hygiene)

Notice that resilience is a flexible, relative concept. It does not occur in an all-or-none fashion but exists on a continuum:

Complete helplessness and vulnerability	Surviving	Resilience (optimal coping)	Perfection, invulnerability

While everyone is resilient to some degree, no one is perfectly resilient, or resilient in all circumstances. Resilience does not mean invulnerability, because anyone can be overwhelmed when circumstances are severe enough. Rather, resilience is about generally working, playing, loving, and expecting well (Werner 1992) and functioning at our best possible level in any given situation. As the legendary coach John Wooden taught his highly successful basketball players, success is doing *your* personal best; sometimes the other team will simply be better on a given day.

Resilience can even vary within an individual depending on many internal and external factors, such as how rested and nourished one is, one's training and experience, or the nature of the situation. As you train, your aim is to grow your resilience to a level that is greater than the challenges you'll face.

Nearly anyone can learn how to be resilient at any age. Ideally, we can develop resilience before crises strike. Sometimes adversity causes us to summon and apply strengths we didn't know we possessed. And sometimes, looking back, we learn from difficult experiences and "get it together" later in life, recognizing weaknesses and turning them into strengths.

A Word About PTSD

PTSD is the most complex of the stress-related psychological conditions. It typically occurs with at least one of the other conditions listed in table 1 and has many common risk factors. Not everyone reading this book is experiencing PTSD. However, if you understand the nature and treatment of PTSD, you'll understand much about the nature, prevention, and treatment of the other stress-related conditions. This is why I frequently reference PTSD in this workbook.

See Where You Are Now: The Resilience Checkup

Resilient people are aware of, and use, their strengths. The following resilience checkup will assess your strengths, providing you with a starting point from which to measure your progress as you practice resilience skills. The process of taking the checkup will also begin to reinforce some of the goals of resilience training: each item on the scale suggests a resilience strength, and thus a goal. And it will be reassuring to know that you already possess some measure of resilience to build upon. There is nothing tricky about this assessment, nor does it matter how your scores compare with others. So relax, and be as honest as you can.

Please rate from 0 to 10 how much you believe each of the following statements. A rating of 0 means you don't believe it at all, and 10 means you think it is completely true.

Statement	Rating
1. I generally feel strong and capable of overcoming my problems.	
2. When I get stressed, I usually bounce back fairly quickly.	
3. I generally function well in the various areas of life: job or school, relationships, and play.	
4. I generally stay calm and steady when the going gets tough.	
5. I am generally flexible, meaning if my usual way of doing things isn't working, I readily try something else.	
6. I am in a good mood most of the time.	
7. I think well of myself and like who I am inside.	
8. Difficult times don't change the way I feel about myself.	
9. I believe that if I try my best, things will usually turn out well.	
10. I am good at reaching out and connecting with people.	
11. I usually try to solve my problems, but I know when to bend if something is beyond my control.	
12. I anticipate difficult situations, make a plan, and carry out my plan.	
13. I enjoy life and am satisfied with what I am contributing to the world.	
14. I am good at coping with strong negative emotions.	
15. I am good at separating myself from people who get me down or upset me.	
16. I have goals and am optimistic about my future.	
17. I'm involved in a variety of activities that I enjoy.	
18. I don't have self-destructive habits.	
19. I feel at peace with myself and my past. I've grown stronger from what I've experienced.	
20. I don't beat myself up when my best efforts don't succeed.	
21. I know when to seek help, and where to find it.	
22. I stay focused and think clearly under pressure. I am persistent, determined, and resolved.	
Total score (add the scores from statements 1–22):	

Next, rate your overall resilience, according to how resilient you generally feel.

0   100

Total lack of resilience   Extremely resilient

Your response: _____

How often do you feel restricted in your daily activities because of difficulties with resilience?

1	2	3	4	5
Always	Often	Sometimes	Rarely	Never

Your response: _____

Activity: Resilience Awareness

To increase your awareness of what is possible, and to recognize strengths in others and yourself,

- notice resilience traits in others over a two-day period, and

- notice resilience strengths in yourself for two days after that.

Can Resilience Change?

Resilience *can* grow. Research at the University of Maryland (Schiraldi et al. 2010; Sullivan, Brown, and Schiraldi 2013) found that practicing resilience skills leads to significant gains in resilience, along with increased happiness, optimism, self-esteem, and curiosity—and significantly decreased symptoms of depression, anxiety, and anger. This is very good news indeed!

About the Skills You'll Learn

This workbook is highly experiential. Your success at developing resilience will be determined by how much you practice and apply the principles and skills we explore.

We'll explore many tools to keep you strong. The tools are drawn from both traditional and positive psychology. *Traditional psychology* fixes problems and helps us move from negative to neutral in terms of mood and performance. Eliminating negative thought patterns and managing distressing emotions are examples of traditional psychology methods. *Positive psychology* focuses on strengths and growth, moving us from neutral to positive emotional states and closer to peak functioning. Interestingly, happiness skills, which are tools of positive psychology, also help to prevent and treat stress-related conditions.

This workbook follows a logical sequence. Most will find it beneficial to work through it from the beginning to the end. Others may choose to skip around. Most people will find value in most, if not all, of the skills if they give them a fair trial. However, you may wish to bypass skills that don't seem right for you. You'll likely have success early on with many skills. Initial success often indicates that a skill will be a useful addition to your coping toolbox, although other skills might "click" only after repeated practice.

Attitude is important. Try to keep an open mind. Assuming that resilience skills will quickly or perfectly solve all problems can lead to disappointment. On the other hand, cynicism can prevent us from giving skills a chance. Try for the middle ground, the beginner's mind that says, "With practice and mastery, this skill might help." Then see what happens.

The Resilience Model

Building resilience follows a simple conceptual model: the resilience model.

Optimize brain hardware. First, to understand the resilience model, compare the brain to a computer. The brain *hardware* refers to the number, health, and function of the brain's neurons and supporting tissues. The *software*—resilience skills—will not work well if the hardware is sluggish. So strengthening brain hardware is where resilience building starts. When you take care of the brain, you're also taking care of your body, mind, and spirit.

Optimize brain software. Resilience skills can be likened to the *software*, or programming, that helps us heal and cope with life's adversities. These skills fall into five important categories:

1. Regulating arousal (your body's response to stress)

2. Managing strong distressing emotions

3. Increasing happiness

4. Thriving: peak functioning and adaptive coping

5. Preparing emotionally for difficult times

How Long Will Resilience Building Take?

Take whatever time you need to cultivate resilience at your own pace. You may wish to select the skills that resonate with you and practice each for several days to give them a fair trial. You may prefer to work on these skills individually, in a study group, or with a therapist. After completing this workbook, make a plan to continue practicing your favorite skills in order to maintain your skill level.

Each Person Makes a Difference

Resilient people are everywhere. They are sometimes famous, such as Christopher Reeve, Mother Teresa, or Arthur Ashe. Sometimes they are ordinary people living nearby.

Most people are not familiar with Rick Rescorla (Stewart 2002). As a boy in England during World War II, Rescorla fell in love with the Yanks. He later volunteered to serve with American troops in Vietnam. There he not only demonstrated unusual tactical competence, but also great social intelligence. Rescorla had a knack for knowing how to buoy his troops, whether with song, banter, or words of encouragement.

Fast-forward to 9/11. Rescorla was then the head of security for Morgan Stanley Dean Witter at the World Trade Center. He had predicted the 1988 bombing of Pan Am Flight 103 over Lockerbie, Scotland, and the bombing of the World Trade Center in 1993, so officials at the company backed his recommendation to create an action plan in case of a terrorist attack. Rescorla assumed that average people, when properly led, would capably care for one another and execute the plan well. Pushing through the resistance of workers who didn't want to be interrupted during the workday, Rescorla did the unpopular thing: he overtrained the entire company, drilling employees in his escape plan frequently and without warning, until they could carry it out efficiently.

After the first tower was hit, Rescorla was seen with his bullhorn, walkie-talkie, and cell phone implementing the evacuation plan, only this time for real. After his tower was hit, he instructed others, "Be silent. Be calm...watch your partner" (257–8). He sang into his bullhorn the same Cornish songs he'd sung to his soldiers in Vietnam. Of nearly 2,700 employees working for his company, all but seven made it out safely from the tower that day. He was among the fallen, remaining to the last to ensure the safety of his charges, just as he had remained in the World Trade Center in 1993. In his last communication, he phoned his wife, saying, "If something should happen to me, I want you to know I've never been happier. You made my life" (259).

We assume that Rescorla was not a master in resilience as a boy, but that he, like each of us, became more resilient with experience.

Before Beginning

There are a couple of things to consider that can help you have a more successful experience with this workbook. First, have yourself screened for unresolved mental disorders and treated if necessary. It is very difficult, for example, to feel happiness in the presence of unresolved trauma. We have learned that unresolved emotional upheavals predict a wide range of psychological, medical, and functional impairments. Fortunately, we know that trauma—and other stress-related conditions—can be effectively treated with a wide range of modalities.

Second, develop independence from family dysfunction. Family support is invaluable in the recovery process. However, resilient individuals know how to separate, figuratively or literally, from destructive family patterns. One might acknowledge and accept that "Mom struggled with depression." Another might come to realize that he doesn't have to accept his father's constant criticism and can't fix him or gain his approval. Other individuals might move at least ninety minutes away from dysfunctional family members to gain relief (Wolin and Wolin 1993).

Finding Motivation

Mastery of resilience skills doesn't happen overnight. It takes effort. Before you commit the time and effort required to complete the program, it might be helpful to do a cost-benefit analysis, just as a manager might before implementing a new plan. Below, list the disadvantages and advantages of embarking on resilience training. I provided a few examples to get you started.

Cons: The bad thing about resilience training is…	Pros: The good thing about resilience training is…
• I'll have to commit the time for regular practice. • People might look more to me for leadership. • I'll have to be responsible. • I'll have to stop feeling helpless or giving excuses for passivity. • _____ • _____ • _____	• I'll handle my emotions better. • I'll feel better mentally and physically. • I'll enjoy life, home, and work more. • I'll feel the satisfaction of doing my best. • _____ • _____ • _____

Another motivating strategy is to complete the following sentence stem in as many ways as you can:

The positive consequences of becoming more resilient are...

_____

_____

_____

_____

_____

_____

Conclusion

Everyone can benefit from developing resilience. You already have within you the strengths to do so, like seeds capable of being grown. Applying the skills in this workbook will help you grow these strengths.

Are you ready to begin the rewarding journey of building resilience? Chapter 1 is the logical starting point—strengthening the brain.

Part 1

RESILIENCE BASICS

Chapter 1

Readying Your Amazing, Adaptable Brain

Resilience starts with the brain. Most people do not fully appreciate how the physical conditioning of the brain profoundly affects mental health and functioning. This chapter will explore how to optimize your brain *hardware*, which refers to the size, health, and functioning of neurons (nerve cells) and supportive tissues. Future chapters will then focus on the *software*, which is the programming—or the learning of resilience skills. To better understand how we can optimize brain hardware, let's start by getting acquainted with the marvelous structure that is the brain.

Brain Overview

The resilient brain functions at optimal efficiency. It learns, remembers, sizes up problems, follows instructions, plans, executes decisions, and regulates moods. And it does all this relatively quickly, even under duress. The resilient brain also resists and reverses cognitive decline and brain cell death.

The brain consists of 100 billion neurons, or nerve cells. Each gets input from thousands of others before it fires. The brain is the consistency of Jell-O or tofu, suggesting the need to protect it from physical trauma. We'll explore four key regions related to resilience (figure 1.1).

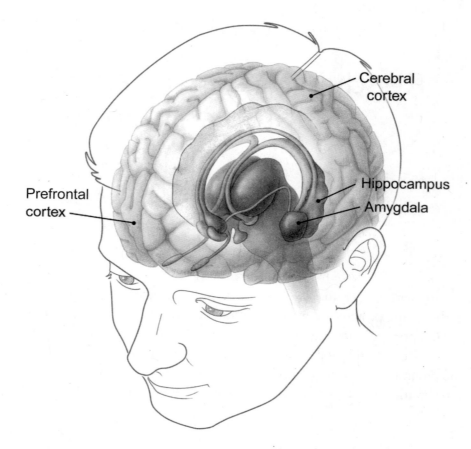

Figure 1.1: The resilient brain (Harderer & Müller 2004)

The *cerebral cortex*, the outer shell of the brain, is the seat of conscious thought, logic, and reason. Consciously recalled portions of memories, which are stored in neural networks that spread throughout the brain, primarily reside here.

The *prefrontal cortex* (PFC) sits just behind the forehead. If the brain is the headquarters of the body (literally *corporate* headquarters), then the PFC is the CEO. The PFC organizes mental and physical activity and enacts all executive functions. Weaving together what is happening around you with facts and memories stored elsewhere in the brain, the PFC judges, predicts, plans, solves problems, initiates action, and regulates impulses and emotions. The PFC helps to keep excessive emotions in check so that you can function. The PFC typically delays decision making until the decision feels right—that is, when facts and feelings come together. Emotional input comes from the next two structures, the amygdala and the hippocampus.

The *amygdala*, which takes its name from the Greek word for "almond," picks up nonverbal cues, especially negative and frightening cues, and immediately trips the stress response and emotional reactions. Thus, another's facial expression, posture, or tone of voice—or even our own negative memories, sensations, or thoughts—can arouse strong, distressing emotions and cause the physical changes of stress. All of this occurs without conscious thought or words. Thus, we might jump or run away from a frightening situation only to think about it later. The amygdala informs the PFC of feelings and body sensations, without which the PFC's decision making stalls. It also picks up memories with similar emotional content and sends these to the PFC to further inform decision making. These feelings in turn get woven into new memories, which helps the memories to be retained.

The *hippocampus* plays a key role in learning and memory. A bigger hippocampus is associated with resilience. This is easy to appreciate when we consider its roles. The hippocampus complements and balances the amygdala. Whereas the amygdala deals in strong emotions and promotes quick and unthinking reactions, the hippocampus deals in cold facts and promotes cool, rational thought.

The hippocampus links the PFC with long-term memory networks. Say you are walking down a path and see a large snake. If acting alone, the amygdala would automatically hit the panic button and send you running. However, the hippocampus calmly pulls up your memories of snakes, which allows the PFC to realize that this snake is different from the rattlers you've encountered in the past. In fact, it looks more like a harmless garden snake. It's as though the hippocampus were saying, "Let's see the whole picture before jumping." Once the situation is deemed safe, the hippocampus dampens the amygdala and the stress response that it initiated.

Should you learn a way to cope with a problem, the hippocampus sends this learning to be stored along with appropriate emotion in long-term memory, and it connects this new memory to related memories and beliefs that are already stored. Thus, as you practice an escape plan, you might learn to move deliberately and calmly to a certain exit during a terrorist attack. Practicing with concentration and some emotion (in other words, moderate activation of the amygdala, but not too much) helps you store and retrieve this memory optimally.

The hippocampus gives context and reality to learning. This enables us to know what happened where, how, and when and is very important for the proper storage of traumatic memories. When the hippocampus is properly functioning, the fragments of a memory hang together in a way that makes sense. Thus, a rape survivor can recognize that a rape happened ten years ago. It had a beginning and an end. Although the rape can be remembered, the memory does not intrude with undue emotion as if the rape were happening now. The perpetrator was a man named Joe, but not all men named Joe—so not all men—are untrustworthy. In other words, the hippocampus allows us to store, think about, and talk about memories in an emotionally cool and rational way.

When Things Go Wrong

The amygdala can get us moving quickly, automatically, and with strong emotion. This can be lifesaving. Usually, however, resilience is better served when strong emotions are checked and directed by cool thinking. The hippocampus and PFC temper the intense emotions of the amygdala, allowing thoughtful, rational decision making to prevail. These three structures must work together. However, when this delicate balance is upset, the brain becomes less resilient.

Excessive stress is one factor that can upset this balance. One of the hormones secreted under stress is cortisol. Moderate amounts of cortisol sharpen thinking in the short term. However, excessive amounts disrupt brain function in several important ways.

Overactivates the amygdala. This can lead to excessive anxiety that hinders learning and makes thinking more emotional and negative. The hyperactive amygdala also imprints memories with excessive, intense emotion rather than details. Thus, a threat that triggers a distressing memory might cause you to overreact with excessive fear or the freeze response. The amygdala is typically hyperactive in people with PTSD. This hyperactivity gives traumatic memories their strong emotional charge.

Shrinks or impairs the functioning of the hippocampus, or both. Recall that the hippocampus tempers the amygdala's response to stress, calmly recalls existing memories when needed (*Where was that emergency exit?*), and stores traumatic memories in a cool, integrated way.

Disrupts PFC function. When this happens, creative thought, problem solving, emotional regulation, concentration, and the ability to shift attention quickly and effectively are probably degraded.

This story demonstrates how excessive stress can disrupt normal memory storage:

> *Marco survived an earthquake when he was traveling through Central America. Although he felt terror during the earthquake, he seemed to be all right when he returned home. Two years later, however, while riding the train to a play in the city after a stressful day at work, the rumbling of the train caused him to break out in a cold sweat. It felt to him that the earthquake was recurring as the terror returned.*

Marco's overactive amygdala caused the first extremely emotional memory to intrude inappropriately and be confused with the rumbling of the train. An unimpaired hippocampus would have enabled Marco to think, *What's happening today is a totally different time, place, and event.*

Aging is a second factor that interferes with optimal brain functioning. The brain typically starts to decline in size and function by age thirty, and, with aging, we usually see a shrinkage that begins with the hippocampus and spreads to the PFC. Similar changes are seen with Alzheimer's disease, with shrinkage and damage spreading from the hippocampus to other areas of the brain involved in memory, language, or decision making (National Institute on Aging). Declines in the brain due to aging can be slowed and possibly reversed. The same healthy lifestyle strategies that protect the brain against age-related decline also optimize brain functioning and might even lower the risk of Alzheimer's disease

Two Important Findings

Two intriguing recent findings about the brain give us great hope for improving resilience. First, the brain is plastic (Doidge 2007). This means that it changes structure and function in response to new experiences throughout an individual's life span in ways that can improve resilience. We now know that new neurons can grow in the hippocampus and other key areas, replacing old ones or those damaged by stress. This growth rate, as well as the size and health of neurons, can be affected by the key factors that we'll discuss shortly. We also know that neurons can link together, forging new neural pathways as we learn adaptive coping skills. The more we practice these skills, the stronger and more efficient these neural connections become. Conversely, neural connections can deteriorate with disuse, and practicing poor coping skills reinforces maladaptive pathways.

Second, brain health equals heart health (Gardener et al. 2016). What kills the body kills the brain. What keeps the heart healthy keeps the brain healthy. Thus, it is important to

stay lean (being overweight doubles the risk of dementia; abdominal fat is particularly risky);

keep blood pressure, blood sugar, total cholesterol, and triglycerides (a type of blood fat) low; and

keep good (HDL) cholesterol high.

The Eight Keys to Optimal Brain Health

Eight keys work together to optimize brain health: regular exercise; brain-healthy nutrition; sleep; minimizing substance use; managing medical conditions; restricting anticholinergic medications; minimizing pesticides, preservatives, and air pollutants; and managing stress. We'll take a look at each one in this section, but first consider what these keys accomplish:

- Increase the volume of, the number of neurons in, and the supportive tissue of the brain—especially in the hippocampus and prefrontal cortex

- Increase the health and functioning of the neurons

- Reduce inflammation and oxidative stress, which impair the brain

- Clear out harmful proteins that are found with Alzheimer's disease

- Strengthen the blood–brain barrier, which protects the brain from damaging toxins and inflammatory agents

- Improve mood

- Enhance cognitive function (concentration; ability to learn, remember, and reason; creativity; productivity; and speed of thinking and of switching focus from one situation to another)

Regular Exercise

Many studies document the ways exercise, particularly aerobic exercise, benefit mood and brain function. Exercisers have sharper brains at all ages. Exercise produces master molecules in the brain that normally decrease with stress and aging. These master molecules increase blood flow to the brain, strengthen and grow neurons, increase antioxidants, and prime neurons to learn new coping skills. Exercise particularly seems to grow the PFC and hippocampus. Exercise reduces tension, anxiety, and depression, often as well as prescribed medications do and without side effects, while improving sleep and increasing energy. When started gradually and done in moderation, regular exercise usually strengthens joints and reduces pain. It has been found to even reduce PTSD symptoms.

Most research on this topic indicates it's best to start by gradually building an aerobic base. A reasonable goal is at least 150 minutes of moderate aerobic exercise a week. This might mean thirty minutes of brisk walking, cycling, swimming, or slow jogging five or more days per week. "Moderate intensity" means you can just carry on a conversation as you exercise. If you can't speak at all, you might be overdoing it. To avoid discouragement, start by doing less than you think you can at a slower pace, increasing exercise time by 10 percent each week until you reach your goal.

Outdoor exercise in the morning can be helpful. Morning workouts seem to help people stick to exercise programs, and ten to fifteen minutes of sunlight a few times a week raises vitamin D levels, which improve brain function in many ways.

You can boost benefits by adding flexibility and strength training—light weights, elastic bands, push-ups, or the like—to your aerobic base. A reasonable goal for strength training is ten repetitions of each exercise two to three days a week. Flexibility exercises, such as stretching, can be done most days to keep limber. You might consider exploring high-intensity interval training, once your physical fitness has improved. This type of training involves alternating bursts of vigorous exercise with periods of easier exercise. Interval training improves many indicators of heart health and brain function in less time than continuous exercise.

Complex motor movements bring additional brain benefits. Yoga, tai chi, dance, racket games, juggling, rock climbing, or playing an instrument all establish beneficial neural pathways. New challenges, such as learning a language, developing a hobby, reading a good book, completing puzzles, taking art classes, or traveling, also sharpen the brain.

Brain-Healthy Nutrition

A growing number of studies have shown that a Mediterranean-style diet greatly promotes longevity, brain health, and sharper brain function. This type of diet emphasizes fruits and vegetables (fresh or frozen), fish, whole grains, nuts and seeds, beans and peas, and olive oil; moderate amounts of poultry, eggs, and low-fat dairy; and minimal red and processed meats (beef, lamb, pork, hot dogs, sausage, salami, and other lunch meats), butter, stick margarine, cheese, pastries and sweets, and fried or fast food. Here are some other helpful nutrition guidelines.

Maximize the intake of brain-friendly antioxidants. These protect neurons from damage caused by stress and aging. Antioxidants are found in colorful fruits and vegetables—such as leafy green vegetables, berries, tomatoes, apples, oranges, or cantaloupe—and even pale plants, such as pears, white beans, green grapes, cauliflower, and soybeans. In your diet, emphasize fresh or frozen plant foods. Antioxidants are also plentiful in nearly all spices, such as turmeric, cinnamon, oregano, ginger, pepper, garlic, and basil. Store spices in a cool, dark place, and use them within two years of purchasing. Chocolate contains antioxidants and is also beneficial—if eaten in moderation.

Aim to eat at least two to three servings of fish per week, totaling at least eight ounces. The omega-3 fatty acids in fish are critical components of the brain's neurons. These fatty acids improve brain health and function, while reducing depression and possibly even stress in traumatized people. Restrict the amount of fried fish you consume, since frying adds unhealthy fats and cancels the omega-3s' benefits. Fish oil supplements can be helpful. Look for supplements that provide five hundred to one thousand milligrams of the omega-3s DHA and EPA daily, as opposed to total milligrams of fish oil.

Choose good carbohydrates. The brain functions best with a steady supply of blood sugar. Plant foods, as nature packages them, contain fiber, which slows the absorption of sugars and provides that steady supply of sugar. Conversely, processed carbohydrates (such as white flour, sweets, sugary sodas, white rice, or processed cereals) result in spikes in blood sugar, followed by a rapid fall in blood sugar. This is why a candy bar might provide a quick energy surge, followed by fatigue, hunger, and slip in mood. Processing also strips plants of antioxidants and other nutrients. So emphasize whole grains and fresh or frozen plant foods, which will also help you stay lean.

Choose good fats. Saturated fats, especially when eaten with refined carbohydrates, impair brain health and function—even after a single meal. Think of a hamburger on a bun made from refined white flour, with a sugary soda and dessert. A single such meal can impair brain function. Replace saturated fats, and the trans fats found in processed and fast foods, with healthy fats found in plant foods. Healthy fats include olive oil, avocados, nuts, and canola oil. Also, choose low- or no-fat, instead of full-fat, dairy products.

Hydrate. Neurons are mostly water. Mood and mental functioning can be impaired by consuming too little liquid. Assuming normal eating, you will likely need to drink nine to sixteen cups of liquid a day to properly hydrate—or even more if you are large or active, even in cooler conditions. Drink throughout the day. Water is a great choice. Two cups before meals promotes leanness. Unsweetened fruit juice contains antioxidants and can be taken in moderation (perhaps half a cup a day). You can tell if you've been drinking enough liquid if the urine that collects in the bottom of the toilet bowl from the first void of the day is the color of pale lemonade.

Spread out protein intake throughout the day. Start with a good breakfast, which sharpens the brain, promotes a sense of fullness throughout the day, and promotes leanness. Protein can come from low- or no-fat unsweetened yogurt, egg whites, poultry, seafood, beans, nuts, peanut butter, or protein powder.

Eat enough, but not too much. If you follow the *2015–2020 Dietary Guidelines for Americans* you can get the nutrients you need for optimal brain health and functioning. These guidelines are consistent with the Mediterranean-style diet and mostly avoid calorie-rich, nutrient-poor foods. The food choices in the Mediterranean-style diet also tend to reduce anxiety and promote calmness. The combination of consuming needed nutrients but not overeating appears to help neurons rest and regenerate.

Minimize added salt and sugar. These are typically found in processed foods.

It's easier to follow these guidelines if you grow your own produce, purchase fresh or frozen produce, and prepare your own meals. Restaurant foods, fast foods, and processed foods typically are high in salt, sugar, and unhealthy fat. Visualize a plate where meat is a small side dish, and the rest of the plate is filled with plant foods, and a brain-healthy meal plan will be easy to follow. You won't have to worry about what *not* to eat when you focus on what *to* eat.

RESILIENT EATING

The *2015–2020 Dietary Guidelines for Americans* specifies the number of servings individuals who are nineteen years or older need each day from the various food groups in order to feel and function their best. The guidelines below are quite consistent with the Mediterranean-style diet and apply to most adults. The greatest need for the average American is to increase servings of fruits and vegetables. (The MIND diet is another type of Mediterranean-style diet that has been found to be brain healthy. To read more about it, visit http://www.newharbinger .com/39409.)

Food Group	How Much Is Needed Each Day	What Counts As…	Comments/Provides
Fruits	1½–2 cups	**1 cup** In general, 1 cup of fruit or 100% fruit juice 1 large banana/orange/peach, 1 medium pear, or 1 small apple ½ cup dried fruit	Fruits and vegetables provide fiber and energy and many vitamins, minerals, and phytochemicals that reduce the risk of various diseases (for example, potassium lowers the risk of high blood pressure).
Vegetables	2–3 cups	**1 cup** In general, 1 cup of raw or cooked vegetables or vegetable juice, or 2 cups of raw, leafy greens 1 cup of dry beans and peas (black, garbanzo, soybean/tofu, split peas, lentils, and so forth). Count these here or in the protein group, but not both.	Seek a variety of colorful fruits and vegetables—green, red, orange, yellow, and white. Berries and green leafy vegetables are very brain healthy. Several times a week include cruciferous vegetables, such as broccoli, cauliflower, cabbage, brussels sprouts, and kale.

Food Group	How Much Is Needed Each Day	What Counts As...	Comments/Provides
Grains	5–8 ounce-equivalents	**1 ounce-equivalent** 1 slice bread or mini bagel 1 cup ready-to-eat cereal (check label) ½ cup cooked rice, pasta, or cereal 3 cups popped popcorn 1 pancake (4½ inches) or 1 small tortilla (6 inches) ½ English muffin	Most servings should be *whole grains*, which reduce the risk of obesity, heart disease, and other diseases. Whole grains contain fiber, B vitamins, antioxidants, minerals, and various plant chemicals. Whole grains include oatmeal, whole wheat, bulgur, whole barley, popcorn, and brown or wild rice.
Protein	5–6½ ounce-equivalents	**1 ounce-equivalent** 1 ounce of cooked fish, poultry, or lean meat 1 egg ¼ cup cooked dry beans and peas 1 tablespoon peanut butter ½ ounce of nuts or seeds	Most or all days should include nuts, seeds, and/or cooked dry beans and peas (for example, pinto beans, kidney beans, lentils, soybeans/tofu, or other soybean products). Note that ½ ounce of nuts equals 12 almonds, 24 pistachios, or 7 walnut halves. The fats in fish are particularly beneficial for the brain. Aim for at least 2 to 3 servings of fish per week, totaling at least 8 ounces.

Dairy	3 cups	**1 cup** 1 cup of low-fat or fat-free milk, yogurt, or calcium-fortified soymilk 1½ ounces of low-fat or fat-free natural cheese, such as Swiss or cheddar 2 ounces of low-fat or fat-free processed cheese (American)	Dairy is a major source of calcium, potassium, protein, B vitamins, and other vitamins and minerals.
Oils	5–7 teaspoon-equivalents (an allowance, not a food group)	**1 teaspoon-equivalent** 1 teaspoon vegetable oil 1 teaspoon soft margarine 1 teaspoon mayonnaise 1 tablespoon salad dressing ½ tablespoon peanut butter	Oils provide needed unsaturated fatty acids and vitamin E. Olive and canola oils are particularly beneficial. Avoid trans and hydrogenated fats found in commercially made snacks, baked goods, stick margarine, and fried fast foods.
Empty Calories (mostly saturated fats and/ or added sugars)	Not needed or recommended. Try to limit to 10% or less of your total caloric intake. Many prefer to "spend" these calories on other food groups.	**Calories in typical serving sizes** 12 ounces of a sweetened soft drink or fruit punch = 150 calories 1 slice of cheesecake (⅛ of a 9-inch cake) = 620 calories 1 tablespoon of jelly or jam = 50 calories 12 ounces of light beer = 110 calories 2-ounce candy bar = 250 calories 1 cup of ice cream = 400 calories 1 ounce of corn chips = 152 calories 1 jelly donut = 290 calories	

* Adapted from *2015–2020 Dietary Guidelines for Americans*. See https://www.ChooseMyPlate.gov for more detailed guidelines and a wealth of practical information about nutrition and physical activity. Except for dairy, the amounts above depend on age, sex, and level of physical activity. The amounts needed assume you expend 1,600 to 2,400 calories per day. Males who are younger or more active, for example, might need to consume amounts in the higher range, or sometimes more.

Sleep

Can you remember that last time you got a good night's sleep and the world seemed brighter and people more pleasant? Sleep energizes and refreshes the brain. A good night's sleep also reduces oxidative stess and helps clear toxins from the brain. Yet most of us do not fully appreciate how even a little sleep deprivation significantly impairs mental health and performance. Most adults require between 7 and 8¼ hours of sleep per night to feel and function their best. Less than that amount worsens mood and functioning. The harmful effects of sleep shortage, which are particularly pronounced with six hours of sleep or less per night, include

brain shrinkage (sleep deprivation is a stressor that stimulates cortisol secretion, which seems to particularly impact the hippocampus);

impaired ability to remember, make decisions, problem solve, settle traumatic memories, and perform tasks requiring speed and accuracy;

increased stress-related conditions, such as depression, anxiety, PTSD symptoms, and substance-use disorders; and

medical problems, ranging from weight gain to cardiovascular disease, diabetes, ulcers, and autoimmune disorders, all of which impair brain function.

THREE PRINCIPLES OF GOOD SLEEP

There are three principles to be aware of that can help you get good sleep: amount, regularity, and quality. In terms of amount, strive for seven to eight hours of sleep per night, or even a little more. Sufficient sleep usually helps people accomplish more during the next day. Regarding regularity, try to go to bed and arise at the same time, even on weekends. Consistency helps the brain regulate sleep cycles and improve sleep. Should you need to change your schedule, try to shift the time you go to bed by less than one hour from one night to the next. The quality of your sleep is important, as this list of variables to consider highlights:

- Light and noise disrupt sleep even when we don't think they do. Blue light from electronic devices is particularly disruptive. Shut down light sources at least an hour before going to bed. Ensure that light and noise are blocked in the bedroom (try curtains or shades that block morning light, eyeshades, earplugs, or a white-noise machine).

- Give yourself an hour or more to wind down before going to bed. Turn off arousing media. Instead try soothing music, relaxation, pleasant reading, or journal writing.

- Napping can partially offset sleep loss. Successful nappers regularly nap in a quiet, dark place for 20 to 120 minutes. If napping interferes with your ability to sleep at night, avoid it to consolidate nighttime sleep.

- Avoid a heavy meal or excessive fluid intake before bedtime. Digestion can override the brain's tendency to fall asleep, and a full bladder can wake you up. Try not to eat *anything* for at least four hours before retiring. If hunger awakens you during the night, a small snack of protein and carbohydrates before bedtime might help you maintain sleep (for example, warm milk and honey, yogurt, cereal and milk). Other small snacks that might be useful include a banana, walnuts, almonds, an egg, avocado, tuna, and turkey.

- Early-morning exercise helps regulate sleep rhythms. Tai chi and yoga usually help. Avoid exercising within two hours of bedtime.

- Cut back on caffeine, nicotine, and alcohol, which interfere with sleep, especially when taken in the hours before bedtime. Caffeine and nicotine are stimulants. Alcohol facilitates falling asleep, but then it has a stimulant effect.

- If possible, get off shift work, which is linked to a variety of mental and physical disorders, including shorter and more disturbed sleep. If shift work is necessary, try to move from earlier shifts to later shifts, and stay on the same shift for as many weeks as possible to help the brain regulate sleep rhythms.

- Challenge distressing thoughts that heighten arousal. Such thoughts might include, *It's awful if I don't get a good night's sleep. I've got to get a good night's rest.* Instead, try to think, *This is inconvenient but not the end of the world.* If you don't fall asleep within twenty minutes of going to bed, simply get up and do something relaxing. Go back to bed when you feel sleepy.

- Seek professional help for conditions that interfere with sleep. These include sleep apnea and other sleep disorders, mental disorders (such as depression, anxiety, PTSD, and substance-use disorders), thyroid conditions, heartburn, arthritis, diabetes, cardiovascular disease, hypertension, respiratory conditions, pain, and urinary problems.

- Avoid sleeping pills as a general rule. These can have adverse side effects and can actually increase insomnia in the long term. Try nonpharmacological steps first, which are generally at least as effective.

Minimize Substance Use

Nuclear brain imaging reveals the effects of substance use on brain function years before structural damage is apparent. Figure 1.2 shows the brains of two sixteen-year-olds. The brain on the left is a healthy, drug-free brain in which all areas are functioning well. The brain on the right is the brain of a sixteen-year-old who has been using marijuana for two years. A similar scalloping or Swiss-cheese effect is seen in the brains of young people after just a few years of excessive use of alcohol, cigarettes, inhalants, cocaine, or methamphetamines.

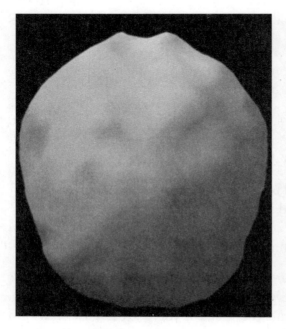
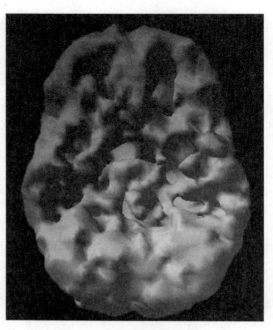

Healthy, Drug-Free Brain,
Age 16

2 Years of Marijuana Use,
Age 16

Figure 1.2: The effects of substances on brain function (Amen 2005)

Consider the following facts.

Smoking greatly increases the risk of depression, anxiety, and panic attacks. It also impairs memory and increases the risk of dementia. Like tobacco, marijuana decreases blood flow to the brain and impairs memory.

Alcohol intake is inversely correlated with resilience. It may even shrink the brain when taken regularly in small amounts described as "mild" or "moderate" drinking.

Excessive caffeine can interfere with brain function by restricting blood flow to the brain, and it can cause insomnia, anxiety, and excess arousal. Up to four hundred milligrams of caffeine a day—about the amount in four cups of coffee—appears to be safe for most healthy adults. This amount can easily be exceeded by drinking energy drinks, caffeinated sodas, or more than four cups of coffee.

Manage Medical Conditions

There are numerous medical conditions that affect brain health and function.

Sleep apnea typically occurs when the airway closes up during sleep, depriving the brain of oxygen. It is marked by snoring, the stoppage of breathing, and loud gasps for air as people partially awaken during the night to breathe. The pattern of blocked breathing and partial awakening can repeat itself scores of times throughout the night. One awakens deprived of both sleep and oxygen, feeling mentally sluggish and tired, and often has problems with memory and mood. Sleep apnea increases the risk of heart attack, stroke, high blood pressure, headaches, and nightmares. Most people with sleep apnea have depression, and sleep apnea is very common in people with PTSD. Fortunately, it is very treatable, and proper treatment often reduces the psychological symptoms that accompany it. Discuss with your doctor treatment options that keep the airway open. Losing five to ten pounds of weight and limiting alcohol, sedatives, sleeping pills, and muscle relaxants might also help.

Elevated cholesterol levels in the blood can sometimes cause depression. Exercise, proper eating, stress management, and medications can help.

Thyroid disorders are called the great mimic because they can cause or worsen so many symptoms of stress-related conditions (including anxiety, depression, or PTSD) as well as unexplained symptoms such as sluggishness, sleep problems, and weight gain. Problems can arise when the hormone thyroxine is slightly above or below normal ranges. Typical blood tests can measure levels of thyroxine in the blood. However, an inexpensive thyroid-stimulating hormone (TSH) test is more sensitive. TSH, which is secreted by the brain, stimulates the thyroid gland to secrete thyroxine. If, for example, thyroxine is in the low normal range but TSH is elevated, this indicates that the brain is trying to stoke a sluggish thyroid. Elevated TSH is associated with decreased blood flow to the brain, especially in the prefrontal cortex, as well as memory and concentration problems. Get a TSH test if you experience a mental disorder, memory loss, elevated cholesterol, or other unexplained symptoms. If you are taking thyroid medication, monitor TSH and thyroxine levels to ensure that the dosage is correct. Avoid smoking, which can interfere with proper thyroid functioning.

High blood pressure can cause microbleeds in the brain. Blood pressure can usually be lowered through a combination of brain-healthy eating, exercise, sleep, and possibly medication.

Type 2 diabetes increases the risk of cognitive impairment, dementia, cardiovascular disease, and hippocampal shrinkage. Reduce the risk of type 2 diabetes by following the guidelines in this chapter. If you have diabetes, keep it under the best control possible through proper treatment and blood sugar monitoring.

Gum disease can produce toxins that enter the bloodstream, leading to inflammation and harm to the brain. This is an argument for regular brushing, flossing, and dental cleanings; if you have gum disease, get professional treatment. Avoiding tobacco, getting sufficient sleep, drinking lots of water, and eating a quarter cup of yogurt containing live bacteria each day might also help reduce the risk of gum disease.

Restrict Anticholinergic Medications

Acetylcholine is an important chemical messenger in the brain. Even with occasional or short-term use, anticholinergic medications block acetylcholine and have been linked to brain shrinkage, slowed activity in areas associated with memory, and dementia (Nelson 2008). These medications include antihistamines, sleeping pills, over-the-counter sleep aids, tranquilizers, muscle relaxants, ulcer medications, and tricyclic antidepressants. Ask your doctor or pharmacist if your medications are anticholinergic. If so, discuss using the smallest dose for the shortest amount of time possible. Or ask about switching to an alternative medication or trying a nonpharmacological treatment.

Minimize Pesticides, Preservatives, and Air Pollutants

Pesticides, preservatives, and air pollutants are toxic to neurons. Pesticides are found on produce and are brought into the house when we walk through outdoor areas treated with weed killers. Growing your own produce, thoroughly washing store-bought produce, buying organic produce, and restricting the use of processed foods reduces pesticides and preservatives. Reduce exposure to air pollutants by avoiding tobacco smoke, by recirculating air in your car if you are stuck in traffic, and by using good filters (such as in the furnace) in the home.

Manage Stress

As we've discussed, excessive or chronic stress can disrupt brain health and function. It can also sap energy and joy. Fortunately, there are many effective ways to manage stress. Much more to come about this later.

Activity: Make Your Plan for a Resilient Brain

Many people have reported that making and sticking to an exercise, nutrition, and eating plan were among the most helpful aspects of resilience training. Make a health plan that you can maintain as you work through this workbook and beyond. Describe your plan below.

Exercise: Aim to get at least 150 minutes of aerobic exercise (such as brisk walking or cycling all or most days) per week. You might also add strength and flexibility training to further sharpen the brain.

_____

_____

_____

_____

_____

Sleep: I'll get _____ hours of sleep per night (a little more than I think I need), going to bed at _____ and getting up at _____.

Nutrition: Eat at least three times per day, selecting brain-healthy choices from the dietary guidelines in the section "Resilient Eating." Using the form in appendix A, make a sample menu that is consistent with these guidelines: Does your plan provide sufficient servings from each food group in order to ensure you're getting needed nutrients? Are you varying foods within each food group, which also helps ensure you're getting all the needed nutrients? (The federal government has an excellent, free online tool to help plan and assess how well your dietary and physical activity choices compare with recommended amounts. Visit https://www.ChooseMyPlate.gov and then locate SuperTracker.)

Activity: Track Your Progress

Using the form in appendix B, track your progress over a fourteen-day period; then make helpful adjustments and continue to follow your plan as you move through the workbook.

Activity: What Else Might Help?

After reviewing this chapter, consider the following, and then make a list of any factors that might be impairing your ability to feel and function at your best:

Unhealthy substance use: Note that abruptly stopping substance use might make the symptoms of psychological problems more troubling. You might wish to find a program, such as Seeking Safety, that gently helps one reduce substance use while preparing to address PTSD symptoms (see recommended resources).

A physical exam: This can help you rule out or treat medical conditions.

Sunlight: We need sufficient sunlight or high-intensity artificial light to feel our best.

Recreation and lifelong learning: These activities lift mood and improve brain function.

Once you've made your list, indicate the steps you plan to take to address these factors. Filling in the chart below can shed light on helpful steps.

What's interfering with my health, mood, or functioning?	What would help?	What steps will I take?	When will I take these steps?

Conclusion

This chapter explored eight ways to strengthen the brain hardware, readying the brain for the resilience skills in the following chapters. You'll likely find that following the recommendations in this chapter will also improve your mood, energy level, and mental functioning. Give yourself time to put a healthy brain plan in place. When you are ready, proceed to the next two chapters, which will help you manage your body's response to excessive stress, or arousal.

Chapter 2

Regulating Arousal: The Basics

This chapter and the next one will help you regulate your body's response to stress so that you can feel and function at your best. We'll explore some very simple and effective skills that will reset your nervous system so that your stress levels will be neither too high nor too low. Let's start by looking at what happens in your body during difficult times.

Understanding Stress and Arousal

When the brain perceives a threat, it triggers changes in the body called the *stress response*, or just *stress*. These changes prepare us to move—to fight or flee. The brain becomes sharper. Stress *arousal* increases, meaning muscles tense and blood pressure, heart rate, breathing rate, and blood sugar increase to get more fuel to the muscles. Ideally, the body moves, expends energy, and then returns to normal. Problems occur, however, when arousal is *dysregulated*. Usually this means that arousal rises too high or remains elevated, though arousal can also drop below optimal levels. Dysregulated arousal is common to the stress-related conditions mentioned earlier, such as depression, anxiety, panic attacks, PTSD, substance-use disorders, and problem anger.

Have you ever felt too aroused to think or talk straight? Conversely, have you ever felt too numb or exhausted to do so? Excessive stress changes your biology. Understanding this will help you to normalize dysregulated arousal and know how to manage it. Let's start by understanding optimal arousal levels.

Optimal Arousal: The Resilient Zone

Figure 2.1 depicts optimal levels of arousal, sometimes called the *resilient zone*. The horizontal lines indicate that arousal is neither too high nor too low. When arousal levels are in this zone, we feel and function at our best. All parts of the brain and the organs of the body are working harmoniously. Breathing and heart rates are slow and rhythmic. Muscles are relaxed, or just tense enough to function well. We feel grounded—secure, centered, whole, connected to our bodies, and aware of bodily sensations.

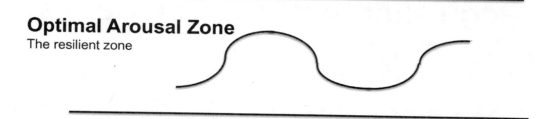

Optimal Arousal Zone
The resilient zone

Figure 2.1: Optimal arousal zone (Heller and Heller 2001; see also Porges 2011, Miller-Karas 2015, and Ogden, Minton, and Pain 2006)

In this zone, arousal fluctuates smoothly and without extremes because there is balance among the branches of the nervous system. Thinking and behavior tend to be flexible and effective. Challenges are typically met with appropriate emotions and social engagement. Thus, we might reach out to others—seeking or offering support, resolving differences, or negotiating with threatening people without being overcome by extreme emotion. This is the ideal place to be when confronting challenges. However, extreme stress can bump us out of the resilient zone, as shown in figure 2.2.

Hyperarousal Zone

Trauma or other emotional upheavals can overwhelm our coping capacities. These events can occur at any time in life and can be particularly disruptive when they occur in the early years. A single severe event or series of events can bump us out of the resilient zone.

If we cannot think or talk our way out of difficulty, as we are hardwired to do in the resilient zone, then the brain automatically kicks us to the *hyperarousal zone*. This is a condition of extreme fight or flight, the purpose of which is to prepare us to physically battle something or someone or run away to safety. Heart and breathing rates become rapid and erratic. Muscles become overly tense. Perspiration increases to cool the body. Preoccupied with survival, regions of the brain concerned with logic and language go off-line, and alarm centers become overactive. We might say that in this zone we are too wired to think or talk straight. Negative thoughts (such as *I can't take it*, *I'm a loser*, and others described in chapter 5), worries, and concentration problems are common in this zone.

Regions of the brain that give us a sense of being one with our bodies also go off-line. We might begin to lose awareness of normal bodily sensations—or we might become overly sensitive or troubled by intense sensations such as pounding heart, heavy breathing, or pain. Strong emotions, such as anger, irritability, anxiety, and even panic are common, as are nightmares and sleep disturbance.

Hyperarousal can serve a protective function during an emergency, but it is problematic when the brain's alarm stays on and the symptoms of extreme arousal persist.

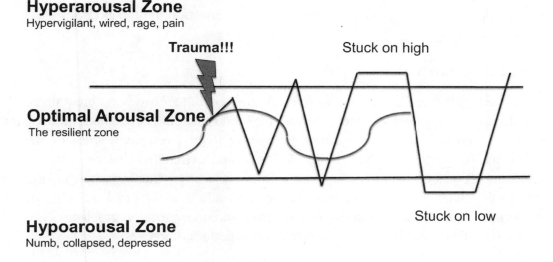

Hyperarousal Zone
Hypervigilant, wired, rage, pain

Trauma!!!   Stuck on high

Optimal Arousal Zone
The resilient zone

Hypoarousal Zone
Numb, collapsed, depressed

Stuck on low

Figure 2.2: Hyperarousal and hypoarousal (Heller and Heller 2001; see also Porges 2011, Miller-Karas 2015, and Ogden, Minton, and Pain 2006)

Hypoarousal Zone

What if you've been on high alert for so long that you feel exhausted or numb? Or what if the normal action of the fight-or-flight response is thwarted? For example, a child may not be able to run away or fight back when being abused, and trying to do so might incite further violence. When fight or flight is blocked or leads to exhaustion, the brain is hardwired to elicit *hypoarousal*, a state of numbness, exhaustion, shutting down, immobilization, or collapse. Sometimes playing dead is the best way to survive, or numbing might temporarily protect one from emotional or physical pain. However, when you're stuck in hypoarousal, you feel disconnected from self, others, and your body. You're too shut down to think or talk straight. Outwardly, you might exhibit a slumped posture, a downward gaze, glazed eyes, weakness, a collapse of normal defenses, or a flat or depressed expression. Some people even feel as if the world is not real, or that they themselves are not real.

Some people alternate between hyper- and hypoarousal. Others, prior to transitioning to the hypoarousal zone, will experience *alert immobilization*, in which the arousal alarm stays on as one also experiences exhaustion.

What You Can Do

The more you practice the simple skills below, the more likely you will be to stay in the resilient zone or return to it readily when stressed. All of these arousal regulation skills involve *tracking*, which is paying very close attention in a curious and nonjudgmental way to what you sense in your body. Tracking brings back online those areas of the brain involved in regulating arousal, thinking effectively, and restoring a sense of connection to one's body.

Breathing Skills

We'll start with three short but effective calming techniques involving breathing. When we're under stress, our breathing often becomes rapid and shallow as we tighten muscles in the throat, chest, and abdomen in preparation for fight or flight. Even subtle shifts in breathing can result in less oxygen reaching the brain, heart, and extremities—along with a shift in blood acidity. Scores of symptoms can result from these stress-induced changes, including anxiety, panic attacks, a feeling that you or your surroundings are not real, exhaustion, headaches, sleep disturbance, unsteadiness, racing heart, and concentration problems. As breathing calms, the ability to think, speak, remember, and perform improves.

THE RESET BUTTON

When you find yourself running around, and your mind is racing, this two-minute technique provides a refreshing, restful pause.

1. Sit comfortably erect in a chair, with feet firmly on the ground, and hands resting unclasped in your lap. Close your eyes if doing so is comfortable. Otherwise, let your eyes drop downward to about forty-five degrees, so that you are looking at the floor.

2. Be aware of your breath. Follow it and notice what happens in your body as you breathe. You might notice the rib cage expand and a feeling of energy or lightness on the in-breath. On the out-breath, you might notice a feeling of settling and comfort. When agitated water settles, it becomes very clear. Similarly, as you pause to let your mind settle in your breath, it too becomes clear.

3. As thoughts, worries, or plans arise, just notice them without judgment, and gently bring your mind back to the breath and the sensations in the body.

4. Feel a sense of connection to yourself and others.

CALM BREATHING

Abdominal breathing has been a mainstay of arousal regulation for centuries. Even small, stress-induced shifts in normal breathing can profoundly affect mental states, medical symptoms, and functioning.

1. As before, sit comfortably erect in a chair, feet flat on the floor, with hands resting in your lap but not touching. Let the back of the chair support your back.

2. If it is comfortable, close your eyes (or drop your gaze) and sense what your body is feeling now. Notice, without judging, areas of the body carrying stress or tension.

3. Now take a moment to consciously relax the muscles of the mouth, jaw, throat, shoulders, chest, and abdomen. Place your hands over your navel. Imagine that the stomach fills with air on the in-breath, so that your hands rise, and empties of air on the out-breath, so that your hands fall. Upper-chest breathing is inefficient and stressful, so keep the chest and shoulders relaxed and still. Breathe naturally and comfortably—no gasps or abrupt movements—for one to two minutes.

4. Track what happens in your body.

TACTICAL BREATHING

This adaptation of calm breathing, developed by Lieutenant Colonel Dave Grossman (Grossman and Christensen 2004), has been widely taught to members of high-risk groups, such as the military and police.

1. Relax your shoulders and upper body.

2. Breathe in through the nose for a count of four, expanding your belly.

3. Hold the breath for a count of four.

4. Breathe out through the lips for a count of four.

5. Hold for a count of four.

6. Repeat steps 2 through 5 about three times. Track what happens in your body.

Activity: Breathing Skills

Try either the reset button, calm breathing, or tactical breathing seven times a day for a week. Try the skill when awakening, before going to bed, before meals, and two other times during the day. Keep a log for how effective each attempt was physically and emotionally, using ratings from 1 (not calming at all) to 10 (very calming).

Seven days will give you an idea of how well a particular breathing skill works for you. Appendix C is a log sheet for resilience strategies. Photocopy it (or download it from the website for this book, http://www.newharbinger.com/39409) and use it to keep a record of the resilience strategies you try. After the seven days, look for patterns in your log. Did its effectiveness improve with practice? Was its effectiveness greater at certain times of day? Going forward, how might you see yourself practicing and applying this skill? You might wish to continue practicing the same breathing skill or experiment with a different one.

Body-Based Skills

Most of psychology works in a top-down way. That is, language and logic are used to calm the body. When we are bumped out of the resilient zone, however, it is often more effective to work from the bottom up. In this way, we first calm the body and the lower regions of the brain that are concerned with mobilizing the body for stress. In the process, we regain composure and feel safer and more secure. Once arousal returns to the resilient zone, regions of the brain concerned with logic and language come back online so that we can think and talk more effectively. Body-based master clinicians Patricia Ogden (Ogden and Fischer 2015; Ogden, Minton, and Pain 2006), Bessel van der Kolk (2014), Peter Levine (2010), and Elaine Miller-Karas (2015) have pioneered the body-based skills that follow. These skills have been taught around the world and, because they are so simple and effective, have even been used in developing countries following natural disasters. Try them and see if you think they are powerful. All of the body-based skills emphasize tracking, which is sensing the inner world of the body in a curious, nonjudgmental way. This helps to bring the structures of the brain that regulate arousal back online and to restore a sense of connection to one's body and self.

MOVEMENT

The stress response is designed to get us moving and expending energy. Movement strategies help to release the bottled-up energy of stress. They also help to counter the immobilization of the hypoarousal state. Besides these exercises, the slow movements of yoga, tai chi, and qigong, coupled with tracking, are also excellent ways to return to the resilient zone.

Kneading: Squeeze or knead one arm, up and down, noticing sensations as you go. Track sensations both on the surface and deep within the arm. Experiment with different types of touch—firmer or softer pressure, quick or slow, deep or shallow, soothing or mechanical. After going up and down one arm several times, pause and compare the feelings in the arm you just squeezed versus your other arm.

Moving the arms: Gently and slowly stretch your arms up toward the ceiling as you breathe in. As you breathe out, slowly and gently return your arms to your sides. Track the sensations—such as flexibility, muscles relaxing, lightness, circulation, and so on—in the arms, shoulders, and hands. Then track what is happening in the rest of the body.

Gesturing: Think of your favorite gesture that you associate with pleasant feelings. The gesture might be smiling, waving hello, slowly rubbing your earlobes or forehead between the eyebrows, positioning the hands palms up in a welcoming gesture, folding your arms across your body with one hand resting on the side of your body and the other on the opposite arm (self-hug), placing a hand over your heart, throwing a ball, or some other pleasant movement. Think of one, take a deep breath, relax your muscles, and then make the gesture. Track what happens with your breathing, heart rate, muscle tone, facial expression, posture, and other visceral sensations.

Resistance: While standing, place one foot behind the other, feet firmly on the ground. Bend the knees, feel the strength in your legs and core, and push slowly but strongly against a wall. Track: sense how your body feels as you actively move. Take your time.

Changing the posture: Emotional upheaval or trauma might have taught you to look down, hunch your shoulders, and slump over. Try to exaggerate these movements and track what happens as you do. Now notice what happens when you straighten your spine, lift your chin, expand your chest, and look confidently ahead. Track how that feels. Go back and forth between these two extreme postures. Notice how changing your posture in pleasant ways gives you a sense of control over your inner experience.

GROUNDING

Grounding anchors us safely and securely in the present moment. Remember the importance of tracking, which pleasantly restores that sense of connection to self and body.

Standing grounding: Stand with feet shoulder-width apart, firmly and securely planted. Unlock your knees, soften your feet, and track sensations in your feet and legs. Slowly rock forward, sensing weight over the balls of your feet. Then rock backward, sensing the weight shifting to your heels, and return to center. Slowly rock to the right, sensing the weight on the outer portion of the right foot and the arch of the left foot. Notice the opposite sensations as you rock to the left. Return to a secure balance point, and pause to track.

Now sense how it feels to stand tall, with relaxed shoulders, straight spine, uplifted chin, and expanded chest.

And now imagine that your legs are the trunk of a tree, and roots grow deeply into the ground from your feet, wrapping around rocks and roots and giving you a sense of security. You might imagine that your arms are branches swaying in the breeze, while your trunk is firmly rooted. You might even slowly move your arms upward and outward before bringing your arms back to your sides. Don't forget to track, noticing things like breath, heart rate, and muscle tension. Notice subtle, pleasant shifts in emotions.

Grounding in the body: Place one hand on the middle of your back so that the fingertips almost reach the spine. For a few moments, sense your rib cage move as you breathe, and track sensations, thoughts, and emotions as you do so. Now place the other hand over your heart, experimenting with different kinds of touch—firm, soothing, and so forth—until you sense which kind of touch feels best. You might move your hand from the back and place it over your heart, your belly, or elsewhere on the body that feels pleasant. Take your time to track sensations, emotions, and thoughts.

RESOURCING

A *resource* is anything that helps you feel a pleasant feeling, such as joy, peace, comfort, love, confidence, or eager anticipation (Miller-Karas 2015). A resource can be a favorite person, place, memory, or pet; a cherished value or inner strength; an accomplishment; a favorite hobby or activity; God; or imagining a pleasant time in the future. Write down three of your favorite resources. Pick one and describe it in writing in as much detail as possible, using all five senses, inner bodily sensations, and emotions. Read your description slowly and track what happens in your body as you curiously hold this resource in mind. Take your time.

Activity: Use a Body-Based Skill

Practice a body-based skill involving movement, grounding, or resourcing. Practice it twice a day for at least three days to give it a fair trial, and record your experiences on a log sheet, such as appendix C. If your experience was positive, try practicing the skill longer, or experiment with another body-based skill to increase the number of tools in your coping toolbox.

Conclusion

The skills we explored in this chapter can be very effective for regulating the nervous system. Contrary to most psychological approaches, these skills work by first calming the body so that the higher regions of the brain can come back online and function better. Master them so that you can use them before difficult events, when you are under pressure, or after a difficult time when you need to recover. In the next chapter we'll explore two additional skills that are very effective for regulating arousal in a bottom-up fashion.

Chapter 3

Advanced Arousal Regulation Skills

In this chapter we'll explore two additional body-based skills that can effectively bring arousal back into the resilient zone. These skills are heart coherence and progressive muscle relaxation.

Heart Coherence

The description of heart coherence that follows and the accompanying figure are adapted with permission from Childre and Rozman (2003, 2005) and the HeartMath Institute®, which has been researching emotional resilience for more than twenty-five years.

We experience emotions primarily in the body, not the head. Think of all the ways we describe emotions experienced in the body: "butterflies in my stomach," "sick to my stomach," "lump in my throat," "he's a pain in the neck," and so forth. Now think of the many ways we describe emotions relating to the heart: heartfelt affection, brokenhearted, "my heart skipped a beat," or "a heart overflowing with gratitude."

The brain communicates with the heart, but far more messages go from the heart to the brain than vice versa. The heart "speaks" to the brain via nerves, hormones, blood pressure, and electromagnetic messages. What do you think would happen if you could calm your heart? Thanks to advances in computer technology, we now know that calming the heart profoundly affects the mind, mood, performance, and the rest of the body.

Generally, a lower resting heart rate is linked to better health and performance. However, the patterns of heart rhythms are even more important. We can now record beat-to-beat changes in heart rate, which allow us to track *heart coherence*: the heart's ability to adjust heart rates smoothly and quickly as needed. Figure 3.1 depicts the hearts of two different people, each person having the same average resting heart rate in beats per minute (represented by the horizontal line). The heart on the left is *coherent*—increasing and decreasing speeds like a world-class athlete who easily accelerates or slows down as the situation requires. The branches of the nervous system responsible for increasing and decreasing arousal are operating in balance. The heart on the right is erratic and struggling to maintain balance.

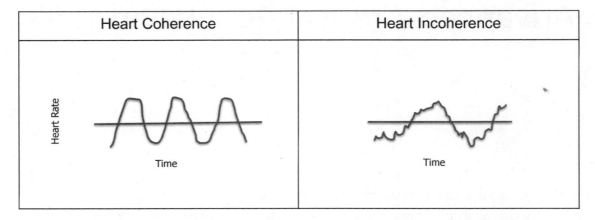

Figure 3.1: Heart coherence versus heart incoherence (Childre and Rozman 2003)

Heart coherence is associated with fewer symptoms of PTSD, depression, anxiety, anger, and stress; a greater sense of well-being; reductions in sleeplessness, fatigue, blood pressure, pain, cortisol, and weight; and improved concentration, thinking, listening ability, and productivity (see, for example, the review by McCraty and Tomasino 2004). Fortunately, with practice most people can achieve heart coherence in a matter of weeks. The basic principle is that any positive emotion experienced at the heart level promotes heart coherence. The quickest and most effective pathway to heart coherence is through the experience of mature love (as opposed to, say, infatuation; Childre and Rozman 2003). Try this experiment to see if the basic heart coherence technique, called Quick Coherence® (reprinted with permission from Childre and Rozman 2005), is effective for you. For example, after practicing the heart coherence skill, you might notice that you feel mentally or physically calmer, or that your mood shifts in a positive way.

Preparations

These four steps will help you to activate a positive feeling, which is an important step in cultivating heart coherence. You'll start by recalling times that stir positive feelings, and use one of these feelings in the activity that follows.

1. Sit quietly and comfortably. Focus on your breathing for a few moments.

2. Identify the person you have loved the most. Think about why that person is important, and how the person has made you feel.

3. Identify other people who have made you feel loved and appreciated. Think about each one for a few moments.

4. Think about times that you have appreciated: perhaps moments in nature, holding a sleeping child, the satisfaction of accomplishment or a fine performance, or something you are grateful for.

5. Select one of the memories above to work with, recalling that love is a particularly powerful way to effect heart coherence. If you have trouble recalling love, then recall another positive emotion. If a positive emotion is difficult to activate, then simply let your heart go to neutral as you practice the technique below, which only takes a minute.

Activity: The Quick Coherence® Technique

1. Begin with heart-focused breathing. Focus your attention on the area of the heart. Imagine your breath is flowing in and out of your heart or chest area. Breathe a little slower and deeper than usual.

2. Activate a positive feeling. Make a sincere attempt to experience a regenerative feeling, such as appreciation or care for someone or something in your life.

Take your time. Let your breathing and heart rhythms settle. Then allow time to let the positive feeling settle in the heart region. *Experiencing* the feeling in the heart is more important than *thinking about* the details of a memory.

Practice this skill several times a day, for several days. Initially try it in calm moments. Eventually, you might try it before a somewhat stressful situation. Log your experience using the form in appendix C.

Progressive Muscle Relaxation

Besides the heart, we also experience emotions in our muscles. When the alarm system of the brain is stuck in the "on" position, muscle tension remains chronically high. Excessive tension is typically uncomfortable, sometimes even painful. Paradoxically, increasing tension levels helps to reset the brain and return arousal to the resilient zone. When we relax, muscles elongate, soften, and warm as blood flow increases. Progressive muscle relaxation is a practice of tensing and then relaxing various muscle groups, paying close attention to (tracking) the difference between the sensations. It's an effective strategy for nearly everyone who tries it.

Practicing this method daily can reduce baseline arousal. Done before bedtime, it may also help you sleep better. Remember that tracking reduces arousal, and tracking while practicing progressive muscle relaxation also helps retrain the brain to detect and reverse the first hint of tension. As relaxation spreads throughout the body, you'll feel calmer as well. Notice this as you track. To practice progressive muscle relaxation, you can read the instructions below as you do it, or you can make an audio recording of the instructions and listen to it.

Activity: Progressive Muscle Relaxation

Practice this skill once or twice a day for at least a week and record the results using the form in appendix C. To prepare, loosen tight clothing. You may wish to remove glasses and shoes. Then, sit comfortably or lie on your back. (In these instructions, we'll assume you are lying down. Obvious adjustments can be made for a seated position.) Breathe abdominally for a few moments until your breathing settles. Without judging, just notice what parts of your body feel pleasant. What parts feel tense? Then proceed.

1. Bend your feet at the ankles so your toes move toward your head. Sense the tension along the outer part of the legs, below the knees. Relax and notice the difference. Take your time.

2. Point both of your feet and toes away from your head at the same time. Notice tension in the calves. Relax and notice the contrast in those areas.

Continue this pattern of tensing, noticing, relaxing, and noticing.

3. Tense the quadriceps on the front of your thighs by straightening your legs and locking your knees. Leave your feet relaxed.

4. Tense the back of your legs by pressing the back of your heels against the floor or bed, as if you are lying on your back at the beach and digging your heels into the sand. Keep the toes pointing skyward. Sense the tension along the backs of your legs.

5. Squeeze your buttocks or seat muscles together while contracting your pelvic muscles.

6. Tense your stomach muscles by pulling them inward. Notice how a tight gut impedes breathing.

7. Tense your back muscles along both sides of the spine by slowly arching your back, pulling your chest up and toward the chin, while leaving your shoulders and buttocks rooted to the surface.

8. Shrug your shoulders, noticing tension above the collarbones and between the shoulder blades.

9. Tense the muscles in the top of your forearms. With palms down on the surface beside your body, pull the relaxed hands back at the wrists, with fingers pointing upward.

10. Tighten your fists and biceps, drawing the hands to the shoulders, as if lifting weights (curls). Notice tension in the fists, forearms, and biceps.

11. Very, very slowly rotate your chin to the right as if looking over your right shoulder, noticing tension along the right side of your neck. Slowly return to center, and then rotate to the left.

12. Gently press your head back against the surface you are lying on, while raising your chin toward the ceiling. Sense tension at the base of the skull, where it meets the neck.

13. Lift your eyebrows and furrow your brow, sensing tension across the forehead.

14. Frown, pulling the corners of your mouth down, sensing tension on the sides of the chin and neck.

15. Grit your teeth and sense tension from the angle of the jaw up to the temple.

16. Grin ear to ear and sense tension around the cheekbones.

17. Spend a few more moments just sensing your breathing and how your entire body feels.

Chapter 4

Rapid Relief Techniques

With skills in hand to manage your body's response to stress, we turn now to skills that will help you manage troubling emotions. At some time or another, we all experience strong, distressing emotions, such as fear, panic, anxiety, sadness, grief, shame, disgust, or anger. If we lack skills to handle them, these emotions can build up like a pressure cooker that eventually explodes. Over time they might erode mood, health, and functioning. Chapters 4 through 9 will teach you practical skills to manage difficult emotions. This chapter will help you recognize painful emotions, and it provides two skills to help you gain rapid relief from *moderately* upsetting experiences.

Painful Emotions Are Normal

Present difficulties often stir up painful emotions, which often stir up similar emotions and unresolved memories from the past. Pain from the past, in turn, can fuel worries about the future. It's reassuring to realize that distressing emotions are common to everyone, and that they usually make sense when we consider one's life experience. Perhaps you can take a moment to consider your own life experience. Please check any adversities below that you've encountered. Without any judgments, simply notice if any emotions arise as you do.

_____ Everyday strains (overwhelming time demands, critical leaders or family members, financial concerns, pressures to excel, ongoing conflict with family or coworkers)

_____ Serious illness or injury in yourself or those you care for

_____ Rejection, betrayal

_____ Humiliation, criticism, feeling inadequate

_____ Losing your job

_____ Loss (death of a loved one or friend, end of a relationship, loss of income)

_____ Infidelity

_____ Divorce (your own or that of your parents)

_____ Failure

_____ Trauma (experiencing, witnessing, or sometimes even learning about overwhelming events such as combat, terrorism, natural disasters, riots, crime, traffic accidents, domestic violence, physical or emotional abuse, or sexual trauma; rape, abuse, and molestation are particularly distressing)

_____ Other: _____

Pause to reflect, again without judging. Do any of these events stir up emotions that seem strong or unsettled? Might there be connections between your everyday emotions and past experiences?

If unresolved, emotional upheaval from the past can keep present emotions highly charged, disrupting mood, physical health, and functioning. We now understand that childhood adversities—such as physical, sexual, or emotional abuse; neglect; or living in a home with domestic violence, mental illness, suicide, substance abuse, or a missing parent—can lead to a wide range of psychological, medical, and functional problems in adulthood. Most adults have experienced at least one such adversity. The more childhood adversities one has experienced, the more likely one is to experience psychological, medical, and functional problems (Felitti 2002). We also know that nearly every kind of trauma, particularly if it has not been resolved, is linked to increases in diverse medical conditions, ranging from the flu to even heart attacks and cancer (Prigerson et al. 1997).

This understanding underscores the importance of processing and settling past emotional wounds—the sooner the better. Fortunately, there are many ways to do this. Many effective strategies have been developed to help people heal from trauma. A skilled trauma specialist can help trauma survivors settle overwhelming experiences. This chapter and chapters 5 to 9 can help you gain relief from less disturbing emotional upheavals by confronting, rather than avoiding, distressing emotions. Also, see _The Post-Traumatic Stress Disorder Sourcebook_ (Schiraldi 2016a) for details on trauma treatments. If dealing with difficult experiences seems daunting, see a skilled mental health professional. You might discuss the skills in this chapter with a therapist and consider using them to complement treatment.

Avoiding Emotions Usually Doesn't Help

Avoidance is a common thread in the stress-related conditions. It is _natural_ to want to avoid painful emotions, memories, or situations. However, as figure 4.1 suggests, the problem with avoidance is that nothing changes, and sometimes the very things we do to avoid pain create their own set of problems. The following lists ways that people avoid. Do any of these describe your typical response to stress? Check those that apply.

_____ I don't think about troubling thoughts, emotions, situations, or memories and thus do little to modify them.

_____ I deny anything is wrong, or I minimize the pain. ("It doesn't really bother me. It used to, but now it doesn't.")

_____ I numb my emotions. (When we numb negative emotions, we also numb positive emotions.)

_____ I dwell on physical pain or symptoms to avoid emotional pain.

_____ I withdraw from people, places, or situations that are distressing.

_____ I keep feelings to myself and don't tell others what is going on inside.

_____ I wish I could erase painful memories. (This is not possible, and trying to do so only creates tension.)

_____ I try to escape or block out negative emotions with:

_____ Drugs

_____ Painkillers

_____ Excessive humor

_____ Workaholism

_____ Intellectualizing (habitually thinking, complaining, worrying, or being stuck on "why" questions while not acknowledging underlying emotions and trying to resolve them)

_____ Overconfidence or overachieving (an attempt to compensate)

_____ Compulsive gambling, shopping, sex, or other addictions

What do you notice? Do you see any patterns? Might avoidance be working for or against you? Avoidance takes a lot of energy and is exhausting. It keeps us stuck emotionally and prevents us from enjoying many of life's satisfactions. Please note that habitual avoidance is not the same as healthy, temporary distractions, such as wholesome recreational activities or vacations. We are talking about habitual avoidance patterns like those listed above that do not change our *response* to pain. These patterns offer short-term benefits, and people engage in them because they haven't yet learned a better response to pain. Fortunately, there is a better strategy.

Figure 4.1: The emotional avoidance detour (Ciarocchi and Mercer, no date)

The New Strategy

We have learned from the study of trauma that each time we bring a painful memory into complete awareness, the brain has a chance to change it. Thus, a survivor of a difficult divorce tells his or her story to a safe and respectful listener, and this enables the brain to incorporate feelings of safety and respect into the painful memory. If that survivor reduces arousal while telling the story, then calmness and comfort might begin to replace agitation.

The better strategy acknowledges pain and actively moves toward it. Rather than battling the pain ("I can't stand this; I need a drink"), or avoiding it in passive resignation, we turn toward the pain with compassion and acceptance. We allow ourselves to stay in contact with distressing emotions, thoughts, memories, and bodily sensations long enough to process them. This helps to reduce symptoms of post-traumatic stress, anxiety, depression, and general distress. For example, Carrie tried very hard to forget a difficult childhood experience by keeping busy, drinking, and partying. Eventually, she learned to turn toward the pain and to allow it in, without judging the pain as bad or good. She realized that she was stronger than she thought and that she no longer needed to run from her memory.

This part of the workbook will help you modify painful memories and your emotional response to difficult times. We'll start with two techniques that often bring rapid relief from intense, distressing emotions, which can arise from a range of events, from an argument with a family member to something traumatic. For traumatic events, it is usually wise to try these techniques with a trauma specialist. For events involving moderately intense emotions, you might experiment with these on your own.

Eye Movements

Dr. Larry D. Smyth (1996), of the Sheppard Pratt Hospital, developed this useful adaptation of eye movement desensitization and reprocessing (EMDR), which is a comprehensive treatment for PTSD and other stress-related mental disorders. The following technique helps about two-thirds of people who try it.

1. Identify a past or present situation that distresses you and is difficult to shake. Remember, go easy. When first trying this technique, do not pick a situation or memory that is extremely intense for you. Rather, pick a moderately distressing situation to gain confidence in the technique. While this technique does not usually have negative side effects, there is always the possibility that one might be overwhelmed by trying to go too fast too soon. In a moment you will think about the situation to the point that you feel 5 to 6 subjective units of distress (SUDs), where 0 means you feel pleasantly relaxed, with no distress, and 10 is the most intense discomfort you could possibly feel.

2. Imagine the upsetting situation. Notice the emotions and bodily sensations. Now add any images (such as someone scowling at you) and thoughts that go along with the memory (such as *I can't take this… Why did this have to happen? What's wrong with me?*) until the SUDs level reaches 5 or 6. Don't allow the SUDs level to go higher, because we don't want this process to become overwhelming. A level of 5 to 6 is moderately distressing—uncomfortable but tolerable. At this level you can think clearly.

3. With eyes open and head still, move two extended fingers back and forth in front of your eyes. Your hand should be about fourteen inches in front of your eyes, and the back-and-forth movement should cover a distance of about two feet. Watch your fingers move back and forth for about twenty-five cycles.

4. Notice where your SUDs level is now. Typically it drops to 4 or 4½. Notice any shifts in the thoughts, images, bodily sensations, or emotions. People often notice that they change or lessen in intensity. For example, an image might shrink or fade, or the gut might feel less tense. If your SUDs level dropped a little, then this technique may be useful for you. Repeat the back-and-forth movement of the fingers.

5. If you wish to use this in places where back-and-forth hand movements are inconvenient, be creative. Try picking two spots on the wall or on your knees and move your eyes between those spots. You can also move your eyes back and forth with your eyes closed, or with your hand over your eyes as if you are in deep thought.

6. If this technique dropped your SUDs level, practice it several times a day for a one-week period to master the skill. Use it as a rapid stress reducer when you want to soothe your nerves, or perhaps before returning home from work.

Thought Field Therapy

Thought field therapy (TFT) is another simple technique that can bring rapid relief from strong and distressing emotions. Its originator, Dr. Roger Callahan (a WWII veteran), described it as a self-help technique that can decrease emotional distress related to anxiety (including panic, phobias, worries, and fears), depression, stress, troubling memories, guilt, grief (for example, from a death or a broken relationship), fatigue, and embarrassment. He noted that it also dramatically improves heart rate variability (which is similar to heart coherence), typically within minutes, while helping to reduce pain and symptoms of certain chronic diseases, such as fibromyalgia and asthma. There are, he stated, no apparent risks or side effects—it either works or it doesn't.

When using the technique, one does not have to talk about, analyze, or disclose any details regarding the adversity. You can easily learn the technique and teach it to others. Preliminary research in Kosovo, Rwanda, and elsewhere appears to support the favorable clinical impressions regarding its use (Johnson et al. 2001; Sakai, Connolly, and Oas 2010). The instructions that follow are an adaptation developed by Dr. Robert L. Bray (2017) (used here with permission). In this technique, you will tap solidly with the tips of two fingers of either hand—firmly but not so hard as to be uncomfortable. To prepare, locate the tapping points (it does not matter which side of the body you use):

1. **Side of hand:** This is the fleshy part where one would strike when doing a karate chop.

2. **Under nose:** Between the top lip and the nose.

3. **Beginning of eyebrow:** Just above the bridge of the nose.

4. **Under eye:** On the bone about an inch beneath the pupil (when looking straight ahead).

5. **Under arm:** On the side of the torso, about four inches below the armpit.

6. **Under collarbone:** Place two fingers at the notch at the base of your neck. Drop them down an inch and slide them over about an inch.

7. **Little finger:** Along the nail line on the inside of the finger (next to the ring finger).

8. **Under collarbone:** Same as step 6.

9. **Index finger:** Along the nail line on the side of the finger near the thumb.

10. **Under collarbone:** Same as step 6.

Finally, there's the *gamut spot*, so named because you carry out a sequence of activities while continuously tapping there. To locate it, make a fist, then place the index finger of the other hand, which will tap, between the knuckles of the little and ring fingers. Slide the index finger an inch down the back of the hand, toward the wrist. That's the gamut spot.

Here are the instructions for TFT:

1. Remember and think about a situation that had a moderately negative impact on you. Using the SUDs scale described with the previous technique, rate the situation from 1 to 10. If you can't remember a situation, focus on a distressing image, feeling, sensation, or sound.

2. In succession, tap each of the ten major points about six to ten times:

    a. Side of hand

    b. Under nose

    c. Beginning of eyebrow

    d. Under eye

    e. Under arm

    f. Under collarbone

    g. Little finger

    h. Under collarbone

    i. Index finger

    j. Under collarbone

3. While continuously tapping the gamut spot, do the following:

    a. Close eyes

    b. Open eyes

    c. Look down and left

    d. Look down and right

    e. Whirl eyes in a circle

    f. Whirl eyes in a circle in the opposite direction

    g. Hum aloud any tune

    h. Count aloud to five

    i. Hum aloud again

4. Repeat step 2.

5. Rerate your level of upset. Repeat the whole sequence (steps 2 through 5) until there is no further drop in the level of upset.

6. End with a floor-to-ceiling eye roll if the SUDs rating is 2 or less. That is, while tapping the gamut spot and holding your head level, rotate your eyes on a vertical line from floor to ceiling over a period of six to seven seconds.

Why Do These Techniques Work?

Various theories might explain why these techniques can be effective. First, both techniques help us to confront pain. Exposing ourselves to distress is the first step toward desensitizing the nervous system, whereas avoidance maintains memories and the resulting arousal. The actions involved in both exercises stimulate both sides of the brain, which helps the brain process distressing memories that are stuck. (It is likely that the brain already contains thoughts and images that help to neutralize distressing memories; these techniques can blend these healing thoughts and images into the distressing memory.) Both techniques disrupt racing and worrisome thoughts, and focusing on bodily sensations—either by noticing them or by tapping—tends to ground one in the body and help to calm oneself down. Moving the eyes and tapping might also help to release energy that is bottled up or stuck.

Activity: Practicing a Rapid Relief Technique

Select either of the rapid relief techniques and try it out for four consecutive days in response to a moderately distressing event. Keep a log of its effectiveness using the form in appendix C.

Conclusion

This chapter introduced the idea of facing, rather than avoiding, what hurts. Doing this in a kind, nonjudgmental way (meaning no thoughts such as *I hate this! This is awful!*) reduces suffering. The eye movements and tapping techniques often provide rapid relief from distressing emotions. You can practice them preventively or in response to a troubling event. Chapters 5 to 9 will broaden your skills for settling troubling emotions.

Chapter 5

Calm Thinking

Our habitual ways of thinking profoundly affect our emotions for good or bad. Say you make a mistake. You might think, *I should have known better. I always mess things up! I'm so stupid.* Or, you might think, *I think I can do better. I wonder how I could improve.* These two thinking styles lead to very different emotions. This chapter will help you manage emotions by learning how to replace thoughts that promote distressing emotions with calmer, more upbeat thoughts.

In the 1960s, a new form of treatment, cognitive therapy, was developed to help depressed people identify, challenge, and replace distressing thought patterns. Since that time, cognitive therapy has become a mainstream treatment for anxiety, post-traumatic stress disorder, low self-esteem, and many other stress-related conditions. When the skills of cognitive therapy are taught outside of clinical settings, as we'll do now, the method is called cognitive restructuring. This method has great utility for managing distressing emotions in everyday life.

The ABC model of cognitive restructuring developed by psychologist Albert Ellis is straightforward and logical:

$$A \longrightarrow B \longrightarrow C$$

Adversity   Beliefs (or self-talk)   Consequences

The A stands for "adversity," or a challenging situation. Most people think that A leads directly to C, emotional "consequences." In reality it is B, the "beliefs" or thoughts we tell ourselves, that has the greater influence.

Beliefs are sometimes called *automatic thoughts* because they arise so quickly that we hardly stop to notice them, let alone test them for reasonableness. When automatic thoughts are unreasonably negative, they are called *distortions*. (Psychiatrist Aaron Beck originated the terms automatic thoughts and distortions, originally described the distortions we'll discuss, and developed the daily thought record.) Distortions commonly cause or maintain stress symptoms. Because we are human and imperfect, we've all picked up some distorted thought patterns from family, friends, media, school, and so on. Through practice we can learn more productive ways of thinking—resulting in less emotional disturbance and better health and functioning.

The good news is that there are only a handful of distortions linked to everything from traumatic stress to everyday stress. When we get skilled at quickly recognizing our own distortions, challenging them, and replacing them, we gain much control over our emotions. This also helps to regulate arousal.

The Distortions

Here are the distortions, along with calmer replacement thoughts. Learn these distortions well, so that under pressure you can readily catch yourself using them and then quickly replace them with calmer, more functional thoughts.

Flaw fixation: Zooming in on what is wrong, or what went wrong, and ignoring the positive aspects (*All I can think about is my screwup. How can I enjoy this day when I messed up? Look at what you did wrong!*). Instead, try thinking more functionally: *I won't allow a negative element to overshadow all the good fortune around me.* Ask yourself: "Is it really the negative element that is ruining things for me, or my choice to dwell on it? What could I focus on that I enjoy? What would I see if I were having a better day? What *isn't* wrong?"

Dismissing the positive: Negating the positives that might otherwise lift your mood and self-esteem (for example, saying "Oh, anyone could have done that—it's no big deal," rather than "I did a good job under the circumstances."). Instead of "Yes, but I could have done better," say thanks, and think, *Yes, I really do deserve some credit for juggling so many demands, getting all these difficult tasks done, working hard, and getting some things right.* See which approach motivates you more.

Assuming (or jumping to conclusions without testing the evidence): There are two types of assuming.

- *Mind reading.* Instead of thinking *I know he's angry at me*, ask! Check it out with the other person. Think to yourself, *Maybe it isn't so; I won't know until I ask. Maybe there's another possibility.*

- *Fortune-telling.* Rather than predicting extremes—that you won't enjoy the party or that you'll do poorly—expect the middle ground. Think to yourself, *I won't know for sure until I experiment. I'll probably have some success and enjoyment, as opposed to none. I might even surprise myself.* If you tell yourself that things will never get better, try thinking, *They might.*

Labeling: Giving yourself or another a name or label, as though a single word could describe a complex person completely—"always" and in "every" case ("I *am* a dud"; "He *is* a loser"). Instead, rate behavior, not the person ("He is *driving* poorly"). Remind yourself that no one is always anything (dumb, rude, inept, and so forth), and the person is probably already suffering from her own faults. Ask yourself why someone's faults should bother you or why you should punish the person further by applying a label. Apply the same standard to yourself.

Overgeneralizing: Concluding that your negative experience applies to all situations ("I *always* flop"; "I *never* succeed"; "*Everybody* hates me—*nobody* loves me"; "*Nowhere* is safe"; "*Nothing* means anything"). When you draw conclusions like this, challenge yourself with questions: "What is the evidence that I never do well and always do poorly?" "What's the evidence that all people fit this negative profile?" Use words like "sometimes," "often," "generally," "usually," and "yet" ("I haven't mastered this *yet*"). Test the notion that you never do well; experiment and see how well you do (your *performance* is likely to be somewhere between 0 and 100).

All-or-none thinking: Evaluating yourself or others with extremes—allowing for no middle ground ("I'm a hero or a loser"; "I'm on top or a flop"). Instead, rate *performance* or *behavior*, not people ("I only batted .300 today—my *performance* wasn't so hot"). A baby has worth, even though he or she doesn't perform well. Ask yourself, "Why *must* I bat 1000?" Accept the fact that those who don't win gold medals are not worthless, just human. (In fact, it has been found that athletes who aim for an excellent job perform better than those who shoot for perfection.) Remember that all people have both strengths and weakness at the same time, and yet they still have worth. Enjoy the satisfaction of knowing you did your best, even if the outcome falls short of perfection.

Unfavorable comparison: Magnifying another's strengths and your weaknesses, while minimizing your strengths and another's weaknesses ("Bill is brilliant. I'm just average. Sure, he has a drinking problem and lots of people like me, but he's the one who *really* gets things done"). To counter this distortion, don't compare yourself with others. Allow that each person is different and contributes in unique ways according to unique strengths. The contribution of a frontline soldier; a nurse, or a homemaker is no less valuable than that of a commander, doctor, or CEO, it's just different.

Catastrophizing: Making things much worse than they really are. ("This is awful and horrible. It couldn't be worse. I can't stand this!") Instead, you might think: *Things really could be much worse, and I can bear this, even if I don't like the inconvenience. If I choose to face the difficulty of this challenge instead of avoiding it, I'll probably figure out a way to deal with it.* To counter catastrophizing, ask yourself questions: "What are the odds of this 'awful' thing happening? If it does happen, how likely is it to do me in? How well am I preparing for coping with this situation?" Remind yourself that you're probably coping somewhere in the middle, not at 0.

Emotional logic: Believing your feelings "prove" that things are as bad as they seem ("I feel too bad, inadequate, or tired to move. Therefore, I must be inadequate, incapable, unlovable, a loser," and so on). Remember that emotions are signals of upset, not statements of fact. Acknowledge the feelings, and remind yourself that feelings change. Think to yourself, *Isn't it interesting that I'm experiencing this strong emotion. Don't go ballistic. It might change with rest, exercise, time, or experience.* If you feel worthless or bad, try to put a number to the reality. For example, asking yourself, *What would 100 percent worthless or bad be?* helps you avoid all-or-none thinking.

Should statements: Making rigid, unchallenged demands of ourselves and the world (He *should* know better. He *must* not behave that way. I *ought* not to tire, be imperfect, get depressed, or be afraid and stressed about this.). Challenge this type of thinking: *At least some of the problem is my expectation that the world agree with my perfectionistic expectations. People really are just the way they should be, given their beliefs, distortions, experience, and upbringing, and it's foolish to demand they be otherwise. It would be nice if they were different, and maybe I could influence them to change. In fact, maybe I would motivate myself more effectively if I used more "woulds," "coulds," and "want-tos"* ("I *would like to* improve, and *want* to, rather than I *should*").

Personalizing: Seeing yourself as more responsible or involved than you really are ("It's all my fault that my son is failing in school"; "That guy is trying to irritate me"). Distinguish influences from causes. Look realistically for influences outside of yourself. Instead of thinking *What's wrong with me?* try thinking *The test was hard* or *I didn't prepare adequately* or *I was tired from working overtime*. In other words, focus on behavior and externals without judging yourself. Also, try to depersonalize ("Maybe I'm not the central figure in the other person's drama today").

Blaming: Putting all responsibility on externals, which makes us feel helpless ("This job is ruining my life and turning me cynical"; "I'm the way I am because of my crummy childhood"). Acknowledge outside influences, but take responsibility for your own welfare. ("Okay, I understand how these things have influenced me. Now I commit to get back on track and move on." Or, "Nothing makes me do anything—I choose how I respond.")

Did you notice any distortions that you frequently use? Were there any you've heard your family members use? Perhaps you could circle those distortions above that you commonly use or heard growing up.

Identify-and-Replace Drill

The first column in the following table lists thoughts that might go through your mind. As an exercise, cover up the second and third columns and see if you can first identify the distortion in the thought and why it's problematic, and then replace the original thought with a calm thought. The third column lists only some calm thoughts. There might be others. Working alone or with a partner, see if you can discover more options that might be useful under pressure.

Thought	Distortion and Comment	Calmer Replacement Thoughts
My worth equals my wages. (If I don't earn a certain amount, my worth is in question.)	**All-or-none thinking** This can lead to excessive overtime, which strains the family, or materialism, which is linked to depression.	My worth as a person is innate and independent of my salary.
It's awful to be mediocre.	**Catastrophizing** This can lead to fear-driven anxiety and perfectionism.	Half of all spouses, parents, cops, soldiers, and brain surgeons are below average. I'll be the best I can and not worry about keeping score.
I'm invincible.	**Labeling** (albeit a positive one) What happens when you realize you're not?	I'm a vulnerable, fallible human—and still capable of very good work.
A mistake means I'm inept.	**All-or-none thinking** It's impossible to live without making mistakes or upsetting people.	A mistake makes me human, just like the people I admire most. I'll do my best and not get too attached to the outcome.
Nobody can relate to what I've been through.	**Overgeneralizing** This isolates us and keeps us from allowing others to support us.	*Some* people might understand. Others might try and perhaps support me imperfectly.
God won't forgive me for what I did.	**Mind reading** This leads to hopelessness.	Where is that written?

Thought	Distortion and Comment	Calmer Replacement Thoughts
I should have stopped him from mistreating me.	**Should statement** This gives the illusion of control that we might not have.	I only have the power to do my personal best.
Either I protect all of my charges (family, troops, and so forth), or I'm a failure.	**All-or-none thinking** This can create unending sadness and self-recrimination.	I'll feel satisfaction in knowing that I do everything that I can to protect them, and I recognize that I can't control everything. Sometimes bad things happen despite all we try to do.
Your dissing me is personal.	**Personalizing** This increases anger.	Maybe this is more about his pain and less about me. I don't need to prove myself to him.
I'm not as capable or brave as Mary.	**Unfavorable comparison** Perhaps, but constant comparisons are exhausting.	Why compare? I have different strengths. It would be better to concentrate on doing *my* best, rather than being *the* best.
I can't bear to think about my friend's death.	**Catastrophizing** Then you might not ever grieve your loss and heal.	I'll carry on, and then deal with my grief later, when it's appropriate.
I feel so bad about what happened. I must have done something wrong.	**Emotional logic** This can lead to unreasonable guilt.	I feel *sad* about what happened, but I did my best.
That trauma screwed up my life.	**Blaming** This creates a helpless victim mentality.	That was a difficult time. I'm going to make the best of that experience.

My anger feels justified. It must be.	**Emotional logic** This allows the anger to persist.	Maybe I'm not justified in taking my anger out on everyone, or excusing my bad behavior.
I feel so anxious, I must be going crazy.	**Emotional logic** Even those who reach their breaking point usually recover with time and rest.	It's just a feeling. Feelings change.
I must not show fear. I should do better.	**Should statements** Fear happens. It's normal. Some fear might enhance judgment and performance. Judging the fear doesn't usually help.	Courage is acknowledging fear and then going ahead. Even if I freeze, I'll breathe and focus on what I intend to do. All I can do is my best.
To function effectively, I must smother all feelings.	**Should statements** It's not possible to smother feelings. Trying to do so wastes much energy.	I can acknowledge feelings, suppress or calm them when I must perform, and then deal with them later.
Either I'm the Energizer Bunny and put my children's needs first all the time, or I'm a bad mother.	**All-or-none thinking** This can be exhausting.	If I don't take care of my physical, emotional, and spiritual needs, I won't be of much use to anyone. I'll strike a balance between their needs and mine.
People always let you down.	**Overgeneralizing** This leads to pessimism and distrust.	*Sometimes* they don't.
It's my fault that my wife hasn't confided in me since she was assaulted—and that I can't help her.	**Personalizing** Many trauma survivors keep things inside for fear of being judged, or they confide only in those who can relate to what they experience.	She may be trying to spare me from worry, or she might fear rejection. I didn't cause her trauma and I can't fix it. I can only be as supportive as I can.

Activity: The Daily Thought Record

Remember that distortions pass through our minds automatically and habitually. We have to slow things down in order to catch and replace the distortions. When you feel disturbed by an event, try filling out a daily thought record—a core skill in cognitive restructuring.

On a sheet of paper, make a simplified daily thought record that looks like this. (Figure 5.1 shows a completed daily thought record. Visit http://www.newharbinger.com/39409 for a blank thought record, item 3, that you can photocopy.)

Adversity: _____

Consequences: _____

Thoughts	Distortions	Calmer Replacement Thoughts

First, at the top of the page, describe the adversity that triggered your distressing emotions. Then list the emotional consequences—all the feelings you experienced, such as sadness, anger, anxiety, guilt, or disgust. If you are using more than a single word, you're probably describing thoughts, not feelings. Rate each feeling from 1 to 10, with 10 being as distressing as possible.

In the thoughts column, list each upsetting thought that went through your mind during the event or goes through your mind now as you think about the event. If you find yourself writing questions, convert them to statements; it will be easier to identify distortions that way. When this is done, in the middle column label each distortion that you identify. In the third column, write a calmer replacement thought for each distortion. Then rerate the emotional consequences to see if their intensity decreased somewhat. Even a small shift in intensity is meaningful and can spell the difference between being disturbed (for example, clinical depression or overwhelming sadness) versus feeling upset (such as appropriate sadness).

You can fill out this record at the end of the day, or any other time when things settle down. It can be very effective to try this in pairs, with a partner asking questions, such as "What happened?" "How did that 'make you' feel?" "What thoughts went through your mind?" "And what else went through your mind?" "Are any of these thoughts possibly distortions?" "Could this thought possibly be a _____ distortion?" Your partner can then help brainstorm replacement thoughts. In this partner exercise, both individuals get better at replacing distortions with calmer thoughts.

Figure 5.1: Simplified daily thought record

Adversity: __The boss unfairly reprimanded me and reassigned me.__

Consequences: __Angry 10 → 7; worried 9 → 6; afraid 7 → 5; frustrated 6 → 4__

Thoughts	Distortions	Calmer Replacement Thoughts
I'm consumed by the boss's unfairness, to the exclusion of the good things about him and the agency. It's all I can think about.	Flaw fixation	What's left? I can still enjoy other aspects of my life and job.
He shouldn't be that way.	Should statement	He is as he is. It would be nice if he were different, but I'll make myself crazy by getting stuck on the unfairness.
He's messing up my life. I'm going to stop trying. I'll get even.	Blaming	I won't justify my cynicism or bad behaviors by blaming him. The effects of cynicism and loss of integrity will live on long after I retire.
He has it in for me.	Personalizing	Maybe he doesn't.
I can't stand this!	Catastrophizing	It will be an adjustment to get used to this new assignment. I'll view it as a challenge to do some good in a difficult environment.

Getting to the Bottom of Things: Core Beliefs

According to cognitive theorists, replacing distortions lessens psychological *symptoms*, but the *cure* for emotional disturbance is replacing what are called *core beliefs*. Core beliefs typically are acquired early in life, lead to the common distortions, and come in three varieties:

1. I'm incapable (inadequate, incompetent, inept, powerless, out of control).

2. I'm worthless (unworthy, bad, of no value, useless, flawed).

3. I'm not lovable (because I wasn't loved in the past).

For example, Jann was constantly told by an abusive parent that she was trash by the side of the road. To compensate for the painful feelings this caused her, Jann became a driven overachiever. Her thoughts were: *It's awful to fail. I must not show weakness. I should be perfect.* Sadly, her driven pursuit of perfection did not relieve the pain or self-doubt caused by her unchallenged core beliefs.

Core beliefs are uncovered by investigating a distorted automatic thought. For example, Jann chose to work with the persistent thought *I should be perfect*, asking herself questions, such as

"What does that mean?" (Answer: "I can't make a mistake.")

"And what would that mean?" (Answer: "People will think less of me. They'll reject me.")

"Assuming that's true, why would that be so bad? What does that say about me?" (Answer: "I am inadequate.")

Perhaps you noticed the mind reading and overgeneralizing distortions that became evident in the questioning process. By questioning her thought, Jann uncovered the core belief *I am* (meaning always and in every way) *inadequate*, which she could then challenge. She might, for example, identify times in the past when she showed considerable competence in difficult situations. She might also consider her likable traits, and the fact that many imperfect people are nevertheless loved in a healthy way.

Try to uncover your core beliefs. From a completed daily thought record, pick a particularly troubling thought, and ask yourself questions until you ultimately get to the question, "What does that say about me?" This usually leads to the core belief. Then challenge both the core belief and the initial responses to your questions. It can be very useful to do this exercise with a partner, as both of you can gain mastery from the practice.

Conclusion

Isn't it interesting that only about a dozen distortions cause so much trouble! Once we take the time to notice them, we can persistently replace them with more reasonable thoughts, resulting in less emotional disturbance. This is a skill that anyone can master with practice.

Chapter 6

Mindfulness

Cognitive restructuring is helpful for nearly everyone who tries it. However, there are times when reason alone is insufficient to soothe troubling emotions. For these situations, there is a complementary skill that, like cognitive restructuring, helps reduce emotional and physical distress across a wide range of conditions. This skill is called *mindfulness*, and it works in a very different way.

In 1979 Dr. Jon Kabat-Zinn introduced mindfulness to Western medicine. As the director of the Stress Reduction Clinic at the University of Massachusetts Medical School (now the Center for Mindfulness), he was sent patients with diverse medical conditions who were not responding to traditional medical treatments. Treating them with what he called mindfulness-based stress reduction, he found that psychological and medical symptoms of suffering decreased by 30 percent, irrespective of patient diagnoses. Since that time, mindfulness training has been taught in psychology and medical centers, universities, and even prisons throughout America and around the world. And evidence has shown that mindful people seem to have a better ability to manage strong negative emotions.

Although mindfulness comes to us from Eastern psychology, it easily blends with nearly everyone's perspective. Mindfulness assumes that each of us is of two minds (see figure 6.1). The wisdom mind, sometimes called our true happy nature, is who we really are at our core. The wisdom mind is kind, wise, calm, patient, cheerful, and hopeful—the traits we associate with resilience. The ordinary mind surrounds and camouflages our wisdom mind, keeping us from experiencing our true happy nature and causing much suffering. Swirling, racing, effortful thoughts (signified by the arrows in figure 6.1) characterize the ordinary mind, which obsesses, worries, plans, ruminates, stews, hurries, judges, resists pain, and fights against the way the world is (*Why do I have this pain? I can't stand it. I have to stop it. What if it doesn't end?*). Such thoughts lead to anxiety, depression, anger, greed, and other troubling emotions. When we say that someone is beside herself (with worry, anger, and so forth), we are saying that she is pulled away from her true happy nature and locked in a battle in the ordinary mind. In the mindfulness view, the thoughts are the problem. The more we engage or fight the thoughts, the more distressed we become. The mindfulness solution is to simply acknowledge distressing thoughts and then go underneath them, returning to our peaceful, natural happy state. A thought is just a thought. It's not necessarily true, and it needn't be given excessive attention.

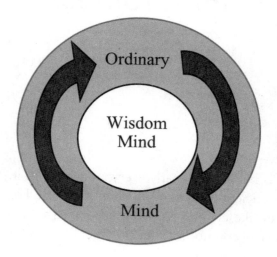

Figure 6.1: The dual nature of the mind

Cognitive restructuring counterpunches, or fights back, against the distortions that lead to emotional distress. For example, one might counter the thought *I'm inadequate* by marshaling evidence for competence. Yet sometimes fighting thoughts can create more tension. Can you imagine what might happen if instead of fighting against the distressing emotion, you simply sat with that emotion and soothed it, much like a loving parent would embrace and soothe an injured, crying child? Eventually the ache diminishes, and the child returns to play. This suggests how mindfulness will teach you a new way to respond to distress.

The Mindfulness Attitudes

In certain Eastern cultures, the word for "mind" is the same as the word for "heart." Mindfulness training cultivates attitudes of the heart. Here are six of the most essential attitudes.

Compassion: This means sorrow for the suffering of others, plus the desire to help and to soothe the pain. In the context of mindfulness, "compassion" also means that we feel the same way toward our own pain. All that is done in mindfulness brings kind, gentle, friendly awareness to each moment of suffering—and to each pleasant moment as well.

Curious, nonjudgmental equanimity: In the West, we typically dislike pain. We often judge and label it as bad and use painkillers to try to escape it. This battle typically increases the pain. In mindfulness practice, we simply observe the pain without judging it as good or bad. We simply watch it the same way we might watch a pleasant emotion. This stance—changing only our *response* to pain—often helps to diminish the intensity of the pain.

Acceptance: This means simply acknowledging the way things are in the moment, without immediately trying to fix, change, or fight them. The attitude of acceptance says, "Whatever I feel is okay. Let me feel it." In dropping the battle with emotions, the emotional intensity often shifts. Not that you try to make this happen. You simply notice what shifts.

Vastness: The wisdom mind is broad and deep enough to take in your suffering. You might liken the wisdom mind to the vast ocean. From the depths of the ocean, the wisdom mind watches suffering rise and fall like the waves on the surface. The ocean absorbs the suffering without being changed by the suffering. Likewise, you can embrace suffering without fear or tension, knowing that it comes and goes, and you are vast enough to cope with it.

Good humor: Much of our suffering comes from being overly serious. We approach mindfulness with an almost playful, cheerful attitude.

Beginner's mind: Experts assume they already know, and so learn little. Like a child, the beginner is open to learning from new experiences. With mindfulness, we remain open to new attitudes and to experiencing our true happy nature. We approach mindfulness practice with the attitude that it might be beneficial, rather than pessimistically assuming it won't be.

The Mindfulness Training Sequence

Imagine that you have chronic pain and are beginning an eight-week mindfulness training. You are first asked to slowly eat a raisin and do nothing else. You might notice that thoughts flood your mind: *What does a raisin have to do with easing my pain? I don't like raisins—Mom put them in my oatmeal. I hate oatmeal. I wonder what's for lunch. I have things on my to-do list.* These thoughts pull you out of the moment to the extent that you don't experience eating the raisin. If you simply notice the thoughts without judging them, and gently bring your attention back to eating the raisin, you might notice rich flavors and other sensations you usually miss when hurriedly eating raisins. You might also notice that you are more relaxed when you pay attention to the physical sensations of eating—just calmly noticing without judging or reacting with strong distressing emotions. In other words, you are beginning to experience the essence of mindfulness practice.

Next, you're taught mindful breathing. Without actually trying to make anything happen, you practice simply watching yourself breathe. With beginner's mind, you notice that each breath is unique. You notice changes in your body as you rest in the breath. When the mind wanders, or thoughts arise, you practice simply noticing, without judging, and gently escorting attention back to the breath. You might notice how calming it is to rest in the breath and to cease fighting against thoughts that come and go.

Then the body scan skill teaches you to simply notice what the body is sensing, without judging particular sensations as good or bad. You're taught to breathe into body regions, and then gently move awareness around the body in a curious way. You continue to practice responding with equanimity to thoughts that arise, returning awareness to the body. Both mindful breathing and the body scan teach you to rest in the body, beneath the distressing thoughts.

These and other skills are blended into the powerful meditation that follows, sitting with distressing emotions, which is a new way to respond to intense negative emotions and to take care of yourself. If this meditation seems useful, you might continue to practice it, or seek additional training (see "Mindfulness" in the recommended resources).

Activity: Sitting with Distressing Emotions

This meditation teaches us to be calm and nonreactive in the presence of whatever emotions arise, be they pleasant or unpleasant. Rather than trying to fight or suppress pain, we turn gently toward pain with kind awareness—relaxing and softening into it. Softening our response changes the way we experience pain. It is recommended that you practice this meditation for thirty minutes or more each day for at least a week.

1. **Assume the meditator's posture, sitting comfortably erect, with feet flat on the floor and hands resting comfortably in the lap.** The spine is straight like a stack of golden coins. The upper body is relaxed but comfortably erect, sitting in graceful dignity like a majestic mountain. (The dignified mountain is secure and unchanged, despite the changing conditions around it.) Allow your eyes to close. Let your breathing help you to settle into your peaceful wisdom mind.

2. **Remember especially the attitudes of compassion, acceptance, good humor, and vastness.** Remember that you are already whole. Use the beginner's mind as you explore a new way to experience feelings.

3. **Be aware of your breathing.** For several minutes let your belly be soft and relaxed, paying attention to its rise and fall as you breathe in and out. Notice the movements and sensations in the abdomen, chest, nose, throat, and rib cage. For example, you might notice the rising and stretching of your abdomen on the in-breath, or the air flowing in and out of your nostrils. Just notice, without judging or trying to make anything happen. Just allow whatever is happening to happen as you rest in the breath, noticing with kind curiosity. And when thoughts arise, just notice them, then gently, patiently, and repeatedly bring awareness back to your breathing.

4. **Be aware of any feeling in your body, any sensation as it comes and goes, without judging or trying to change it.** For example, you might notice where your leg meets the chair, or where your hands rest in your lap. Pick a region, such as the belly. Breathe into and out of that region. Imagine that your mind is resting in that region. Just notice what you sense, without judgments, such as *I don't like discomfort.* Simply notice sensations with kind acceptance and allowance. Sometimes sensations change when we bring kind awareness to them—they come and go. Nevertheless, just watch what happens without trying to make something happen. When you are ready, take a more intentional in-breath, breathe out, and then let attention dissolve from that area as you bring attention to another region of your body, such as your chest. Notice what you sense in the region around your chest. If there is any discomfort or anxiety, simply notice that. Breathe into that area. Think of your breath as carrying kindness and acceptance to that area. Breathe into and out of that area, just noticing the changing sensations in that area. When you are ready, take a more intentional in-breath, breathing into that area. On the out-breath, let awareness of that area dissolve as you bring awareness to another area of your body, such as your hand. Breathe into and out of that area, just noticing what you sense in that area. When you are ready, take a more intentional in-breath, and as you breathe out let awareness shift to your body as a whole.

5. **Whenever you find your mind wandering, congratulate yourself for noticing this.** This is just what the ordinary mind does. Remember that thoughts are just thoughts and not who you are, and bring your awareness gently back to breathing and sensing your body. You are not trying to stop your thoughts, only to notice them calmly and then gently escort awareness back to your breathing and body.

6. **And now recall a difficult situation, perhaps involving work or a relationship, and the feelings that arise, such as unworthiness, inadequacy, sadness, or worry about the future.** Make a space for this situation. Give deep attention to these feelings. *Whatever* you are feeling is all right. Greet these feelings cordially, as you would greet an old friend.

7. **Notice where in the body you feel the feelings.** It could be your stomach, chest, or throat, for example. Let yourself feel the feelings completely, with full acceptance. Don't think *I'll tighten up and let these feelings in for a minute in order to get rid of them.* This is not full acceptance. Rather, create a space that allows you to completely accept the feelings.

8. **Breathe into that region of the body with great compassion.** Think of fresh air and sunlight entering a long-ignored and darkened room. Follow your breath all the way down through the nose, throat, lungs, and then to the part of the body where you

sense the distressing emotion or emotions. Then follow the breath out of your body, until you find yourself settling. You might think of a kind, loving, accepting smile as you do this. Don't try to change or push the discomfort away. Don't brace yourself against or struggle with it. Just embrace it without judging it—with real acceptance, deep attention, peace, and the goodwill and kind feelings toward all people that are known as *loving-kindness*. Let the body soften and open around that area. The wisdom mind is vast enough to hold these feelings with great compassion; love is big enough to embrace, welcome, and penetrate the discomfort. Let your breath caress and soothe the feelings as you would your adored sleeping baby.

9. **Remember that you are vast enough to embrace the pain with kindness.** If you find it helpful, think of loved ones who remind you of loving-kindness—and let that loving-kindness penetrate your awareness as you remember that difficult situation. Simply notice what happens to the feelings without trying to change them.

10. **When you are ready, take a deeper breath into that area of the body, and as you exhale, widen your focus to your body as a whole.** Pay attention to your whole body's breathing, being aware of the wholeness and the vast, unlimited compassion of the wisdom mind that will hold any pain that comes and goes. Expand your attention to the sounds you are hearing, just bringing them into awareness without commenting or judging. Simply listen with a half smile. Feel the air against your body; sense your whole body breathing. Notice all that you are aware of with a soft and open heart.

11. **To conclude, say the following intentions silently to yourself:** "May I remember loving-kindness. May I be happy. May I be whole."

12. **Be mindful of what you are now experiencing.** With curiosity and good humor, just notice how your body feels. What emotions are you feeling? Is there calmness, peace, or a feeling of being settled? Are you upset? Whatever you feel, it's okay. Just let yourself be aware.

If you are interested in exploring mindfulness further, you might read *10 Simple Solutions for Building Self-Esteem* (Schiraldi 2007), from which this meditation was adapted, or consult other mindfulness aids in the recommended resources section.

Activity: Sitting with Core Beliefs

Cognitive restructuring, described in chapter 5, taught you a way to uncover and dispute distressing core beliefs. This can often be very helpful. However, core beliefs typically are embedded in our minds in the early years and might be difficult to completely soothe with logic. Mindfulness teaches a different way to deal with distressing core beliefs that relies more on the heart than the head.

Let's say that your core belief is *I'm inadequate*. This is normal. Nearly everyone feels that way at times. No one likes to feel that way, of course. So you might get locked in a battle against that thought, thinking *I'm not inadequate. That's too painful a thought. I can't let anyone know I feel that way. I'll become so competent that no one will ever accuse me of being inadequate.* Or you might simply keep thinking about reasons why you are capable. Perhaps the core belief originated when you were criticized severely as a child. As an adult, the battle continues, along with much distress.

Mindfulness assumes that the thought *I am inadequate* is just a thought that we fight in the ordinary mind. What would happen if you were to simply allow that thought to be without fighting it? What would happen if you were to notice where in your body you sense the emotion linked to that thought and embraced the emotion with compassion? Can you see that this approach changes only your *response* to the situation? Paradoxically, this approach cultivates a security that allows us to grow, unencumbered by the exhausting mental battle.

For this activity, select a troubling core belief, such as *I'm inadequate*, *I'm unlovable*, or *I'm worthless*. Rather than fighting thinking with thinking, drop the fight against the core belief. You'll notice where in your body you experience the core belief (or more correctly, the associated emotion). You'll breathe into the discomfort without judging it, and then you'll let awareness of the discomfort dissolve. As you fail to react emotionally but respond compassionately, the neural pathways associated with negative thoughts and feelings degrade through disuse. Instead you'll strengthen the pathways associated with the wisdom mind. Practice this meditation for several times over the next few days, and notice what happens.

1. **Sit comfortably in the meditator's posture, sitting comfortably erect, with feet flat on the floor and hands resting comfortably in your lap.** Breathe softly, resting in the wisdom mind.

2. **Bring the core belief into kind awareness.** Without judging the thought, simply notice where you sense the thought and associated feelings in your body, and breathe into that area with loving-kindness and complete acceptance.

3. **Occasionally, if it is helpful, mindfully remind yourself:**

   It's just a thought.

   Holding that thought in kind awareness.

   Feeling compassion.

4. **Keep breathing into the area of the body where you sense the thought.** Take your time, breathing into the area until you are ready to release your awareness of that area.

5. **Take a deeper, more intentional breath into that area.** On the out-breath, let awareness of that area dissolve as you become aware of your environment. Or, shift to the smile meditation (this meditation can be found with item 9 at http://www.newharbinger.com/39409).

Conclusion

Mindfulness offers a refreshing alternative to the battles we often fight with our thoughts. Paradoxically, by kindly accepting whatever we feel, we find that the intensity of negative feelings often subsides. The next three chapters offer specific applications for bringing kind acceptance and awareness to difficult circumstances.

Chapter 7

Self-Compassion

This chapter explains how to use the skill of self-compassion, a short and simple way to deal with difficult emotions and suffering. It extends the practice of mindfulness in a way that softens and helps us bounce back from the pain of personal setbacks.

Do you tend to be hard on yourself? When you encounter difficult times—making a mistake; failing to achieve a goal; being mistreated, rejected, or harshly criticized—are you highly self-critical? Do you fixate on what's wrong with you and drive yourself to immediately "fix it"? Do you beat yourself up with harsh self-talk in order to keep yourself in line and motivate yourself to do better? Is the way you treat yourself perhaps reminiscent of the way you were treated in the past?

We think we protect and motivate ourselves with such a stern stance. Research is finding, however, that a kinder approach is less stressful and leads to greater growth and resilience.

Dr. Kristin Neff has led the way in self-compassion research. She explains that *self-compassion* is the Golden Rule in reverse—that is, treating yourself as you would treat a loved one or a good friend when the chips are down and bringing understanding and kindness to difficult times. Three components comprise self-compassion (Neff 2011):

- **Mindful awareness of distressing emotions:** In a calm, nonreactive way, we simply notice what is going on inside of us in the moment. There are no judgments, only acceptance. We actively turn toward the pain, which is the only way we can heal the pain. This is similar to the mindfulness principles we discussed in the previous chapter. To these Dr. Neff adds the two following unique features.

- **Sense of common humanity:** This is the realization that we all suffer; we're all in the same boat. Walk down any street and behind every door we will find suffering. Each of us yearns to be happy and to not suffer, yet we all stumble at times. We all feel the pain of disappointed dreams, our own imperfections, or the loss of goodwill. Understanding this, we feel a bond with others and realize we are not being singled out. This helps to put our suffering into perspective. We feel less isolated.

- **Being kind to and supportive of yourself:** Rather than harsh criticism or self-condemnation for being imperfect, we respond to our own pain with deep caring, patience, understanding, warmth, and encouragement. It is the stance that says, "You are not alone; I am here for you." It is more motivating to lead with a carrot than a stick. Fear does not lead to the best performance and growth in the long run.

Can you think for a moment about the kind, caring feelings you might feel toward a close friend who lost a loved one? Or a person on the side of the road, injured in an accident? A dear family member who was humiliated by another? A suffering child? Can you imagine directing this type of kindness toward yourself when times are tough? What would that feel like? The following skill, adapted from Dr. Kristin Neff's excellent website, http://www.self-compassion.org, is very effective for difficult times that trigger emotional pain or suffering.

Activity: Self-Compassion

1. **Select a moderately difficult event from the past that triggered emotional distress, such as sadness, anger, frustration, shame, self-criticism, rejection, isolation, and so on.** (Once you gain comfort with this skill, you can try it with more upsetting situations, or with situations as they occur.)

2. **Permit yourself to bring into full awareness all the difficult emotions and sensations.** Don't brace against them or try to push them away. Just allow them in with a soft and open heart, remembering this phrase: "Whatever it is, let me feel it." Place your hands warmly over a part of your body that holds the pain, such as your heart or abdomen. As you breathe in, imagine that compassion flows down your body and penetrates and soothes the area that holds the pain. Notice the sensations as you breathe, such as the rising and falling of your abdomen and chest.

3. **With a soft and kind facial expression, perhaps like that of a loving parent, slowly and deliberately repeat these four statements, either silently or aloud:**

This is a moment of suffering.

Suffering is a part of life.

May I be kind to myself in this moment.

May I give myself the compassion I need.

4. **Repeat the four statements several more times.** As you continue to notice your breathing, feel soothing understanding and kindness filling your heart and body with each breath.

5. **When you have finished, notice if the present moment is somewhat less distressing than a few moments ago.** Paradoxically, sometimes this happens when we don't try to make it happen.

Activity: Practicing Self-Compassion Statements

Memorize these four statements so you can say them in any difficult situation: (1) This is a moment of suffering; (2) Suffering is a part of life; (3) May I be kind to myself in this moment; (4) May I give myself the compassion I need. Notice that the first statement refers to mindful awareness, the second to one's sense of common humanity, and the last two to being kind to and supportive of yourself. If you prefer, you can replace some of these statements with those of your own choosing, such as those in the following table (Neff 2011).

Mindful Awareness	Sense of Common Humanity	Being Kind to and Supportive of Yourself
This is really difficult, and I'm in need of care. Yes, there is pain. This is hard for me right now.	Many others have suffered like this. Suffering is part of being human. It is normal to feel this way.	May I bring kindness and caring to this pain. I'm so sorry you're in pain. May I be as understanding with myself as possible. May I accept myself as I am.

Try using the four statements you've chosen in response to difficult situations you encounter during the week, following the five-step pattern described in the "Self-Compassion" activity. You might record your experience on the log in appendix C.

Conclusion

The self-compassion skill builds upon mindfulness meditation, in that you place your hand over the area of the body that holds emotional pain, and then repeat four self-compassion statements: one that acknowledges and locates the pain, one that reminds you that we are all in the same boat, and two that offer you kind support. This skill offers a kind, gentle way to navigate difficult life circumstances.

Chapter 8

Expressive Writing

Are you troubled by memories of difficult times? Do you worry over current concerns? This chapter will explore another very useful strategy: using writing to help settle negatively charged memories and worries. You might think of expressive writing as experiencing compassion through journaling. This strategy involves more verbalizing than those in the previous two chapters do.

The Effects of Unresolved Trauma and Emotional Upheavals

Research has clearly shown that old emotional wounds don't necessarily heal with time. Left unresolved, they can exert an influence that affects present health and functioning. For example, the number of adverse childhood experiences is directly correlated with an adult's likelihood of suffering from obesity, diabetes, heart disease, depression, suicide attempts, tobacco and intravenous drug use, alcoholism, unintended pregnancy, and poor job performance (Felitti 2002). Often we focus on the smoke (the psychological, medical, or functional symptoms) without addressing the flame (the underlying emotional wounds). Recognizing the relationship between childhood trauma and suffering in adulthood offers people a great opportunity to heal.

Writing What's Wrong

The psychologist James W. Pennebaker (1997) reasoned that "keeping it all inside" was not healthy. He asked various groups, ranging from students to survivors of the Holocaust, the San Francisco earthquake, the Gulf War, and job firings, to simply write about their most difficult adversities. He instructed them to put down their deepest thoughts *and* feelings surrounding the event, writing continuously for fifteen to thirty minutes for four days. Pennebaker was surprised by the number of traumas experienced by people who appeared "normal" on the outside. The traumas were wide ranging, from rape, physical and sexual abuse, suicide attempts, and accidentally causing deaths to being blamed for parents' divorces. People were least likely to confide childhood traumas—especially sexual traumas—but those were also the ones most likely to cause illness later in life. Understandably, moods slipped during the four days of writing. But afterward, those who confided in writing showed better physical and psychological health. They showed less depression, anxiety, and stress and experienced greater self-esteem, stronger immunity, and fewer illnesses. Those who wrote about losing their jobs found new employment more quickly.

Pennebaker and Smyth (2016) and other researchers have linked writing about past adversities to improved sleep, job satisfaction, memory, and grades and reductions in pain, fatigue, general distress, PTSD symptoms, arthritis, and asthma. Undisclosed wounds that are not processed and expressed verbally often intrude painfully into awareness and are expressed in bodily and psychological symptoms, including nightmares. They also compete with attentional resources, interfering with daily functioning. Slowing down to put painful memories into words helps the brain organize, neutralize, complete, and settle them. People who write about their troubling memories often report that they understand them better and are less troubled by them, finding it easier to move on. The process is like opening a bullet wound in order to help it drain and heal. People realize that they can express their feelings, even with tears, and then return to a stronger "normal."

Confiding in writing seems to particularly help those who have never told anyone about a distressing event (for example, for fear of embarrassment or punishment) but wish they could have. Keeping secrets is fatiguing and tends to isolate people. You might try confiding in writing for any past trauma or adversity that still troubles you, including the loss of a loved one, a breakup, moving, a parents' divorce, or anything else you'd like to forget, avoid, or resolve. It is comforting to realize that we can confront what we have run from, and in so doing overcome our aversion to the memories.

The following guidelines for disclosing in writing are adapted, with permission, from Dr. Pennebaker's website (https://liberalarts.utexas.edu/psychology/faculty/pennebak#writing -health).

1. **Preparing to write.** Find a neutral place to write where you won't make unwanted associations. Ideally, pick a time at the end of your workday or before you go to bed. Promise yourself that you will write for a minimum of fifteen minutes a day (fifteen to thirty minutes usually works well) for at least three or four consecutive days. Write continuously, and don't worry about spelling or grammar. Ideally, you should write about something you have not talked about with others in detail. If you run out of things to write about, just repeat what you have already written. You can write with a pen or pencil or type on a computer. If you are unable to write, talk into an audio recorder. You can write about the same thing each day or something entirely different. It is up to you.

2. **Choosing a topic.** What's affecting your life in an unhealthy way? Have you been avoiding something for days, weeks, or years? Do you dream about something from the past regularly? What are you thinking or worrying about? Choose one topic or write about them all.

3. **Writing.** Here are the instructions generally given in Dr. Pennebaker's research.

   Over the next four days, I want you to write about your deepest emotions and thoughts about the most upsetting experience in your life. [Start by describing the facts, then the emotions and thoughts.] Really let go and explore your feelings and thoughts about it. In your writing, you might tie this experience to your childhood, your relationship with your parents, people you have loved or love now, or even your career. How is this experience related to who you would like to become, who you have been in the past, or who you are now?

   Many people have not had a single traumatic experience, but all of us have had major conflicts or stressors in our lives and you can write about them as well. You can write about the same issue every day or a series of different issues. Whatever you choose to write about, however, it is critical that you really let go and explore your very deepest emotions and thoughts.

   Warning: Many people report that after writing, they sometimes feel somewhat sad or depressed. Like seeing a sad movie, this typically goes away in a couple of hours [or more rarely, a day or two]. If you find that you are getting extremely upset about a writing topic, simply stop writing or change topics.

4. **What to do with your writing samples.** The writing is for you and for you only. Its purpose is for you to be completely honest with yourself. When writing, secretly plan to throw away your writing when you are finished. Whether you keep it or save it is really up to you. Some people keep their samples and edit them. That is, they gradually change their writing from day to day. Others simply keep them and return to them over and over again to see how they have changed. If you wish, you might burn or erase your writing, or tear it into little pieces and flush them or throw them into the ocean or let the wind take them away.

Tips for Expressive Writing

In addition to the basic writing guidelines, these considerations might also be useful. They are adapted from the writings of Pennebaker and his colleagues (Pennebaker 1997, Pennebaker and Evans 2014, Pennebaker and Smyth 2016)

Use a rich range of emotions, both negative and positive, as you write. Naming emotions calms the amygdala. Rather than using slang, try to name genuine feelings (for example, "sad," "disappointed," "hurt," "humiliated," "lonely," "angry," "caring," "eager," "excited"). You might find that using statements such as "I feel like my world shattered," or "I was so scared that…" helps you more fully describe your feelings. If you are not used to expressing emotions, you might experiment to see if this technique becomes more comfortable with practice.

Try to understand why you feel as you do. Try to add insight words (for example, "realize," "know," "understand") and causal words (for example, "reason," "because") to your writing, which encourage reflective thinking.. The benefits are greater when expressing emotions is tied to reflective thinking.

It is good to write about adversities that you can't control. This is especially true if you can accept having imperfect control. However, don't use writing as a substitute for action, when change is possible, or for needed professional help. Note that expressive writing can be a useful complement to therapy.

If you feel distressed after writing, remember to try the strategies you have learned so far. For example, abdominal breathing, body-based skills, progressive muscle relaxation, heart coherence, eye movements, or thought field therapy can help you reduce your stress.

Remember, if writing is overly distressing, ease up. Approach the event gradually or write about a different topic.

On the fourth or fifth day, you might discuss in writing how you have benefited or could still benefit from the adversity. What good can come out of this experience? What lessons have you learned? What advice would you give an imaginary friend dealing with a similar adversity? Were there bright spots in the darkness? Did you somehow persevere and show certain strengths? Did you or others demonstrate nobility of character? Could you give the story a new twist? For example, could the event signal a new beginning with a positive ending?

If writing about a traumatic event doesn't help, see a mental health professional who specializes in treating trauma. A trauma specialist will help you learn other healing strategies (see the recommended resources). As with the other techniques in this book, you might also seek the help of a mental health professional if you feel that remembering the event might be too overwhelming.

Don't push yourself. If your life is chaotic, or if the upsetting event is very recent or raw, you may wish to wait until things settle down before trying expressive writing. Instead, try exercising or using the other skills you've learned so far.

Be your own scientist to find your best writing schedule. You may prefer writing for four consecutive days. Others may prefer writing once a week for four weeks.

Writing about present-day concerns (worries) has also been found to be very useful. If simply trying to relax and stop worrying isn't working, try writing about what is worrying you (describing the facts) and what you are feeling and thinking. During the day, postpone worrying until your next "worry period," when you can write about your worries for about thirty minutes.

Conclusion

The bottom line is this: If you want to reduce distress, try keeping a journal that no one but you will see. Write down the facts, thoughts, and feelings regarding either past adversities or present worries. It is rare for such a simple, inexpensive strategy to be so effective. Remember to add this tool to your coping toolbox.

Chapter 9

Managing Distressing Dreams

Recurring nightmares are common in people who have experienced emotional upheavals or traumas. For example, even the well-adjusted WWII veterans that I interviewed still struggled with nightmares of liberating the concentration camps decades after the war ended. Many veterans with PTSD still have several nightmares a week decades after returning from combat. You might have frequent, troubling nightmares related to any number of difficult experiences, and this chapter will help you manage them.

Nightmares simply signal that there is memory material that the mind is trying to sort out. Normally, dreams help the brain process and settle distressing memory material. However, for extremely distressing experiences, dreams can get stuck, replaying without change or resolution.

Recurring nightmares disrupt sleep, leaving people fatigued and less effective the next day. They trip the stress response and increase cortisol secretion, which further affect mood, memory, and performance. Many who suffer from nightmares begin to fear going to sleep, resulting in insomnia. The combination of disrupted sleep and the distress caused by nightmares can increase the risk of several stress-related conditions.

Settling Nightmares

Fortunately, there are steps you can take to change nightmares and lessen their negative impact. In this chapter we'll explore a five-step process that might help you settle your nightmares.

1. **Normalize your nightmares.** Think of your nightmares as simply distressing memory material that needs to be processed and settled, not avoided. The helpful principle is to bring all aspects of the nightmare into calm awareness, changing both your response to the nightmare and the nightmare itself. It can be reassuring to realize that your nightmares contain themes similar to those of others who have experienced difficult experiences. Dream researchers have described the following common themes in nightmares (Barrett 1996):

- Danger, terror, death, fear of death

- Being chased

- Being rescued

- Monsters (who might chase, harm, or frighten you)

- Revenge

- Being punished

- Being alone

- Being trapped, powerless, helpless, or confused (for example, freezing and being unable to fight back or protect yourself; being unable to find a weapon or the weapon doesn't work; being lost)

- Physical injury (for example, losing teeth might symbolize losing control or being wounded emotionally)

- Filth, garbage, excrement (might symbolize disgust, shame, loss of dignity or meaning in life, or evil)

- Sexual themes (for example, following abuse one might dream of good or bad sex, shadowy figures, worms, snakes going into holes, blood, shame, disgust, anger, hurting the assailant, being shunned)

- Violence, gore, killing, injury

- Being threatened again by a person or event that harmed you

2. Confide your dreams. Recall from chapter 8 that verbalizing, telling the story in words, helps to neutralize, integrate, and settle difficult memories. In this step, you bring your dream to conscious awareness so it can be processed and completed. You might describe your nightmare to a supportive person or an audio recorder or write about it in a journal kept beside your bed. The goal is to fully describe all the elements of the nightmare so it has a beginning, middle, and end. Relax and describe the following details:

- Facts (What is the setting? Who are the characters? What is happening? What are you doing? What are the symbols and what are they saying?)

- Feelings (What are you feeling?)

- Thoughts (What are you thinking?)

- Sensations (What are your physical sensations?)

3. Rehearse a different, calmer response. For example, instead of feeling terror, you might imagine calming yourself in the dream by kneading your forearm, breathing slowly, and saying to yourself, "This is just a dream. I'm safe now." Before going to sleep, mentally rehearse this new response so that it is in place should the dream recur.

4. Change the nightmare in any way that feels right. You might give it a new ending. You might imagine finishing business—saying farewell to those who died and seeing them now in heaven, smiling. You might imagine healing the severely injured by moving your hand over injured limbs (anything is possible in imagery). You might see yourself being rescued or protected by good and powerful people. Perhaps you stop and turn toward the monster chasing you and make friends with it. You will know what is needed. The only caution is to not include violence in your new ending, because it does not usually settle nightmares. Write or draw how you want to change your dream; then mentally rehearse the new dream for about fifteen minutes at least once a day for a week.

5. Expect changes in dream content. As you rehearse different responses and changes to nightmares, you'll likely notice shifts in your dream content. Perhaps your dreams of deceased people now contain assurances that they are well off. Or perhaps your dreams now have more positive outcomes. Maybe you realize you did your best under difficult circumstances and now feel somewhat better or brighter about the future.

An Example of Processing Dreams

The following example demonstrates how nightmares can be processed. This case combines the use of drawing with verbal expression. Art can be a very helpful medium for processing dreams in that it can tap feelings, thoughts, sensations, and even creative solutions that might be difficult to capture initially with words. And once the dream is captured on paper, it is often easier to talk about it "out there" at a distance.

One couple hadn't slept throughout the night for four years because their otherwise well-adjusted nine-year-old son Jake burst into their room each night, terrified by nightmares. The boy had merely seen a commercial for a scary movie, but he could not be comforted; he had to sleep in his parents' bedroom with the lights on. When I asked the boy to draw his nightmare, he drew a picture that at first glance didn't appear too frightening. However, the drawing depicted the scary movie character Chucky (see figure 9.1, and notice the eyebrows and the scars). I asked him how he felt when he looked at the picture. He replied, "Scared, mad, sad." I asked what went through his mind as he looked at the picture, to which he replied, "I'm not strong; I'm weak. I can't do anything." He rated the intensity of those feelings and thoughts as 10 on a scale of 1 to 10.

I then asked him to draw pictures of how the dream made him feel in his body, and he drew the figures 9.2 and 9.3. Notice the rating scale for his heart rate in 9.3. I didn't know what that meant, but it didn't matter because it made sense to him. Next I asked him to change the dream in a way that felt good. He drew figure 9.4. Notice that the scars are healed and that Chucky is smiling and friendly. In figure 9.5 Jake depicted the way that the new drawing made him feel in his body. In the drawing, he is saying, "Hi, you wanna play with me?!" Jake said he now felt "strong and recharged," like he could "do almost anything." I then asked him to think about the new drawing and the new thoughts, feelings, and sensations as we did a calming exercise. After doing this, Jake said he felt great and that he didn't think the memory was as scary anymore. The ratings of his negative thoughts and feelings dropped greatly.

The next day, his parents called and said, "You won't believe this, but Jake slept through the night for the first time in four years." Months later he was still sleeping well.

I often share Jake's case in my resilience trainings to show that processing nightmares need not be difficult. On several occasions adults have reported that they successfully used the steps outlined in this chapter with their children or themselves.

Figure 9.1: Jake's drawing of Chucky.

Figure 9.2: Jake's drawing of his emotions.

Figure 9.4: Jake's drawing of
his modified dream.

Figure 9.3: Jake's drawing
of his sensations.

Figure 9.5: Jake's drawing
of his new reactions.

Conclusion

You don't need to be a psychologist or an art therapist to try this skill and process your nightmares. It's not about producing high-quality art; it is about authentic expression of thoughts, feelings, and sensations. Of course, like all other skills in this book, seek an experienced mental health professional if you feel you need additional support.

Before leaving the topic of nightmares, please note that sleep apnea is common among those who experience frequent nightmares. It is thought that apnea starves the hippocampus of oxygen, which interferes with the proper storage of emotionally charged memories. Be sure to get checked for sleep apnea. Treating sleep apnea often reduces nightmares.

Part 2

SPIRALING UPWARD

Growing Happiness and Positivity

Chapter 10

Happiness Basics

In part 1 you learned many skills to strengthen your brain, regulate the physical changes of stress, and manage strong, distressing emotions. You are now prepared for an extremely important part of resilience training: growing happiness. As you'll see, what makes us happier helps us "spiral upward," or flourish, and become more resilient overall. Part 2 will explore many practical, well-researched happiness skills drawn from positive psychology. We'll start in this chapter with happiness basics.

What Is Happiness?

The definition of "happiness" is important and comprises two things:

1. Feeling genuine, heartfelt positive emotions on a fairly regular basis—such as contentment, gratitude, joy, inner peace, satisfaction, inspiration, enthusiasm, hope, awe, amusement, curiosity, and love. The experience of such pleasant emotions is called *positivity*.

2. Feeling overall satisfaction with one's life and self—believing that these are meaningful and worthwhile.

So happiness is more than fleeting emotions that result, say, from getting everything you wanted for your birthday. Rather, happiness reflects a deeper, more enduring inner condition. It is the ability to inwardly enjoy life even amidst outer turmoil. It is the capacity to savor life's beauty and to say, with Winslow Homer, "All is lovely outside my house and inside my house and myself."

Why Is Happiness Important?

Happiness and resilience are closely intertwined. For example, positive emotions help people more quickly reduce elevated arousal and recover from stress. In addition to being correlated with resilience, happiness has been linked to thriving and effective functioning in many areas of life. (See Diener and Biswas-Diner 2008 and Fredrickson 2009 for excellent overviews.)

Psychological thriving: Happiness is associated with

> higher self-esteem, optimism, emotional stability, and self-confidence;

> fewer psychological problems, such as worry, anxiety, depression, hostility, and tension; and

> better coping abilities, such as recovery from depression and grief.

Occupational thriving: Happier people on average enjoy their work more, are more engaged at work, earn more, get more favorable performance ratings, look forward to coming to work, are more helpful to others at work, discover more creative solutions to problems, make better decisions, are more likely to arrive at work on time, and have higher retention rates.

Social thriving: Happy people report greater satisfaction with family, stay married longer, have more friends, are more cooperative, make those around them feel happier, are less aggressive, and commit fewer crimes.

Medical thriving: Happy people live longer; have stronger immunity; are more energetic; and suffer fewer symptoms related to colds, high blood pressure, pain, inflammation, and other medical conditions. The wounds of happy people also heal faster.

How Does Happiness Help Us Flourish?

The broaden and build theory of leading positive psychology researcher Dr. Barbara Fredrickson (2009) explains how happiness helps us flourish. Pleasant emotions expand our view of adversity, helping us see a broader range of coping options. They also motivate us to act on new coping options. Applying a broader range of coping options builds new neural pathways in the brain—and a larger coping repertoire for future adversity. The mechanism may be related to brain biochemistry. Pleasant emotions cause the brain to secrete neurotransmitters such as dopamine and opioids. These chemicals foster one's tendency to approach and solve problems (rather than avoid them) and reinforce or reward coping efforts with more positive feelings. An upward spiral is created whereby positive emotions lead to more effective coping, which increases satisfaction levels and the openness to tackle more challenges. Thus, happiness researcher Sonja Lyubomirsky (2007) has concluded that feeling happier makes people more productive, likable, energetic, healthy, friendly, helpful, resilient, and creative.

Can We Be Happy All the Time?

In an imperfect world, perpetual happiness is an unrealistic expectation. Most would find constant euphoria boring and shallow. Constant happiness does not favor optimal functioning. Down times can send us back to the drawing board to become wiser, stronger, and more compassionate. Strive for greater happiness, but not perfect happiness. The pursuit of perfect or constant happiness can be exhausting and disappointing.

Happy people do experience distress. For example, it is perfectly normal to feel grief and guilt at times. However, happy people spend less time feeling negative emotions, and when they do they know how to bounce back.

How Much Happiness Is Best?

There are times when being too attached to happiness, and not being open to all emotions, can work against us. For example, a person who is overly attached to happiness might minimize medical symptoms or ignore a doctor's advice. However, Dr. Fredrickson (2009) has found that people generally flourish by increasing the ratio of positive emotions to negative emotions they experience. She found that a positivity ratio of at least three to one builds resilience over time. That is, for every unpleasant emotion you experience, you need to experience at least three positive emotions to offset it. Most people fall below that ratio. The ratio can be increased by either reducing gratuitous negativity or increasing the positives. Eliminating distortions is an example of reducing negativity. Being open to the simple beauties around us is an example of increasing the positives.

Where Does Happiness Come From?

Based on a considerable amount of scientific research, Sonja Lyubomirsky (2007) and her colleagues have identified three sources of happiness (see figure 10.1).

1. **Genes:** Up to 50 percent of happiness is inherited. Genes establish a baseline temperament that we tend to return to. Thus, a pay raise or a new car might give you a temporary bump in happiness, but happiness typically returns to baseline once the novelty wears off.

   Circumstances: External conditions such as income, physical attractiveness, where we live, climate, age, gender, race, religious affiliation, marital status, education, and objective physical health combined account for only 10 percent of happiness. So expecting great improvements from changing a particular external circumstance is probably unrealistic.

2. **Intentional activities:** What we regularly think and do accounts for 40 percent of our happiness. The greatest potential for increasing happiness lies here. We can actually program the brain for happiness by practicing the thought patterns, attitudes, values, and activities associated with happiness. Such practices can influence the way genes are expressed.

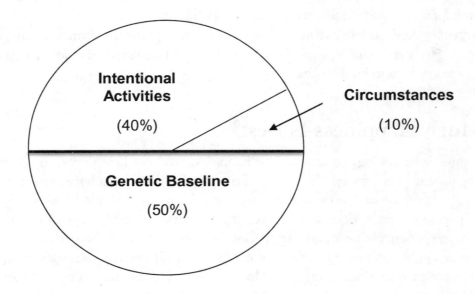

Figure 10.1: The happiness pie: Where does happiness come from? (Lyubomirsky 2007)

Figure 10.2 depicts one way to look at the relationship between genetic baseline, circumstances, and intentional activity when it comes to happiness. External events, such as a promotion, a new car, or marriage, can produce a bump in happiness, which typically returns to the genetic baseline over time. However, regularly and intentionally engaging in activities that promote happiness can raise happiness levels to a new baseline, which can be maintained as long as we continue to engage in happiness-enhancing activities. Let's note the need for balance here. If your genetic baseline is low, acknowledge this with kind understanding, while recognizing that there is still much you can do to grow happiness.

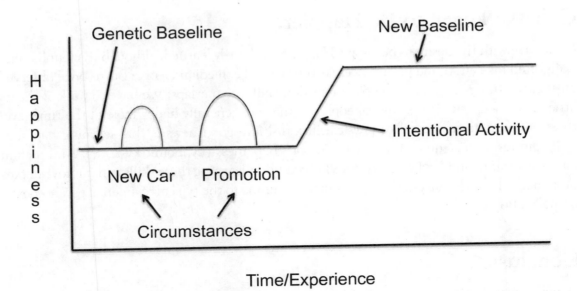

Figure 10.2: Increasing happiness through intentional activity (Kerr, no date)

Who Is Happy?

It is more difficult, though not impossible, to experience pleasant emotions when one lives in dire economic, political, medical, or psychological conditions. Thus, it is important to strive for financial security and to treat medical or psychological conditions. Remember, many conditions that interfere with happiness, such as PTSD, depression, anxiety, apnea, thyroid disorders, and high cholesterol, are highly treatable.

Considerable data show that people on average are happier if they live in an economically developed democracy that respects human rights and actively participate in running their government. Married people are generally happier than those who are cohabitating or single. However, people who are happier are more likely to marry and stay married. In other words, people who remain married were happier going into their marriage. Starting out marriage with steep expectations and fewer relationship skills can lessen the chance of happiness in marriage. Though raising children can be stressful, especially during their teen years, a number of studies link having children with happiness. Children are often linked to other factors associated with parental happiness, such as marriage, morality, stable work, religion, and meaning. (See Brooks 2008 for an excellent summary of happiness research.)

Can We Learn to Be Happier?

We all live with the desire to be happy. Happiness is largely learned, although the foundational skills often take effort and persistence. As the beloved comedian George Burns once observed, most of the things that make people happy don't fall into our laps. We have to work at them a little. The good news is that most people say they are generally happy most of the time, even those suffering from mental or physical illness. More good news is that learning happiness skills can result in significant increases in one's happiness (Lyubomirsky 2007). And preliminary studies (Sin and Lyubomirsky 2009) suggest that learning these skills can improve depression, suggesting the utility of adding happiness training to the typical regimen of psychotherapy or medication.

Conclusion

Happiness is a critical component of resilience. It changes the brain in a number of ways that favor optimal well-being and functioning. The brain is plastic; it has the capacity to build neural pathways associated with happiness. You might wish to review chapter 1 on the brain. Jot down any steps that might strengthen your brain and prepare you to etch new neural pathways for happiness. Even small steps, such as increasing sleep by fifteen minutes, reducing excessive caloric intake by fifty calories per day, adding a serving of fruits or vegetables to your daily menu, or taking a short walk, can reap large dividends. In chapters 11 through 21 we'll turn to developing happiness software—the programming, or habits, that increase happiness at both the brain and heart levels.

Chapter 11

Gratitude

Gratitude, the first happiness skill we'll cover, has received considerable research attention. Practicing gratitude is more than just being polite. It is noticing—and feeling heartfelt appreciation, awe, and wonder for—all of life's good things. In addition to increasing happiness, gratitude researchers such as Robert Emmons and Michael McCullough (2003) have found that the intentional practice of gratitude has been found to improve job and relationship satisfaction, sleep, and health (for example, less pain, fatigue, inflammation, and depressive symptoms). Practicing gratitude has even been found to make distressing memories less troubling and less likely to intrude into awareness (Watkins et al. 2008).

Shifting attention to what is good in life counters the tendency to dwell on problems and is a powerful way to lift mood. The more we practice gratitude, the more we find to enjoy. The habit builds on approaching the day with curious interest and optimism (*I wonder what I'll find to enjoy today*). Feelings of connection to people increase as we remember shared good times and the traits we appreciate in them. Practicing gratitude has even been found to cause beneficial changes in brain and heart functioning (McCraty and Childre 2004).

How Is Gratitude Cultivated?

Two basic approaches to cultivating gratitude have been tested in the research.

Keep a gratitude journal. Each night list up to five things you are grateful for from the previous twenty-four hours. Briefly describe each—how it makes you feel, what it means to you, and what the goodness is that made the moment turn out well (for example, the goodness of nature, others, God, or yourself). The point is to savor the feelings as you reminisce, so don't be overly analytical, intellectual, or emotionally detached. Do this for about five minutes each night over a two-week period. Alternatively, pick one night a week and write about five things you are thankful for from the past week. Keep this up for six to ten weeks or longer. Some find that spreading out the journal writing keeps the process fresher. Experiment to find a frequency that works best for you.

Write about anything that makes you happier or enriches your life, big or small. You might write about:

- Funny or pleasant moments (such as engaging in a hobby, watching a movie, spending time with loved ones or friends, eating meals, having conversations, sleeping, or noticing moments that made you smile)

- Accomplishments or successes (yours and others')

- A scene in nature, beautiful surroundings

- Something you learned

- Uplifting principles

- Things in progress (goals, opportunities, possibilities to anticipate)

- Tender mercies (kindnesses provided by others, nature, or Providence)

- Pride in surviving, personal strengths

- Things that "work" (roads, schools, running water, laws)

- Art and inventions

- Medical care, insurance

- Employment

- Health, parts of your body that function well

To get the ball rolling, does anything come to mind that you might like to write about?

_____

_____

_____

_____

_____

To strengthen your writing experience, you might add photos, letters, quotations, or other mementos to your journal. You might practice heart coherence—experiencing gratitude for a memory at the heart level. During the day, be on the hunt or alert for things you are grateful for, such as sounds in nature, the aroma of food, or a child's innocent facial expression.

Write a gratitude letter to someone who has touched your life for the better. This can be especially profound if you have never properly thanked that person. Read the letter aloud in the person's presence. Writing a gratitude letter tends to give a greater burst of happiness than journal writing, although the happiness boost from journal writing lasts several months longer. This activity makes the other person feel grateful and good, which increases your own happiness.

These are just two of the ways that you can cultivate gratitude. There are many others, such as the following suggestions.

Express gratitude to others frequently. To waitresses, protectors, or people working in businesses, say, "Thanks for your help." Be genuine and specific ("I really appreciated the way you…"). If service is especially good, tell the supervisor. This makes three people feel good: the appreciated worker, the supervisor, and yourself.

Teachers might especially appreciate this story. Mark Medoff (1986), the playwright and screenwriter of *Children of a Lesser God*, returned to his school. He introduced himself to a favorite teacher as a student of hers from many years before. She cocked her head, hoping the angle might jog her memory. He wanted to deliver a perfectly worded message. Instead, all he could say was, "I wanted you to know you were important to me." There in the hallway, this lovely, dignified lady began to weep. She encircled him in her arms and whispered, "Thank you!" before disappearing back into her classroom. Gratitude lifted the spirits of two people that day. The ripple effect undoubtedly benefited the students that day, as well. Remember to thank loved ones often. It strengthens bonds.

Share gratitude experiences with loved ones at the end of the day. It is pleasant to hear about what went well and what has been working. By making time together more enjoyable, this process can strengthen relationships. This is an enjoyable way to tuck children into bed, which also helps them to cultivate the habit of gratitude. You might also ask children how they might thank someone for giving them a gift.

For a short while, give up something that you take for granted. Doing this can help you realize the value of little things. I think of a WWII POW who told me that the deprivation of his prison experience caused him to appreciate a simple piece of chocolate immeasurably. Others told me how being a POW made them cherish freedom even more. Those who "fast" from television often discover greater pleasure in other areas of life.

Increase everyday joy and gratitude. We can build "gratitude inertia" through little efforts. You might try these:

- When "stuck" in a line, in traffic, or in a difficult situation, stop, take a breath, and look around. Notice something to enjoy in your surroundings, such as a face, a smile, a picture on the wall, or clouds.

- Think of something you appreciate, and place that feeling in your heart.

- At the end of the day, sit comfortably, close your eyes, and breathe abdominally. Let your mind become quiet. Feel warmth in your heart, and let a golden light spread to your head. Ponder what you are grateful for.

Try grateful reminiscing. The concentration camp survivor Viktor Frankl imagined the face of his beloved wife to preserve his sanity during his imprisonment. Resilient people often reminisce to get through difficult times. Grateful remembering can elevate mood, self-esteem, and positive feelings toward others, the past, and the future—while diminishing the distress of troubling memories. Start by making a list of good memories, from your childhood to the more recent past. Consider especially warm, nostalgic times with people who mattered to you, significant accomplishments, unmerited favors, simple pleasures, and enjoyable moments in nature. For ten to twenty minutes, relax, close your eyes, breathe abdominally, and then immerse yourself in one pleasant memory. Recall as many details of the memory as you can—sensations (what you saw, heard, smelled, tasted, and felt with your body), emotions (where you feel these in your body), and thoughts. Imagine that you are reliving the experience, with all the sensations, feelings, and thoughts. Recall the expression on your face, and let your face experience that expression again. If a negative thought intrudes, such as about something unpleasant that happened later, tell yourself that you won't let this ruin your experience, and go back to focusing on the pleasant memory. Do this every few days for a variety of memories.

When you finish reliving a memory, you might record the details of the memory in writing. This can help to solidify and reinforce the memory. A written record of happy memories can be a great resource for stressful times. You might find it helpful to refer to reminders of your experience, such as photos or other mementos. You might wish to place these with your written record. If you find that writing becomes too analytical and dampens the emotional experience, then don't do it.

Find gratitude amidst adversity. Resilient people have many tools in their coping toolbox to help them get through life's inevitable adversities. Gratitude can be one such tool. It can change our perspective in a way that lifts our spirits and helps us through difficult times. Some people find gratitude amidst suffering. For example, Viktor Frankl appreciated the sunsets he could see through the barbed wire of the concentration camp.

Gratitude in Adversity

The gracious tennis star Arthur Ashe was dying from AIDS, which he contracted from a blood transfusion during heart surgery. He said, "If I ask 'Why me?' as I am assaulted by heart disease and AIDS, I must ask 'Why me?' about my blessings, and question my right to enjoy them" (Ashe and Rampersad 1993, 326).

Fill out a gratitude reflection sheet. Some people find that a more structured approach helps them to more fully appreciate and savor the good things in life. Using the form below, list a few things you are grateful for each day. Then indicate how each has benefited you and how your life without it would be less rich. (You may also want to visit http://www.newharbinger.com/39409 and see item 13, which offers a strategy for gratefully processing difficult times.)

I'm grateful for...	How this has enriched my life...	How life without this would be different...

Before moving on, please take a moment to ponder these reflections:

Be grateful to those who have made you stumble, for they have strengthened your ability. —Chinese master Chin Kung

He is a wise man who does not grieve for the things which he has not, but rejoices for those which he has. —Epictetus

If you haven't got all the things you want, be grateful for the things you don't have that you don't want. —Anonymous

The pessimist looks at a glass of water and wonders why it isn't full, why everyone else has more water, and why it isn't wine. The grateful optimist thinks, "See how beautiful and clear the water is." —Anonymous

Unless we are grateful for what we have, we'll never be happy with more. —David Rich

Activity: Practice Gratitude

Reviewing this chapter, pick one or more gratitude activities to try. You might, for example, try one structured and one unstructured activity:

Structured activities: Write a gratitude journal, a gratitude letter, or a gratitude reflection sheet or try grateful reminiscing.

Unstructured activities: Express gratitude spontaneously to others, talk about what you're grateful for with others, give up something you take for granted, and be on the watch for things you are grateful for, savoring them during the day or in imagery.

Conclusion

Do you remember the flaw fixation distortion, which keeps your eye on what's wrong? Gratitude widens your focus to include what's right, including life's inexpensive, simple pleasures. Broadening your focus in this way increases happiness, which in turn increases resilience. Gratitude is a great place to start increasing happiness, and the practice particularly relates to the topic of the next chapter, self-esteem.

Chapter 12

Self-Esteem

Being quietly glad to be yourself, feeling securely anchored during the storms of life, knowing that difficult times do not change your basic inner worth—these perspectives suggest why self-esteem is central to happiness and resilience. This chapter will show you what healthy self-esteem is and how to cultivate it.

What Do We Know About Self-Esteem?

Around the world, self-esteem is the strongest predictor of happiness, even in countries where individualism is discouraged, such as Korea and Singapore (Diener and Diener 1995; Zhang 2005). Recall from the broaden and build theory (Fredrickson 2009) that happiness increases resilience. We would expect, then, that self-esteem would be linked to resilience. It is in several ways.

Self-esteem is linked to increased persistence and active problem solving in the face of setbacks (see the review in Barker 2007; Dumont and Provost 1999), to motivation to pursue goals (Harter 1986, 1999), and to competent functioning in children living in extremely stressful environments (for example, Cicchetti et al. 1993). In other words, feeling worthwhile motivates us to try our best and persevere under pressure.

Self-esteem is also closely related to mental health. For example, lack of self-esteem predicted anxiety, depression, and PTSD following 9/11 (Boscarino and Adams 2008; Boscarino, Adams, and Figley 2005). On the other hand, having self-esteem protects people from developing depression in highly stressful times (Hobfoll and London 1986; Hobfoll and Walfisch 1984). Lacking the secure anchor of self-esteem is painful. Thus, the links between self-dislike and drug use, suicidal thinking, and excessive stress arousal when threatened are self-evident.

Difficult experiences, such as living with constant criticism, can change the way we view ourselves. Restoring a wholesome sense of identity and self-esteem, then, is an important part of the healing process.

What Is Healthy Self-Esteem?

How we define self-esteem is critical. *Self-esteem* is a realistic, appreciative opinion of oneself. "Realistic" suggests that we are truthfully aware of our strengths and weaknesses. "Appreciative" implies that we have an overall positive regard or feeling about our self—a quiet gladness to be who we are, despite our imperfections.

Self-esteem does not equal perfection. If it did, no one would have it. Often, people who are neurotically driven toward perfection are trying to compensate for a lack of inner security. Self-esteem is not omnipotence or narcissism—the false security that says one is more worthwhile and capable than others and should be on a pedestal. A brittle sense of worth might lead one to overcompensate by having feelings of grandiosity or entitlement. It has been observed that criminals and bullies appear to think themselves superior to others. However, a large study of ten- and eleven-year-olds suggests that this is not the case: the most aggressive children felt left out and bullied, had a negative self-image, and did not enjoy themselves (Sprott and Doob 2000). This is hardly the picture of one with healthy self-esteem. To be mortal is to be imperfect. We can calmly accept that and enjoy progressing, or we can fight this reality by becoming boastful, conceited, or overly competitive—struggling to prove our worth.

Wholesome self-esteem partners with wholesome humility. A person who feels humility recognizes that all people have worth, unique strengths, different viewpoints shaped by life experience, and something valuable to contribute. To be humble is to recognize that we can learn from everyone, and that there will always be people who are more advanced than we are in certain areas. Like self-esteem, humility is grounded in truth. Humble people recognize and celebrate their strengths (without arrogance or boasting) *and* those of others—while recognizing limitations. Humility readies us to learn from, and cooperate with, others.

Finally, self-esteem is not selfishness. The selfish person cares only for self. The other extreme is to care only for others. A person with wholesome self-esteem has an enlightened "both focus": a healthy regard and respect for self and others. Inner security frees us to be more conscious of others.

The Pillars of Self-Esteem

Self-esteem rests upon three pillars, or building blocks. Each pillar suggests ways to grow self-esteem. The first is equal, unconditional worth *as a person*. While others might have more *social* or *market* worth than you or me, *human* worth comes with birth. Social and market worth might result from externals, such as appearance, health status, education, acquired skills, the house we live in, the car we drive, the clothes or uniform we wear, or the group we belong to. Worth defined by externals can fluctuate—with the stock market, age, popularity, performance, promotions, firings, awards, or the way others treat or label us. By contrast, worth as a person is unchanging and anchored in something deeper—the recognition of who we are at the core. Each person, at birth, comes with a set of core capacities—all the attributes and potential needed to live well. Thus, each person has the capacity to love, learn, sacrifice, enjoy, and contribute. While others might be more advanced in certain areas (for example, math or humor), each individual possesses these core capacities, in embryo, like seeds that can grow. It is the unique mix of strengths that makes one person different from another. Inner worth already exists; it does not need to be created. Fortunate children will learn this from the way their parents treat them. They come to understand that mistakes don't diminish their inner worth—and thus they don't fear "failing." They realize that they are *worthwhile*—literally worth the time to live well and actualize their potential.

Unconditional love is the second pillar. Ponder how effective parents communicate this to a nursing infant. They nonverbally communicate unconditional love to the child through hugs, smiles, gazes, and soothing sounds. They do not say, "Well, I'll only love you if you don't mess your diapers, and by the way I only love you because you will someday represent us in Congress." Unconditional love, along with a sense of unconditional worth, becomes the secure foundation for the child's emotional growth. Note that love from others does not *make* one worthwhile, although it might help one to *feel* worthwhile. A great task in life is to learn to love unconditionally. If you did not learn how to do this from your parents, you can still learn to unconditionally love yourself. Doing so makes life's journey so much more enjoyable. There is no survival value whatsoever in self-hatred.

Growing, the third pillar, is the process of actualizing our strengths—coming to flower, if you will. It is the process of becoming more capable, caring, and productive, and of elevating both self and others. Although fruitful living does not create or increase inner worth, it definitely helps us to feel more satisfied with our self and our life course. So we do not grow in order to make ourselves worthwhile; we already are. Rather, we enjoy growing as an *expression* of who we are. Growing does not mean reaching perfection. Rather, it is the process of doing one's personal best and feeling the satisfaction of trying. When we see that growing *springs from* our worth and is *not a condition for* worth, we become free to grow—to do our best, which is the one thing we can control—with more joy and much less fear of failure. Core worth is the seed; love is the fertilizer.

How Is Self-Esteem Raised?

We cultivate self-esteem by practicing skills that address each of the three pillars. We cultivate a sense of worth by recognizing strengths and capacities that already exist. We increase unconditional love by deciding each day to want and do what is best for self and others. We grow by building upon existing strengths and capacities. The following is a sampling of some of the many effective skills I teach in my courses (Schiraldi 2007a, 2016b; see the general resilience section of recommended resources for additional information on these books).

Activity: Seeing Clearly

People with self-esteem are aware of their present, unique mix of strengths and weaknesses in a way that makes them more sure of themselves. Knowing our strengths leads to confidence and motivates us to contribute. Identifying weaker areas helps us to understand our limitations and know when to seek help or invest the energy to improve. The person with self-esteem observes strengths and weaknesses with nonjudgmental curiosity (*Isn't that interesting: there is a strength, and here is a weakness*). You might think of people as unique portraits in various stages of completion. Different areas might shine more brightly in different portraits, and for some no particular areas may stand out (this might be the case of a person who is versatile and balanced overall, but not necessarily outstanding in any one area). We look at each portrait with pleasure, relishing the process through which the painting is completed. We view less developed areas as those with the greatest potential for development.

The following activity will help you see clearly, and with appreciation, how you are currently expressing your core worth.

Directions

1. To begin, rate yourself on each of the following personality traits that describe human beings. Using the scale from 0 to 10, for which 0 means a complete and total absence of the trait (that is, you *never* demonstrate it in the least degree), and 10 means that the trait is completely developed (that is, you demonstrate it as well as a human being possibly can), circle the appropriate rating. Try to be as fair and accurate as you can in your ratings. Neither inflate nor deflate them. Don't worry if you rate yourself higher for some items and lower for others; this is normal. This is not a competition against others. High ratings do not mean more worth; remember, worth as a person is already a given and is equal in all. You are just noticing unique ways in which your worth is presently *expressed*. All of the benefit comes from being objective. Avoid all-or-none thinking and overgeneralizing.

Circle the appropriate rating:

Intelligence/IQ	Completely lacking									Completely developed
	0 1 2 3 4 5 6 7 8 9 10									

Character (ethics, honesty, morality, fairness)	Completely lacking									Completely developed
	0 1 2 3 4 5 6 7 8 9 10									

Creativity/problem solving	Completely lacking									Completely developed	
	0	1	2	3	4	5	6	7	8	9	10

Judgment/wisdom	Completely lacking									Completely developed	
	0	1	2	3	4	5	6	7	8	9	10

Kindness/compassion	Completely lacking									Completely developed	
	0	1	2	3	4	5	6	7	8	9	10

Humor (initiating or appreciating)	Completely lacking									Completely developed	
	0	1	2	3	4	5	6	7	8	9	10

Respect/regard for others	Completely lacking									Completely developed	
	0	1	2	3	4	5	6	7	8	9	10

Self-regard	Completely lacking									Completely developed	
	0	1	2	3	4	5	6	7	8	9	10

Potential for growth, improvement, and change	Completely lacking									Completely developed	
	0	1	2	3	4	5	6	7	8	9	10

2. Now, list five additional traits that describe the way you contribute to your well-being and that of others. This will not be difficult if you consider the many attributes that describe human beings, including determination, persistence, loyalty, cheer, playfulness, thrift, generosity, gentleness, friendliness, appreciation, gratitude, tact, reverence for human dignity, patience, industry, self-control, prudence, order, organization, sincerity, warmth, justice, cleanliness, tranquility, chastity, acceptance, steadiness, courage, sensitivity, commitment, composure, enthusiasm, courtesy, dependability, and humility. The standard is not that you possess these attributes perfectly, only that you possess them in some measure. Then rate the degree to which you have developed these traits, as you did in the first step.

1.	Completely lacking										Completely developed
	0	1	2	3	4	5	6	7	8	9	10

2.	Completely lacking										Completely developed
	0	1	2	3	4	5	6	7	8	9	10

3.	Completely lacking										Completely developed
	0	1	2	3	4	5	6	7	8	9	10

4.	Completely lacking										Completely developed
	0	1	2	3	4	5	6	7	8	9	10

5.	Completely lacking										Completely developed
	0	1	2	3	4	5	6	7	8	9	10

3. Consider what you have just done. Because humans are so complex and diverse, your rating pattern is undoubtedly different from anyone else's. You were probably higher in some areas, lower in others. You probably also noticed an absence of zeros or tens because such extremes rarely, if ever, exist. This activity reveals a complex and unique personal portrait of attributes at various stages of development. Emerging from this composite is a more certain awareness of core worth. The idea of numerical ratings is not to invite comparisons with others, but to present an image of wholeness and possibilities—and to offer recognition and appreciation of one's unique mix of strengths.

Having completed your ratings, please respond in writing to the following questions:

As you ponder your responses to steps 1 and 2, which attribute (or attributes) do you feel best about?

_____

_____

_____

Let's consider the self-as-a-painting analogy. If an impartial observer were to consider your entire portrait, where would "the light shine brightest"? In other words, if a person were to take the time to see you as you really are at present, what areas would he or she be most likely to appreciate or enjoy?

_____

_____

_____

Which attributes or strengths would you enjoy applying more in your life?

_____

_____

_____

From this activity, I learned that…

_____

_____

_____

_____

_____

_____

_____

_____

Seeing Clearly Through the Eyes of a Child

Sometimes children teach us what is possible. Linda and Richard Eyre (1980, 149–150) relate that a teacher was showing a group of children how to skip. Four of the children just couldn't get the hang of it, and three of them got very upset or gave up. The fourth child, Jimmy, kept watching and trying without the slightest embarrassment or self-consciousness. Afterward, Richard and Linda asked him some questions:

Eyres: Do you like to skip?

Jimmy: Yes, but I can't do it very good.

Eyres: Well, did you wish they'd stop skipping and do something you were better at?

Jimmy: No, because I want to learn how.

Eyres: Do you feel bad because you can't skip?

Jimmy: No.

Eyres: Why not?

Jimmy: Because I'm better at other things.

Eyres: Like what?

Jimmy: Mommy says I'm good at painting pictures.

Eyres: I see.

Jimmy: And I'm 'specially good at keeping my baby brother happy.

Eyres: I see, Jimmy. Thanks for answering our questions.

Jimmy: That's all right. Don't worry. Someday I'm going to be good at skipping, too.

Do you get the sense that this child was secure—in himself as a worthwhile person and in his potential? Knowing what he was good at, this little boy could better accept what he wasn't good at as he continued to try. Is there a lesson for us here?

Activity: The Inner Dialogue of Self-Esteem

People with self-esteem talk to themselves differently than those who dislike themselves. In chapter 5 you learned to eliminate negative, self-defeating self-talk that undermines self-esteem. Now you'll practice the inner dialogue typical of those with sound self-esteem. You might think of this as laying down new neural pathways or installing new software in the brain. Research with athletes has demonstrated that mentally rehearsing in detail can be nearly as effective as actual practice (Verdelle 1960). In this activity you will mentally rehearse thoughts that affirm core worth, enhance security, and motivate growth.

Following is a list of statements representing the inner dialogue of self-esteem.

The Thoughts of Self-Esteem

1. I think well of myself. This is good.

2. I accept myself because I realize that I am more than my current skill levels, shortcomings, or any other externals.

3. Criticism is an external. I examine it for ways to improve, without concluding that the criticism makes me less worthwhile as a person.

4. I can criticize my own behavior without questioning my worth as a human being.

5. I notice and enjoy each sign of achievement or progress, no matter how insignificant it may seem to me or to others.

6. I enjoy the achievements and progress that others make, without concluding they are more valuable than I am as a person.

7. I am generally capable of living well, and of applying the time, effort, patience, training, and assistance needed to do so.

8. I expect others to like and respect me. If they don't, that's okay.

9. I can usually earn people's trust and affection through sincere and respectful treatment. If not, that's okay.

10. I generally show sound judgment in relationships and work.

11. I often constructively influence others by my well-reasoned viewpoints, which I offer and explain effectively.

12. I like to help others enjoy themselves.

13. I enjoy new challenges and don't get upset when things don't go well right off the bat.

14. The work I do is generally of good quality, and I expect to do many worthwhile things in the future.

15. I am aware of my strengths and respect them.

16. I can laugh at some of the ridiculous things I do sometimes.

17. I can make a difference in people's lives by what I contribute.

18. I enjoy making others feel happier and glad for time that we shared.

19. I consider myself a worthwhile person.

20. I like being a one-of-a-kind portrait. I'm glad to be unique.

21. I like myself without having to compare myself with others.

22. I feel stable and secure inside because I rightly regard my core worth.

For this activity, you'll focus on each separate statement in turn, as follows:

1. **Sit in a quiet place,** well supported in a chair where you will be comfortable for about twenty minutes.

2. **Close your eyes, if that is comfortable.** Take two calming breaths, and relax your body as deeply and as completely as possible. Prepare yourself for, and expect, a pleasant experience.

3. **Open your eyes long enough to read the first statement.** Then close your eyes and *concentrate* on that statement. Repeat it to yourself three times slowly, allowing yourself to feel as though that statement were essentially accurate. You might wish to imagine yourself in a situation actually thinking and believing the statement. Use all your senses to experience the situation.

4. **Don't worry if a statement doesn't seem to apply to you yet.** Just think of this as patient practice in creating a new mental habit. Don't allow negative or pessimistic thoughts to distract you or undermine your progress. Accept whatever actually happens, without demanding perfection. If a statement still does not feel right, bypass it and return to it later. Or modify it so that it does feel right, keeping it positive though.

5. **Repeat step three for each statement.** The entire exercise will take about twenty minutes.

6. **Repeat this activity daily** for at least three days.

7. **Each day, after doing this activity, notice how you feel.** Many people notice that with practice, the thoughts begin to feel more and more comfortable, becoming as it were trusted friends.

Activity: Acknowledging Strengths

This especially effective activity fosters a realistic appreciation of one's strengths. It is based on the research of three Canadians (Gauthier, Pellerin, and Renaud 1983) whose method enhanced the self-esteem of subjects in just a few weeks.

To warm up, consider the strengths below. Circle each one that describes you. Circle one if you sometimes are, or have ever been, reasonably:

Accepting of others

Adventurous

Brave, courageous

Cheerful, mirthful, good-humored

Clean

Committed

Complimentary

Composed

Confident, self-assured

Cooperative

Courteous

Creative in problem solving, imaginative

Curious, interested

Dependable, responsible, reliable

Disciplined

Encouraging

Energetic

Enthusiastic, spirited

Ethical, moral, honest

Flexible

Forgiving

Generous

Gentle

Graceful, dignified

Grateful, appreciative

Handy

Humble, modest

Industrious

Introspective

Intuitive, trusting of your instincts

Just, fair

Kind, compassionate

Loving

Loyal

Open-minded

Optimistic

Orderly, neat

Organized

Patient

Persistent, resolved

Persuasive

Playful

Prudent, wise

Punctual

Rational, logical, reasonable

Respectful

Responsive to beauty or nature

Reverent

Self-accepting

Self-controlled, able to regulate emotions

Sensitive

Serene, peaceful

Sincere

Spontaneous

Steady, consistent

Tactful

Thrifty

Trusting

Trustworthy

Warm, friendly

Wise in judgment, sees what is important

Check any of the following roles, or ways that strengths can be expressed, that describe what you are sometimes reasonably good at:

_____ Athlete		_____ Letter writer
_____ "Cheerleader," supporter		_____ Listener
_____ Cleaner		_____ Mate
_____ Cook		_____ Mediator
_____ Counselor		_____ Mistake corrector
_____ Debater		_____ Musician or singer
_____ Decision maker		_____ Organizer
_____ Enjoyer of hobbies		_____ Planner
_____ Example		_____ Requester
_____ Family member		_____ Risk-taker
_____ Financial manager		_____ Smiler
_____ Follower		_____ Socializer
_____ Friend		_____ Storyteller
_____ Helper		_____ Taker of criticism
_____ Leader or coach		_____ Thinker
_____ Learner		_____ Worker

Perfection was not required to circle these items, because _nobody_ plays any of these roles all the time or perfectly. However, if you circled a few and have managed to maintain reasonable sanity in a very complex world, give yourself a pat on the back. Remember, this was just a warm-up. The part of the exercise that follows has been found to be very effective in building self-esteem.

In the following space, write ten positive statements about yourself that are meaningful and realistic and true. You may develop the statements using the lists at the beginning of this exercise, generate your own statements, or do both. Examples might include "I am a loyal, responsible member of my family (or team, unit, and so forth)," "I am clean and orderly," or "I am a concerned listener." If you mention a role that you perform well, try to add specific personal characteristics that explain why. For example, instead of saying only that you're a good manager, you might add that you treat others with respect, are open to new ideas, and are decisive. Roles can change (for example, after a job loss or declining health), but character and personality traits can be expressed across many different roles.

Ten Positive Statements

1. _____

_____

2. _____

_____

3. _____

_____

4. _____

_____

5. _____

_____

6. _____

_____

7. _____

_____

8. _____

_____

9. _____

_____

10. _____

_____

Once you've completed your list:

1. Find a place to relax undisturbed for fifteen to twenty minutes. Meditate on one statement and the evidence for its accuracy for a minute or two. Repeat this for each statement.

2. Repeat this exercise every day for seven days. Each day, add an additional statement in the following space.

3. Several times each day, look at an item on your lists. For about two minutes, meditate on the evidence for its accuracy.

Additional Statements

1. _____

_____

2. _____

_____

3. _____

_____

4. _____

_____

5. _____

_____

6. _____

_____

7. _____

_____

If you prefer, you can write the statements on index cards and carry them with you. Some find cards easier to refer to during the day.

Notice how you feel after practicing this skill, which disputes distortions, such as "I am no good" or "I have no strengths," by substituting appreciative thoughts and feelings. Upon completing this activity, you may have feelings similar to other individuals who have completed this exercise:

Hey! I'm not so bad after all.

I got better with practice. I didn't believe the statements at first. Then I found myself smiling on the way to work.

I feel *motivated* to act on them.

I felt peaceful and calm.

I learned that I have a lot more good in me than I give myself credit for.

Activity: Viewing Yourself with Love

US Army Chaplain N. Alden Brown taught this very powerful way to nonverbally counter feelings associated with long-held negative thoughts. In it, you will look into a mirror and view the core self with kindness, perhaps seeing yourself differently than you ever have before.

Do you ever notice what you see when you look into a mirror? Do you immediately focus on the externals—clothes, hair, wrinkles, or blemishes? Do you notice imperfections, perhaps in a harsh, judgmental way? Or do you first experience your core self with a pleasant feeling?

1. Over the next four days, seek out a mirror several times each day.

2. Look into your eyes in the mirror with love. You might first notice that there is stress in and around the eyes. Look with real understanding and emotion. Try to understand what's behind the stress, and let it subside. As you look deeply with love you will notice a change in your eyes and in your entire countenance.

3. Repeat this exercise often. You can use any mirror, even a car mirror.

Over time, this simple yet profound exercise allows a very wholesome and good feeling to take root and grow. As you look into your eyes and see the core self with kindness, appearances and externals begin to assume their correct (that is, secondary) position of importance. Instead of dreading mirrors, they might come to remind you to experience an appreciative feeling for the core self, a feeling that provides the secure foundation for optimal performance and growth.

In addition, when you do need to check out your appearance in the mirror, focus on what is right rather than what is wrong. Consider how remarkable it is that the body performs so well so much of the time. Notice attractive features and appreciate steadily performing organs (the amazing heart, eyes, ears, lungs, kidneys, and so forth).

Also, notice and appreciate any accomplishments, no matter how small or where they occur. Give back-pats for effective efforts ("Good job." "Well done!" "Wow, I accomplished a lot"), rather than dwelling on what went wrong. Encouragement is generally more motivating than harsh criticism. It is not immodest to take satisfaction in sincere efforts, and we preserve healthy humility by remembering that we all have much to learn.

Conclusion

Comparing ourselves with others is exhausting. It will never provide the inner security that healthy self-esteem provides. Those who practice the skills of self-esteem are often surprised at the difference it makes in their happiness and resilience. And it can be very comforting to realize that self-esteem is a skill you can master, just like the other skills in this workbook.

This chapter helped you recognize your core worth and innate strengths, and to experience yourself with positive feeling. Growing your innate strengths in a way that lifts yourself and others makes life more satisfying. It also makes you more resistant to breaking under stress, just as tempering glass makes it more resistant to shattering from a blow. Future chapters will explore ways to grow your strengths.

Chapter 13

Realistic Optimism

It was Cicero who said, "While there is life, there is hope." Optimism, like self-esteem and gratitude, is strongly related to happiness. Also, like self-esteem and gratitude, optimism is an attitude and a skill that can be cultivated through practice. This chapter explores ways to enhance this important strength of resilience.

What Is Realistic Optimism?

Having realistic optimism doesn't mean that you expect everything to turn out perfectly. Rather, it means you have the view that if you try your best, things are likely to turn out as favorably as possible. It is also expecting that even if things turn out badly, you can still find something to enjoy and look forward to. Think again of WWII concentration-camp survivor Viktor Frankl, who marveled at the beauty of the sunset through the barbed wire, while dreaming of lecturing someday about creating meaningful lives.

What Are the Benefits of Realistic Optimism?

Researchers such as Martin Seligman (2006) have found that optimists are not only happier than pessimists, but they are mentally and medically healthier, are more resistant to stress, are more satisfied with their relationships, and perform better in high-stress environments. Optimists are more likely to anticipate bad *and* good outcomes, plan accordingly, and persist in doing their best. They don't waste time getting bogged down in negativity or fruitless activities.

Beware Unrealistic Optimism

Optimism moves us to action. However, it is important to distinguish between realistic and unrealistic optimism. When we have realistic optimism, we recognize the importance of personal effort: we hope for a good outcome and actively work for it. If one approach doesn't work, we flexibly choose another. While we expect that goodwill generally prevails, we accept times when nothing more can be done.

Unrealistic optimism, on the other hand, causes us to blindly assume that all will be well without fully considering the challenges and effort needed to succeed. We may assume that we are more capable than we are. This false security and overconfidence can leave us unprepared and disappointed. Thus, people with unrealistic optimism might fail to take care of their health or might fail professionally because they didn't sufficiently train. Now let's translate these ideas into learnable skills.

Explanatory Styles

Optimists and pessimists think differently about bad events (Seligman 2006). If you ask a person why a bad event happened and what it means, his explanation indicates how he thinks about himself, his life generally, and his future. Let's say two coworkers, one a pessimist and the other an optimist, fail a promotion test. The pessimist attributes the failure to the three Ps, something that is personal, pervasive, and permanent:

- **Personal:** The pessimist condemns himself and entirely blames himself, attributing the failure to personal flaws at the core. He might think, *What's wrong with me? I'm such an incompetent idiot!*

- **Pervasive:** The pessimist sees the failure as a consistent pattern in all areas of life. He thinks, *I mess up everything. I can't do anything right! My whole life stinks.*

- **Permanent:** The pessimist thinks that nothing can or will change. His thoughts might be *I'll never do well. I'll never get promoted. I'm doomed. I might as well give up.*

In contrast, the optimist has a very different way of explaining things, attributing her poor performance to things that are external, specific, and impermanent:

- **External:** The optimist steps back and sees a bigger picture, allowing for outside influences—critiquing her performance, not herself. She might think, *I studied as hard as I could with the time I had. It was a very difficult test, and I was really tired from cramming.*

- **Specific:** The optimist realizes that this is just one situation. She thinks, *I do mess up sometimes, but I'm certainly not messing up everything. I wasn't up to par that day. Sometimes that just happens.*

- **Impermanent:** The optimist looks at a bad outcome as fleeting and changeable. She thinks, *I can learn and improve. If I rest and study more, I'll probably do better next time. This isn't a signpost for the rest of my life.*

Which explanatory style is more likely to motivate you to feel and function at your best? Notice that the optimist's thoughts are realistic and adaptive. Also notice the relationship between the pessimist's thinking style and low self-esteem. The pessimist's thinking style is more likely to lead to feelings of helplessness, passivity, and depression. Fortunately, we can learn to think more optimistically. Mastering this skill can reap huge benefits.

Activity: Explanatory Style

This activity works well in a group of two or three, but it can also be done individually.

1. Generate a list of bad situations that have happened or could happen. For example, finish this sentence: The worst things that could happen in my job (or family or life) are...

2. Selecting one bad situation, complete the blank explanatory style worksheet (figure 13.1), filling in as many thoughts as you can for what a pessimist would think, and then what an optimist would think.

3. Once the blank form is completed, play the devil's advocate game: Read or have someone read each of the pessimistic thoughts, one at a time. Try to respond to each with a more optimistic thought. For instance, if you hear "I failed because I'm stupid," you might reply, "I failed because I used the wrong strategy"—or "didn't try hard enough," or "because the problem was unsolvable."

Bad Situation (describe something that happened or could happen): _____

_____

Pessimistic Thoughts	Optimistic Thoughts
Personal—*condemns and entirely blames self; attributes outcome to personal flaws at the core*	**External**—*sees whole picture; allows for influence of other people or difficult circumstances; no self-condemnation for poor performance; focuses on improving performance*
Pervasive—*consistent pattern in all areas*	**Specific**—*limited to this situation*
Permanent—*unchangeable*	**Impermanent**—*temporary, fleeting, changeable*

Figure 13.1: Explanatory style worksheet

The Optimist's Inventory

Rather than becoming despondent and giving up, an optimist tends to look at adversity and see a silver lining—some hidden benefit, something that is right, something that could lead to a new chapter in life. Like taking an inventory after a military engagement, the optimist looks at adversity and sees what's left to work with. For example, consider an optimistic young man who was severely injured in an automobile accident. His rehabilitation took years, and yet he remained positive:

> I lost a leg, but it could be worse. At least I didn't lose an eye. At least I didn't die. At least I can still listen to music.

> At least I learned I can survive almost anything (demonstrating survivor's pride).

> At least I learned what is most important in life. At least I still have my goals, my faith, and my sense of humor.

> At least I can still look forward to meeting good people.

Activity: The "At Least" Exercise

This exercise stimulates a constructive shift in the way we respond to adversity. It helps us appreciate what's left to work with. It provokes us to ask how well we can manage despite what happened. It stimulates curiosity about future possibilities. The instructions are to simply identify an adversity and complete the sentence stem "At least..." Write down as many completions as you can. Let the thoughts flow without inhibitions of any sort. Then, put the sentences aside and come back to them after sleeping, to add additional thoughts. When finished, you might ask others to contribute their thoughts.

Strengthening Optimistic Beliefs

Optimistic beliefs can be reinforced in many ways.

Read books that reveal the optimistic thinking of resilient survivors. Excellent examples are the autobiographies of Arthur Ashe (the tennis star who contracted AIDS through a blood transfusion) and WWII survivors Viktor Frankl and Irene Opdyke. (See "General Resilience" in the recommended resources.)

Collect and ponder reflections regarding optimism.

It is a peculiarity of man that he can only live by looking to the future…and this is his salvation in the most difficult moments of his existence, although he sometimes has to force his mind to the task. —Viktor Frankl

Freedom is nothing else but a chance to be better, whereas enslavement is a certainty of the worst. —Albert Camus

The optimist sees opportunity in every danger; the pessimist sees danger in every opportunity. —Winston Churchill

We are troubled on every side, yet not distressed; we are perplexed, but not in despair. —2 Corinthians 4:8

Complete the optimism questionnaire. This questionnaire suggests optimistic thoughts to use when facing adversity. It also reinforces active coping behaviors, which are discussed further in chapter 22. (Visit http://www.newharbinger.com/39409 to download the questionnaire, item 4.)

Use self-instruction training. This works well in groups of two or three but can also be done individually. Anticipate a difficult event (for example, a threat, failure, defeat, or loss) that could happen to you as an individual or to your unit or team. Second, brainstorm realistic optimistic thoughts to use before, during, and after the event. What could you tell yourself? You might use the optimism questionnaire for ideas. Also, put a check beside the ideas below that you could see yourself using:

Before

_____ This could be tough. If I do what seems best, things will probably turn out as well as possible.

_____ The first time through is usually more difficult. Keep goals realistic.

_____ I'll approach this with curiosity, not self-doubt.

_____ I'll recognize if it is time to shift strategies.

_____ Other: _____

During

_____ This is a difficult situation.

_____ Keep calm and steady. I'll probably solve this.

_____ If I try a different strategy, perhaps I'll get better results.

_____ My best is all I can expect to give to this challenge.

_____ Other: _____

After
(Identify thoughts for a good outcome.)

_____ Good job.

_____ All in all, I did pretty well.

_____ I used my strengths and skills and marshaled needed resources.

_____ This gives me confidence to succeed in other areas.

_____ Other: _____

(Identify thoughts for a bad outcome.)

_____ It's water under the bridge; tomorrow is another day.

_____ This challenge revealed both strengths and areas to improve. I'll improve with time and experience.

_____ Next time, I'll try a different strategy, specifically _____.

_____ Some situations are beyond my control.

_____ Even though I came up short, I'm still a worthwhile person.

_____ Other: _____

Create a hope kit or album. If hope has been dimmed, it can be ignited again. You might create an album of things that remind you of hope: photos of loved ones, mementos, inspiring quotes, a record of goals and dreams you've accomplished and plan to accomplish, and how and when you will achieve your goals (Echterling, Presbury, and McKee 2005). Keep your hope kit accessible and refer to it regularly. You might also include reminders of hopeful thinking, such as _I have what it takes to improve_; or _When my efforts fall short, I have what it takes to find contentment_; or _This too shall pass_; or _I look ahead to pleasant times, because I can figure out how to make them happen._

Consider taking a break from television and other forms of entertainment that encourage passivity, violence, and other negative themes. Optimists watch less television than pessimists (Peterson and Bossio 1991).

Creating a Bright Future

Optimists have dreams. They imagine a better life and set goals to create it. As noted, writing about past traumas for up to thirty minutes a day for four days in a row can raise your mood and reduce visits to health care providers; even more impressive results can result from writing for the same amount of time about creating your hoped-for future (King 2001).

Activity: The Best Possible Future Self

Can you imagine a bright future, one in which you have worked hard, overcome obstacles, and achieved the goals you most desire? Are you open to the idea of a better future? The process of describing this type of future life helps you sharpen goals, reminds you of what you're really working for, and motivates and empowers you to achieve these goals. This activity (which combines elements described in Austenfeld, Paolo, and Stanton 2006; King 2001; and Lyubomirsky 2007) involves writing continuously for twenty to thirty minutes on each of four consecutive days. Here are the instructions.

1. Imagine your life in the future. Imagine that everything has gone as well as it possibly could, and you've realized all your dreams. You have worked hard, overcome obstacles, and achieved your goals in the important areas of your life. You might consider, for example, goals in the following areas: profession or education, relationships, recreation and leisure, meaningful causes, spirituality and ethicalness, and health. Think about goals being reached at various points in your life, such as one, five, and ten years from now. Now describe this life in writing. Add details such as what you see and feel. Where are you? How would it feel to be at this place in your life?

2. Describe what you did specifically to achieve these goals. How, specifically, did you overcome at least one major obstacle? (Later in the writing process you might break down goals into subgoals and specific steps needed to accomplish these goals and subgoals. Doing this in writing helps to clarify the process.)

3. Along the way:

Notice and replace pessimistic thoughts, such as *I can't do it*, or *This good thing will never happen.* Instead, you might think, *Maybe I can*, or *Maybe it could happen.*

Pay attention for new insights or directions. (For example, *Perhaps I can be content with less, with excellence rather than perfection, or with something altogether different, such as greater inner peace. Perhaps a new strategy could work better than my old ways. Perhaps I can better appreciate how my strengths and strategies have gotten me this far. Perhaps I can accept what I realistically can't control. Perhaps I see myself forgiving old wounds. Perhaps I see how giving myself kind, wise advice or encouragement could benefit me.*)

Conclusion

Strengthening optimism can counterbalance a difficult past by urging us forward, toward a brighter future. Resilient people keep their dreams for a happier life alive, despite setbacks. When you feel stuck in the negatives of the past, remember to return to the skills in this chapter.

Chapter 14

Altruism

The eighth-century Buddhist monk Shantideva said, "Whatever joy there is in the world, all comes from desiring others to be happy." This quotation beautifully introduces altruism, the focus of this chapter. Altruism is closely tied to happiness and resilience.

What Is Altruism?

Altruism means unselfish concern for the good of others; we wish to give another a leg up. Simply stated, altruism is the practice of offering heartfelt kindness in thoughts, words, and deeds—without concern for our own gain.

What Are the Benefits of Altruism?

Altruism makes us happier, healthier, and more likely to succeed in health, love, and work. For example, in the famous Harvard men's study, George Vaillant (1977) found that an altruistic disposition in college was among five predictors of medical, psychological, social, and occupational success decades later. Happiness researcher Sonja Lyubomirsky (2007) concluded that altruism builds social ties (people tend to like kind people), while altruistic acts distract us from our own cares. Through mirror neurons—which allow happiness to activate similar areas of the brain in both the server and the person served—the lift that we give others through selfless service is reflected in our own brains.

Kindness changes the way we see others and ourselves. We begin to see the person served as one who matters. We see ourselves as more capable, useful, and strong, and we see our lives as more meaningful.

Altruism can inspire others to be kinder and less cynical. For example, a sixteen-year-old named Andrew was devastated by the destruction caused by hurricanes in the south. However, the bravery of emergency workers so impressed him that he began training at night to become an emergency medical technician so that he could help others (Goldman 2005). Psychologist Jackie Lapidus interrupted her private practice to donate five days to work with Pentagon survivors after 9/11. As a result of the experience, she said, "I'm less cynical because I have witnessed so many acts of kindness and courage" (American Psychological Association 2001). Viktor Frankl observed, "We who lived in concentration camps can remember the men who walked through the huts comforting others, giving away their last piece of bread. They may have been few in number, but they offer sufficient proof that everything can be taken away from a man but one thing: the last of the human freedoms—to choose one's attitude in any given set of circumstances, to choose one's own way" (1963, 73). A POW in the brutal Japanese prison camps of World War II told me that he was inspired by a leader who took beatings from his captors to spare his men from being beaten. Other POWs wept as they recounted tales of selfless friends who gave them their own food to save them from death. In a squalid prison in North Vietnam, one sick prisoner inadvertently threw up his dentures into the bucket that served as the toilet. A comrade thrust his arm up to his shoulder in excrement until he retrieved the dentures, inspiring fellow prisoner Larry Chesley (1973) to say that it was an honor to live with such men.

In all age-groups, practicing altruism has been found to improve happiness more than recreational or passive activities, such as watching television or shopping (Seligman 2002). Unlike sensual pleasures, the satisfactions derived from altruism seem to grow over time (as long as we don't overextend). Interestingly, those in three altruistic professions—clergy, firefighters, and special education teachers—ranked among the happiest in both their jobs and their lives. Lawyers, bankers, and others with higher-status jobs score lower in life and job satisfaction (T. W. Smith 2007). Seligman (2002) notes that lawyers are the richest and most depressed professionals, and they experience higher-than-average rates of alcoholism, illegal drug use, and divorce. (Perhaps it is because they are trained to be aggressive, judgmental, adversarial, pessimistic, and emotionally detached. He recommends pro bono or mediation work to increase altruism.) Let's look at two ways to cultivate this special attitude of altruism.

Activity: Kindness Day

Sonja Lyubomirsky (2007) found that doing five kind acts on one day each week for six weeks boosted happiness. Concentrating the acts on one day boosted happiness more than spreading out the acts. To try this, designate one day a week as your kindness day, and plan to do five altruistic acts. Do them with heart—freely, cheerfully, and without expectation of personal reward. If you can, try to interact with the people you help—talk with them, look into their eyes. Do not judge them negatively for needing help. Do not try to do so much that it overwhelms you and takes the joy out of giving. If it becomes drudgery, it's okay to take a break.

To prime the pump, consider the activities below, and place a check beside those you'd like to try. Then plan to do five acts on each of your weekly kindness days over a six-week period. Both anticipating and then doing altruistic deeds can lift the mood.

_____ Babysit for a friend.

_____ Befriend someone who isn't popular.

_____ Bring a friend a simple gift, such as homemade jam for a holiday.

_____ Bring a meal to a shut-in, or just stop in to say hello.

_____ Bring a treat for someone's pet.

_____ Buy dessert for someone at another table.

_____ Buy or provide a meal for a homeless person.

_____ Call just to say hello.

_____ Donate to charity.

_____ Do something unexpected for a family member (cook a favorite food, do a chore without being asked, be patient, listen intently, compliment, share a possession).

_____ Drive an elderly person to an appointment or errand.

_____ Give a larger tip.

_____ Give a massage.

_____ Help a neighbor (take in the trash can, mow the lawn, sweep the sidewalk, share vegetables from your garden).

_____ Help your child with homework.

_____ Host an unexpected birthday party.

_____ Invite someone who is feeling down to lunch, to a movie, or for a walk.

_____ Let a driver get in front of you.

_____ Pay for someone behind you at the toll booth or fast-food drive-through.

_____ Pick up litter.

_____ Say "Thanks for your service" to a police officer or military service member.

_____ Send an "I'm thinking of you" note or get-well card.

_____ Send a thank-you note to a new teacher, custodian, principal, or someone else who makes a difference.

_____ Share your knowledge or skill with a person or group.

_____ Smile or say hello to someone you don't usually greet.

_____ Spend one-on-one time with a family member doing something he or she likes.

_____ Tell someone you appreciate him or her and why.

_____ Tutor someone.

_____ Volunteer for a good cause, such as at a nursing home, at a soup kitchen, at a homeless shelter, at a blood drive, at a school, at an orphanage, for a children's team, or for Big Brothers Big Sisters of America.

_____ Welcome new neighbors with a plate of cookies.

_____ Other (consider neighbors, friends, family, strangers, coworkers):

_____

Guerrilla Kindness

Whereas a kindness day is planned, guerilla kindness is a less structured approach to altruism involving random acts of kindness. A reporter once asked Mother Teresa how he could help her serve the poorest of the poor. She said simply, "Come and see." In other words, kindness does not usually take elaborate planning, training, or effort. Often we simply see what needs doing, and then we do it. All we need to bring is an open heart and the willingness to help. So, we might shovel snow from our neighbor's walk or bring a meal to a sick friend, contributing in our own unique way.

If you keep a journal, you might note the kind things you did for the week. Research has shown that this practice increases happiness (Lyubormirsky and Della Porta 2010).

Two Stories of Kindness

A newspaper some years ago reported this story of altruism and gratitude, as related by Thomas S. Monson (2005, 4):

The District of Columbia police auctioned off about 100 unclaimed bicycles Friday. "One dollar," said an 11-year-old boy as the bidding opened on the first bike. The bidding, however, went much higher. "One dollar," the boy repeated hopefully each time another bike came up.

The auctioneer, who had been auctioning stolen or lost bikes for 43 years, noticed that the boy's hopes seemed to soar higher whenever a racer-type bicycle was put up.

Then there was just one racer left. The bidding went to eight dollars. "Sold to that boy over there for nine dollars!" said the auctioneer. He took eight dollars from his own pocket and asked the boy for his dollar. The youngster turned it over in pennies, nickels, dimes, and quarters—took his bike, and started to leave. But he went only a few feet. Carefully parking his new possession, he went back, gratefully threw his arms around the auctioneer's neck, and cried.

I think of a former student, an undercover narcotics agent for years, who had somehow avoided becoming cynical. When he arrested people, he did so with goodwill and thought, "Something tells me not to judge. This is someone on the downward slope at this time. He's not all bad. I remember many people helping me in my life. Perhaps helpful people could help turn him around, too."

Conclusion

Ask yourself which is more satisfying: doing a kind deed or shopping? Doing good or making money? Most people say that altruistic acts bring more satisfaction than self-focused pleasures. Think about it. If you kiss a dollar bill, it doesn't kiss you back—but kindness lights up the brain. Before moving on to the next chapter, please ponder these reflections on altruism.

When I was young, I admired clever people. Now that I am old, I admire kind people.
—Abraham Joshua Heschel

Sometimes our light goes out but is blown into a flame by another human being. Each of us owes deepest thanks to those who have rekindled this light .—Albert Schweitzer

Let no one ever come to you without leaving better and happier. Be the living expression of God's kindness: kindness in your face, kindness in your eyes, kindness in your smile.
—Mother Teresa

If you want others to be happy, practice compassion. If you want to be happy, practice compassion. —Dalai Lama

Chapter 15

Humor

Rodney Dangerfield once quipped, "My psychiatrist told me I was crazy and I said I wanted a second opinion. He said, 'Okay, you're ugly, too.'" What is humor? What is its relationship to resilience? When is it healthy and useful...or not? Can it be cultivated? These are questions that we'll explore in this chapter.

What Is Humor?

The word "humor" derives from the Latin word for moisture. Indeed, humor can moisten, or lubricate, life. Humor is a rather complex but learnable skill that is most effectively used alongside the other skills in this book.

Specifically, *humor* is the propensity to amuse and be amused (Franzini 2002), the ability to see the comical and find pleasure in many situations. Bigger than joking, humor is a way of looking at life differently—with clarity, acceptance, playfulness, and optimism. When we stumble, humor lets us think, *I may not be great, but I'm a darn sight better than* some *might think!*

Humor allows us to see even bad situations in a new light—with a sense of amusement, inner peace, and hope. Humor lightens us up, countering the overseriousness that is common to the stress-related conditions.

How Does Humor Relate to Resilience?

All of the resilient WWII survivors that I interviewed believed that humor helped them through their tribulations. They couldn't always explain why, nor were they necessarily funny, but they knew that humor had mattered.

We've learned that a wholesome sense of humor is a vital asset of resilient people—one, it is generally agreed, that is necessary for optimal mental and social health. Wholesome humor brings pleasure to life's moments, which increases happiness. Happiness, in turn, opens up the brain such that we see more ways to cope with adversity and brighten up both the bad and the good times. Thus, the upward spiral continues.

A wholesome sense of humor both springs from, and helps to maintain, a happy disposition. There's a Jewish tradition that before kicking Adam and Eve out of the Garden of Eden, God gave them a sense of humor to get them through life with grace and composure. Much like optimism, humor helps us think, *No matter how bad the situation, I can find something to enjoy.*

The Forms of Humor

Humor comes in many guises, such as stories, jokes, pranks, wit, ribbing, banter, bloopers, slapstick, horseplay, and malapropisms (think Yogi Berra's "Nobody goes [to that restaurant] anymore because it's too crowded" or Archie Bunker's "last will and testicle"). The various forms of humor may be broadly grouped as either wholesome or hostile. Nearly all of humor's benefits related to mental health, more satisfying relationships, and better functioning derive from wholesome humor, whereas hostile humor is associated with poorer mental health and less happiness (Martin 2007).

Wholesome humor lifts spirits, puts us at ease, and draws us together. It promotes warm laughter at our common lot in life—our shared silliness—and conveys the feeling that we are all in the same boat. (Notice the similarities with self-compassion.) It might poke fun at something anyone could do, without putting anyone down. It has a good-natured, rather than hostile, tone. For example, Mother Teresa said, with a smile, to her Missionaries of Charity, "Keep smiling, and anyone who doesn't smile, make her smile" (Petrie and Petrie 1986). Carlos Mencia once quipped, "God has a sense of humor. If you don't believe me, tomorrow go to Walmart and just look at people [including ourselves]." This humor style makes someone safe and fun to be around. People with this humor style can also laugh at themselves in a good-natured, accepting way.

As a fifth-grader, I was once annoyed at my favorite teacher over something silly. So I drew a picture of her with measles and frizzy hair. I was so engrossed putting the finishing touches on the caption—"This is Mrs. Mulholland. She has the measles"—that I didn't notice she had walked up to my desk and was taking in my drawing. Horrified, I looked up to see her throw back her head and laugh, "Oh, Glenn, is that what I really look like?" That cemented my adoration of her. Occasionally, wholesome humor can bind group members together when they poke good-natured fun at someone outside of the group. When we are alone, we might amuse ourselves by thinking of the irony of a bad situation, or by thinking of something funny.

Hostile humor belittles people and includes sarcasm, put-downs, teasing, and derisive nicknames. Telling an embarrassing story about someone in order to exclude that person exemplifies this form of humor. If someone is offended or embarrassed or doesn't enjoy an attempt at humor, there is a good chance that it is hostile. Rodney Dangerfield once quipped, "I haven't spoken to my wife in sixty years. I didn't want to interrupt her." If she was not amused, this was an example of hostile humor. If you have to say "just kidding" when challenged by others, you might be using aggressive humor. Hostile humor also includes habitually putting ourselves down in a disparaging way. Whereas we might use wholesome humor to poke fun at ourselves in a lighthearted, accepting way, hostile self-directed humor reveals a deeper self-dislike.

While some comedians make a living with this humor style, this style usually does not wear well in real life. It can bring others down as it reminds them of their own insecurities or the negativity they are trying to rise above. For the teller, this style might reinforce negativity and the habit of trying to cover up real pain and insecurity rather than directly confronting them. Chris Farley, for example, made people laugh at his own expense, but he was deeply unhappy inside and died of a drug overdose at a young age. In short, this style erodes self-respect, invites ridicule, and puts others off.

Developmentally, wholesome humor reflects that one is secure and likes himself or herself and others. Hostile humor tends to reflect the opposite.

Take Your Humor Temperature

Ask yourself the following questions:

- Am I more serious than I need to be?

- Might I have more fun in life?

- Could I laugh more?

- Could I find more amusement in life's comical, ludicrous, ironic, or unexpected moments?

- Could I think of more ways to make others smile or laugh?

- Could I make my moments with others more enjoyable?

- Could I be more playful?

- Are there ways to spend more time with people who enjoy life?

If the answer to any of these questions is yes, please read on.

Comic Relief in the Midst of Adversity

Humor enables us to rise above and survive even the most dire situations. If only for a moment, humor can shrink the pain and infuse adversity with pleasure—reminding us that we still have inner resources and the hope of triumphing. Some of the most profound examples of comic relief have been found in life's darkest moments.

Larry Chesley was imprisoned for many years in North Vietnam, and he provides an example of humor providing levity in dark times:

One of the most significant things that helped us hang on over there was a sense of humor, being able to laugh at each other and ourselves. Towards the end, when we had a little less restriction on our movements, we used to watch one prisoner ride his "motorcycle" around the camp. He would polish it and wash it—he even had a helmet made out of something or other. He had the high handlebars, and he would kick-start the bike and make all the appropriate noises as he rode it around. Of course all of this was imaginary, but he really entertained the other prisoners. The Vietnamese authorities didn't know what to make of him. He had them all flustered. They probably thought he was crazy. One day the camp commander told him he was not allowed to ride his motorcycle anymore because there wasn't room in the yard; and besides, the other prisoners didn't have a motorcycle.

We had some riotous times laughing at some of the silly little things that happened. I think I may have laughed harder in prison than I have ever laughed at anything in my life. (1973, 78–79)

Humor Guidelines and Principles

Before trying to be funny, try noticing the joyful aspects of life. Examples include nature's beauty or seeing others do things well. Dispense compliments and appreciation, rather than criticism, at every honest opportunity.

Simply chuckle at the incongruous, comical, amusing, ironic, ludicrous, or absurd. Such situations are all around us. Will Rogers once said, "I don't make jokes. I just watch the government and report the facts." Simply be aware. If you bring others into the laughter, that's icing on the cake.

Be kind and affectionate. Ensure that humor builds bridges, not walls. Teasing, for example, even when offered in a good-natured way, usually is more upsetting than the teaser realizes. Be especially cautious about sarcasm, humor intended to dominate or demean, or laughing at outsiders. During disagreements, be sure that your humor isn't invalidating another's viewpoint or blocking another person's serious attempt to problem solve. Be especially cautious with humor directed at people who are insecure, anxious, depressed, guilty, or overly serious.

If you are uncertain about how humor is being received, ask. (For example, "I was just trying to lighten things up. Was that okay?") Then listen to the other person's response.

Be yourself. You needn't force humor. Use the humor type you are most comfortable with, whether that is telling a funny real-life story or joke or just enjoying a comical moment with a buddy or small group of friends.

Know when not to be funny. Not every moment needs to be turned into a joke. One who clowns around too much isn't taken seriously. While a light comment might help when someone is in pain, it can often backfire. If a loved one has a genuine concern, trying to make a joke of it can frustrate the person.

Use self-effacing humor sparingly. A secure person can usually laugh at his or her own imperfections and can put others at ease by doing so. However, don't overdo it. Putting oneself down too much can turn people off.

Be spontaneous. Respond in an unplanned and playful way. Most laughter results from spontaneous conversational humor. The second greatest source of laughter results from mishaps when no one is seriously hurt—when a person can think, with humor, *I'm more than my mistakes. I can dance around them even under duress.*

Humor Activities

Discover your humor preferences. Recall what your sense of humor was like as a child. What made you laugh? How would you describe the humor of your closest relatives and friends in childhood? Did they enjoy humor? What kind? Did they initiate everyday humor? Did they initiate humor during stressful times? Who most influenced you and why? Pondering these questions will probably give you insights into the types of humor you most appreciate.

Try humor reminiscing. In a quiet place, relax and recall three funny stories from your life that really made you laugh hard. See the pictures clearly. Reexperience them. Hear yourself laugh. Feel your body laugh. Record the experiences in detail in your journal. Share one experience with someone close to you.

Be more mindful of things that make you smile. Look around you to find five blue objects. Perhaps you'll realize that blue objects are all around you, even if you hardly noticed before. In a similar way you can find things that make you smile if you look for them (A. Klein 1989). You might smile at a beautiful baby or a sunset, or you might find something funny. Record what you find every day for a week. Be ready to smile, laugh, and be playful.

Start off the day laughing. Smiling and laughing activate the pleasure centers of the brain, making the mood more positive. This happens even when the laugh is forced. Try reading this paragraph aloud when you wake up in the morning:

HA HEE HEE HEE, HA HO HA! HA HO HO HO HEE

HO HEE HO HEE HO HA. HA HO HEE HEE HA HA

HO HA HEE HO HA. HA HO HEE HEE HEE HEE, HA

HO HO HO HA HO HO. HA HEE HO HO! (quoted in A. Klein 1989, 112)

This laughter exercise is similar to a Buddhist laughter meditation that has been practiced for centuries. (See also the smile meditation in item 10 at http://www.newharbinger.com/39409. Alternatively, try starting the day thinking *I'm glad to be alive*, rather than thinking negative thoughts.)

When angry, depressed, or anxious, try to find something to laugh about. Do this consciously until it becomes automatic. Remember that you can lighten your own mood without diminishing the seriousness of a situation.

Create a humor collection. List your favorite comedy movies, cartoons, funny books, jokes, comical experiences, and cards. Keep this list handy and refer to it often.

Tell a joke or funny story. Select a favorite, and practice until you can tell it well—especially the punch line. Tell it to various groups and notice the response. Tweak it or try another. Humor in storytelling and jokes is a skill that improves with practice.

Play with language. Language can be fun, as these snippets show: It was when he was trapped in a boxcar that Archie Bunker decided to write his "last will and testicle." A sign read, "Ears pierced while you wait" (McGhee 1999, 150). Jay Leno showed us how to have fun with unintentionally funny newspaper headlines and wedding announcements. Go easy on the puns, though—most don't find them nearly as clever as the punster.

Exaggerate. Laughing at the worst-case scenario makes the problem seem less serious. For example, "I'm so old that I don't buy green bananas anymore."

Laugh at yourself. We have to laugh at ourselves because we all do ridiculous things at times. Be amused, knowing that flaws, weaknesses, and blunders are externals and don't define one's core worth. And when you do laugh at yourself, do so in an accepting way. Overdoing it can reflect low self-regard. Humor researcher Paul McGhee (1999, 203) suggests this activity: Make a list of the things you don't like about yourself. This helps you realize that flaws don't signal the end of the world. Divide the list into things that are changeable or not. Practice poking fun at the imperfections and embarrassing moments you are most sensitive about in a kind way (for example, "My toes are so long that they get to the door two minutes before the rest of me"). Or imagine introducing yourself to a group of imperfect people, à la Alcoholics Anonymous: you say, "I'm John, and I have protruding ears," and they say, "Hi John," with lighthearted acceptance. Do this with the attitude that anyone who would reject you for such imperfections has a serious problem.

Find humor amidst adversity. Consider how you have responded emotionally to adversity in the past, or how you typically respond. Perhaps you get sad or anxious. Consider other options. For instance, you could stay housebound and miserable after a divorce, or you could be like the woman who ran outside, opened her arms, and yelled, "Next!" Ask yourself, *What would _____ do in this situation?*—filling in the blank with someone who shows good humor amidst adversity. You might reframe adversity (for example, "I'm not lost; I'm exploring."). Or you might conjure up a funny memory and superimpose it over a bad one. In Army Ranger school, my buddy and I had to cross a ravine in the pitch black darkness of the night. We found a tree that had fallen across the ravine and were gingerly tightrope-walking across it when, like a trapdoor, it gave way. We plummeted fifteen feet to the bottom of the ravine. After a short silence, I heard my buddy burst into loud laughter. When I realized that neither of us was hurt, I joined in. We both sat there in a crumpled heap laughing for several minutes. When I superimpose that comical memory over difficult memories or present situations, they tend to seem less daunting. As an exercise, write down several funny memories of when you or others found humor in adversity.

Observe humor styles. For several days, observe yourself and others using the wholesome and hostile humor forms described earlier in this chapter. Record these observations in your journal, just to get yourself thinking about these forms. Record the effects the two forms have on you and others.

Connect with playful people. Call or visit someone who makes you smile. Do this weekly or more often.

Conclusion

Wholesome humor can lift both you and those around you. Viewed from this perspective, wholesome humor can be an act of service. The spark of wholesome humor already exists within you. It often springs naturally from, and is nourished by, other resilience strengths described in this workbook, such as optimism, compassion, self-esteem, altruism, and love. Remember, humor is basically about being open to play and amusement. In this regard, humor is quite simple and natural.

Chapter 16

Moral Strength

Living up to our moral capacity breeds happiness, helping us feel inwardly more peaceful and good about ourselves. Recall that feelings such as peace and contentment are related to happiness, and that happiness is linked to resilience. Conversely, regrets and guilt, which are often the result of not living up to our moral capacity, can create unsettling inner turmoil that makes us more vulnerable to stress-related conditions. This chapter will discuss moral strength—what it is, why it matters, and how to cultivate it—and how it relates to resilience.

What Is Moral Strength?

In nearly all cultures around the world, if people are asked what comprises moral strength, the virtues consistently mentioned include honesty, respect, benevolence, courtesy, trustworthiness, responsibility, fairness, and the like. In this chapter, we are not talking about values imposed on us by others. Rather, we'll be talking about inner strengths that already exist within us as capacities that can be developed.

Being moral is simply being good and decent—having good character. Morality seeks the common good—doing what is in the best interest of self and others.

We assume that people want to be good and to do good. Most people realize that there is no lasting happiness to be found in unkindness—either to themselves or to others. Conversely, being good connects us to who we really are at the core, which leads to lasting happiness.

Moral Strength, Happiness, and Resilience

Happy people behave in ways that promote peace of conscience and minimize regrets. They live with integrity, meaning that the way they live accords with their highest values. Just as structural integrity means that something does not break or tear easily, so does moral integrity help us withstand adversity. Living with integrity lets us look back on our lives with satisfaction—and enjoy our memories again.

Peace of conscience does not require perfection. It does require that we do our best—that we strive for moral excellence. This requires a very basic form of courage, since the moral life is not necessarily the popular or easy life.

The idea that happiness is tied to goodness is ancient. Aristotle used the word *eudaemonia*, or "good soul," for happiness, and taught that happiness is derived from virtuous living. Conversely, many writers have described the anguish of transgressing deeply held values. For example, Ed Tick (2005) describes PTSD in veterans as a "soul wound," with moral pain as a root cause. John Chaffee describes a gradual entrapment, or seduction by degrees, noting that "immoral people are corrupted at their core, progressively ravaged by a disease of the spirit" (1998, 341). And Jonathan Shay (2002), an expert on combat-related PTSD, notes that from moral wounds come self-loathing, feelings of unworthiness, and loss of self-respect.

Although morality is seldom improved in a lasting way through compulsion, most would agree that moral strengths are innate and susceptible to enlargement—just as the other strengths of resilience are.

Living up to our moral capacity is within everyone's grasp. Mother Teresa (Petrie and Petrie 1986), when asked what it was like to be a living saint, replied, "You have to be holy in the position you are in just as I have to be holy in the position [I am in]. Holiness is a simple duty for you and me. There is nothing extraordinary about being holy." To be *holy*, which has the same linguistic root as "whole," "heal," and "health," means to have integrity—consistency between one's values and actions. Thus, one can be a holy teacher, parent, trash collector, or firefighter.

In his *Notebook*, Mark Twain (1971, 261–262) wrote, "No man, deep down in the privacy of his own heart, has any considerable respect for himself." It is interesting that Twain suffered from depression. In contrast, resilient people strive to maintain self-respect. If it is lost, they have ways to recover it.

How to Grow Moral Strength

There are essentially three paths to inner peace and self-respect.

1. **Decide in advance to live morally, and then do so.** The best time to make decisions about what you will or will not do is before adversity strikes. Once a moral course has been predetermined, it is considerably easier to act with integrity when you're under duress, tired, or tempted.

2. **Have a system for righting, and making peace with, wrongs that you will inevitably make because you are human.** Starting anew, bouncing back from mistakes or

bad choices, is a critical part of resilience. We might call this moral resilience. In many cultures, religions, and recovery groups, these are the steps:

- *Admit the wrong.* We can't change what we deny.

- *Make amends when possible.* This is the compassionate thing to do as it is healing for the offended party and ourselves. Sometimes a sincere apology is all that can be given.

- *Acknowledge mitigating circumstances* (for example, "I was inexperienced," "I made a decision under pressure," or "I didn't have all the facts"). This is not making excuses, just increasing understanding. I'll always remember my West Point company mate, Doug Madigan, with appreciation. At a class reunion, I shared with him my biggest regret from West Point. Two of my roommates during plebe year flunked out, and I wondered whether, if I had been a better friend, they might have made it. Doug, who was friendly with both of the roommates, said with genuine concern, "What did we know when we were eighteen?" Somehow, that made me feel better. In a more general sense, what do we know when we are thirty or fifty years old? We are all still learning and trying to get the hang of living well.

- *Acknowledge your right to pick yourself up after falling.* Worthwhile people don't lose their worth because of imperfections, nor do they forfeit their right to keep trying to improve.

- *Reconcile with a higher power.* For example, ask for forgiveness, allowing God to take the pain and trusting that forgiveness will come.

- *Forgive yourself.* Some become depressed, dispirited, and even suicidal because of an act or a pattern of transgression. They might conclude they are beyond redemption or can never again be good enough after doing *that.* Following the suggestion of Follette and Pistorello (2007), you might ask yourself, "Have I stopped valuing [honesty, kindness, virtue] just because I strayed from the path, or got turned around once, twice, or even for several years?"

- *Commit to a better course of action, resolving not to repeat the mistake.* Have the wisdom to change course, then do your earnest best. That's all we would ask of our children. And if you then stumble, try again. Growing moral strength is a lifelong process.

3. **Persist in the pursuit of moral excellence.** Recall that people in many cultures value the moral strengths mentioned earlier. These strengths seem to help individuals, families, and groups be happier. The following activity is intended to help you grow these consensus virtues and give yourself credit for progress you've made.

Activity: The Fearless, Searching, and Kind Moral Inventory

This activity is patterned after the moral inventory used in Alcoholics Anonymous. When a grocer inventories the shelves, he simply counts, without judging, what is there and what is not in order to see where he stands. Likewise, in the fearless, searching, and kind moral inventory we simply take stock of our present moral condition. We notice strengths, lest this inventory be only an *immoral* inventory. And we notice what we need to do to grow stronger. The process is fearless, searching, and kind because there is no condemnation or denial—only the intention to grow and be happier at an appropriate pace.

Before starting the inventory, take a moment to meditate on integrity. Integrity brings us self-respect, inner peace, happiness, and trust. Sitting quietly, consider this question: Is there anything that disturbs my peace, damages my reputation with myself, or leads others to distrust me? Now follow these steps to take the fearless, searching, and kind moral inventory:

1. Start by reading the definitions of the character strengths in the first column. Make any adjustments to these definitions that you feel are appropriate.

2. In the second column, rate where you presently stand on a scale from 1 to 10, with 10 meaning you are living this strength as well as a person can.

3. In the third column, describe a time in the past when you demonstrated this strength. This helps to motivate you to improve by reminding you of strengths and potentialities that already exist.

4. In the fourth column, identify specific steps that will bring you closer to moral excellence—to demonstrating a strength better and more often. For example, to increase honesty you might keep an honesty–dishonesty journal for a week. Each day, list the

    lies you hear (How does it feel to hear them?),

    lies (even white lies) you tell (How does it feel to tell them? Does it make you happier?), and

    truths you tell, giving yourself credit for telling the truth when doing so is difficult (How does that make you feel inside?).

At the end of the week, see how you did. Then set a goal for improvement. For example, you might aim to go an entire day (or some other reachable goal) only telling the complete truth—no white lies, no deceit, no excuses to save face. Ask yourself what is the worst that could happen if you told the truth? What is the best thing that could happen?

The Fearless, Searching, and Kind Moral Inventory

Character Strength	Rate Yourself (1–10)	Describe a time in the past when you demonstrated this strength	Describe what you could do to demonstrate this strength better and more often
Courage means persisting in doing the right thing despite the pressure to do otherwise.			
Honesty means you speak only the truth, always. No white lies, half-truths (truth can be tactful and kind), cheating, or stealing.			
Integrity means your behaviors match your values and that you show your sincere, authentic self without pretense.			
Respect means you honor people and treat them as worthwhile and that you are civil and courteous.			
Fairness means you play by the rules, do not take dishonorable advantage of others, and treat others impartially.			
Loyalty, faithfulness, and trustworthiness mean you keep commitments and confidences, don't speak ill of others behind their backs, and are reliable.			

Character Strength	Rate Yourself (1–10)	Describe a time in the past when you demonstrated this strength	Describe what you could do to demonstrate this strength better and more often
Responsible means you are able and willing to respond to valid needs and duties, are dependable, and protect yourself and others.			
Kind and caring mean you are concerned with the welfare of others and desire to help and support their growth; you are considerate, generous, and tenderhearted.			
Sexual integrity means you use sexual expression in the context of love and concern for the other and never in a selfish or exploitive way.			
Tolerant means you are patient with the differences and imperfections of others; you are forgiving.			

Here are two additional ideas that might help to motivate and support you in your efforts to grow moral strengths.

Search for inspiring stories of people who did the right thing despite great peril or inconvenience. For example, during World War II Chiune Sugihara, who was serving as the Japanese consul to Lithuania, wrote visas—in defiance of his government—that saved more than six thousand Jews from the Nazis. As a consequence, he was imprisoned by the Russians and shunned by his government after the war. Influenced by his samurai code, which taught him to help those in need, he and his wife had decided to risk the consequences simply because it was the right thing to do. Their moral courage liberated them from fear of ridicule and rejection, notwithstanding the costs. Arthur Ashe, Joshua Chamberlain (the highly respected Civil War officer), and Viktor Frankl are others who were admired for their quiet moral courage.

Complete a moral strength sentence stem. Think of a moral strength you'd like to grow. Complete this sentence stem with as many responses as you can think of: The positive consequences of my being more _____ (for example, honest, kind, or tolerant) are… This exercise can be very motivating.

A Story of Honesty

Over the course of my career, I've been asked to write many letters of recommendation. I first invite the requesters in for rather searching interviews in order to make the letters more personal. At some point I ask about character. I might lead with, "What would distinguish you and make you valuable to your employer?" One unusually accomplished, self-motivated young woman said, with quiet self-assurance, "I'm honest." I asked her what integrity means. She said, "Doing the right thing even when you don't have to, when no one is watching." I asked her for examples. She said, "I don't take company supplies at work. When we are assigned online closed-book tests, I don't use books." "Anything else?" I asked. "When my class was assigned to attend a concert, my friends left after getting a ticket stub. I stayed for the concert knowing that I would have to say whether or not I attended."

As I was writing the letter, I called her father, a longtime friend, and asked him what he considered his daughter's greatest strength. Without hesitation, he said, "Kelly is honest." I thought, *There's a young woman who can be trusted, and who will have inner peace if she remains true to her values.* It was a pleasure to recommend her without reservation, for she had not only intellectual intelligence, but moral intelligence as well.

Conclusion

Committing to moral living helps to connect us to our true happy nature—our higher self. This commitment promotes happiness and anchors us during difficult times. Before advancing to the next chapter, please ponder these reflections on moral strength.

Happiness and moral duty are inseparably connected. —George Washington

Live a good, honorable life. Then when you get older, and think back, you'll be able to enjoy it a second time. —Dalai Lama

An honest man's pillow is his peace of mind. —Anonymous

Be more concerned with your character than with your reputation, because your character is what you are, while your reputation is merely what others think of you.
—Coach John Wooden

Set your heart on doing good. Do it over and over again, and you will be filled with joy. A fool is happy until his mischief turns against him. And a good man may suffer until his goodness flowers. —Buddha

The real things haven't changed. It is still best to be honest and truthful.
—Laura Ingalls Wilder

There is no friendship more valuable than your own clear conscience. —Elaine S. Dalton

You cannot have a moral holiday and remain moral. —Oswald Chambers

Goodness Can Live with Suffering

The Nazis kept the slender ballerina Edith Eva Eger alive at Auschwitz to entertain them while they killed her family. She forgave them to free herself from the past. "At the end I remember feeling sorry for the German officers and soldiers as I watched them flee through the open camp gates. I remember thinking to myself, 'I will have painful memories of what happened, but they will always have to live with memories of what they did.' I lost my family in Auschwitz. It was very traumatic. But I have integrated the experience, and I'm the person I am because of it" (Siebert 1996, 238).

Chapter 17

Meaning and Purpose

Have you considered lately what gets you out of bed in the morning? What are you enthused about accomplishing? What brings you happiness and makes your life satisfying? Do you feel that your life matters? Questions like these turn our attention to significant aspects of resilience: meaning and purpose. Let's discuss what we know about these topics and how to benefit from them.

What Are Meaning and Purpose?

Purpose refers to what one determines to do—goals one intends to accomplish. *Meaning* implies that one's purposes, actions, or experiences are worthwhile and significant to the person.

How Do Meaning and Purpose Affect Resilience?

People who sense that their lives have meaning and purpose are generally happier and more resilient. What might explain this?

Some of the most profound thoughts on meaning and purpose were expressed by the psychiatrist Viktor Frankl. He based his thinking largely on his experience in WWII concentration camps. Frankl was fond of quoting the German philosopher Friedrich Nietzsche, who said, "He who has a why to live can bear with almost any how." In other words, meaning and purpose can help us survive and even thrive in difficult circumstances.

Frankl observed that those who endured their suffering best had a reason for living—something that life expected of them, something that impelled them to persist, something that lifted their spirits. Some found joy and meaning in serving their suffering comrades in the camps. In fact, at great peril to his own health, Frankl volunteered to care for prisoners who were sick with typhus, applying his much-needed medical skills. He further transcended the misery of camp life by envisioning his beloved wife and by imagining himself in the future giving lectures on the lessons of the concentration camps. He also marveled with consummate pleasure at nature's beauty. From his experience, he declared that your physical freedom might be taken away, but no one can take away your inner freedom—the freedom to choose your attitude toward suffering and your ability to impose meaning on even the greatest adversities. His experience actually helped him develop the school of psychotherapy called logotherapy, which helps people find meaning in their lives. In his own life, Frankl found great satisfaction in helping others find meaning and purpose. He wrote that what human beings need "is not a tensionless state but rather a striving and struggling for some goal worthy" (1963, 166) of them.

Psychologists Philip Zimbardo and John Boyd (2008) further suggest that looking forward to a meaningful future stimulates one to set satisfying goals, make plans, and work hard to succeed and be healthy. These behaviors tend to promote happiness, health, and resilience. And focusing on creating a meaningful and purposeful future helps to protect against post-traumatic stress symptoms and mental disorders generally—perhaps by countering the tendency to get stuck in the negatives of past experiences.

Having Meaning and Purpose Is a Personal Choice

Circumstances in life, particularly difficult ones, will cause you to summon your strengths—your abilities, values, loves, desires, experience, and wisdom. Applying your strengths in a meaningful way is a very personal, creative, heartfelt process: no one else will combine the strengths you have in the same way. When we immerse ourselves in challenging causes that matter, meaning and purpose increase (Nakamura and Csikszentmihalyi 2003). Unlike fleeting material pleasures, the satisfaction we gain from meaningful endeavors tends to persist and even increase with time.

How to Grow Meaning and Purpose

How do we discover, or increase, meaning and purpose in our lives? It can be useful to consider three domains: life in general, work, and crisis.

Meaning in Life

Frankl stressed that each person finds his own unique path to meaning and purpose in his own time. The meaning and purpose checklist (adapted from Schiraldi 2016a), which is based on Frankl's work, lists possible routes to meaning and purpose. As an exercise to stimulate ideas, place a check beside an item that you might be interested in pursuing, either now or in the future. In other words, check those items that you think might increase meaning and purpose in your life. As you complete this checklist, consider what you really want from life and what you want to contribute to the world. The items are grouped in three broad areas. The most satisfied people will generally strike a balance between the three.

The Meaning and Purpose Checklist

Give something meaningful to the world. This area is about contributing in ways that make the world a better place, investing your strengths in ways that matter.

_____ Establish, join, or recommit to a social or political cause that excites you (politics, science, church or synagogue, Mothers Against Drunk Driving, Parents of Murdered Children, urban sanctuaries for children, youth mentoring, strengthening your own family, and so forth).

_____ Create art, poetry, and writing or explore other creative expression that makes something new, beautiful, or useful.

_____ Give money or material support to a worthy cause.

_____ Engage in selfless service, seek self-transcendence, and build up or help others.

_____ Give even in small ways that help or please others, such as by picking up trash by the side of the road; beautifying your yard for your neighbor's benefit, not yours; giving a coworker, spouse, or neighbor an unexpected hand; lifting up anyone in any small way (a smile, a thank-you, a listening ear).

_____ Commit to do your best at your job today.

_____ Simply observe what you do, or can do, to meet others' needs.

_____ Share with others what you have discovered to reduce your own suffering.

Experience and enjoy life's wholesome pleasures and beauties. Being in awe of the world's beauty or being absorbed in simple pleasures reminds us that life is worthwhile. Experiencing positive emotions increases the feeling that our life matters. Enjoy:

_____ Adventure

_____ Cathedrals

_____ Connecting with neighbors

_____ Exercising your body

_____ Faces

_____ Friends

_____ Intimate love

_____ Nature (for example, get up early and watch the sunrise; gaze at the constellations at night)

_____ Noticing what you appreciate in others (tell them)

_____ Recreation

_____ Teamwork

_____ Watching children play (hearing them laugh)

Develop personal strengths and attitudes. This is innately satisfying, and it prepares us to contribute to the world in meaningful ways.

_____ Courage, taking responsibility for your own life (According to Yalom 1980, "I can't" often means "I won't take responsibility for my own life," which is a form of avoidance.)

_____ Improving the mind

_____ Loyalty and honesty

_____ Peace of mind, serenity

_____ Personal growth, holiness, goodness of character, self-actualization

_____ Refraining from criticizing, complaining, whining, backbiting, and other negative behaviors

_____ Understanding, empathy, patience, compassion

Meaning and purpose spring from our deepest values. Before proceeding, please consider these questions: What do you notice about the items you've checked? What do they say about what you value in life? Is there balance among the three areas? Does this checklist suggest actions you'd like to take? Perhaps you'd wish to write about this in your journal, if you keep one.

Meaning in Work

Many people find meaning and purpose in their work. Ideally, find an occupation that you love to do. People who are happy at work tend to be more successful. If you can't have the job you most love, figure out how to love the job you have.

How might you turn your job or career into a vocation in which your strengths are utilized in a meaningful and satisfying way? How might you redefine your job as a calling rather than drudgery? As an exercise, rewrite your job description so that people would want to apply for it. Highlight the benefits. Especially consider those aspects of the job that call forth your strengths, skills, and values—and give you the greatest pleasure, including interactions with others. After you complete this job description, imagine hiring yourself. Keep the new job description handy. Reread it when you get frustrated with your boss or when you wonder why you are doing the work you are doing.

Amy Wrzesniewski and colleagues (1997) found that one-third of a hospital's cleaning staff viewed the work as a calling—a calling to make the hospital experience positive for patients and staff alike. While the other two-thirds complained about the degrading work and low pay, this minority believed that its work mattered. They went beyond their job requirements, bringing flowers and smiles to patients. They reasoned that beautifying the environment would help patients heal and the medical staff to be more effective. Similarly, a customer service representative might turn cynical as she considers the rude people she constantly must confront. Or, she might find meaning in remembering that she gets to help frustrated people feel better.

Each job can be meaningful. In World War II, General George Patton told his truck drivers that without them the war would have been lost. If your whole job is not satisfying, what parts can you find satisfaction in completing? If completing a task is not possible in the near future, can you find satisfaction in the process of making progress?

You might reconsider your goals and expectations for work. For example, a physician might focus on external rewards, such as prestige, income, and pleasing his parents with the status of his job. Alternatively, he might focus on the more intrinsically satisfying goals of serving others.

Meaning in Crisis

Barbara Fredrickson and colleagues (2003) found that *resilient* people feel more positive after crises because they are more likely to find positive meaning from the crises. They suggest that meaning and purpose might be the most powerful ways to cultivate positive emotions during and after crises. (Recall that positive emotions, in turn, help to improve performance under pressure.) It is understandable that we will likely feel negative emotions as we deal with life's difficult situations. However, finding positive meaning can help us to cope better during and after such situations. These researchers suggest the following activity for finding meaning in adversity.

Activity: Finding Meaning in Adversity

Identify a current problem, such as conflict, the end of a relationship, having too much to do, a troubled family member, a move, major life changes, the illness or death of a loved one, or your own illness. Take time to ponder and then respond to these questions in writing.

How could this problem change your life in a positive way?

Which of your strengths does this situation require?

Has anything good come out of dealing with this problem so far?

How might you benefit from this situation in the long term?

How might this situation prepare you for adversity in the future?

How might others benefit in the long term as a result of this situation or the things you've suffered?

What might you learn from this experience?

What can you still feel good about?

What in life is still important to you despite this experience?

Additional questions to consider:

What inner strengths have kept you from suffering more than you might have?

What has kept you going?

What is life still expecting of you?

What keeps you from quitting?

Meaning Making: A Remarkable Story

During World War II, Corrie ten Boom and her sister Betsie were imprisoned in a German concentration camp because they had helped Jews in Holland escape the Nazis. During that terrible ordeal, they, like Viktor Frankl, found ways to give meaning to their adversity. Corrie and Betsie talked of establishing a "concentration camp" for the guards after the war, a home where "people who had been warped by this philosophy of hate and force could come to learn another way" (ten Boom, Sherrill, and Sherrill 1971, 215). This would be a camp without walls or barbed wire, and the barracks would have window boxes filled with flowers that would help to teach about love.

Betsie died in the prison camp, but before her death, she told Corrie, "[We] must tell people what we have learned here. We must tell them that there is no pit so deep that He is not deeper still. They will listen to us, Corrie, because we have been here" (227). After the war, the German government turned over a former concentration camp to Corrie, where from 1946 to 1969 she rehabilitated those in need of rest and care. In Holland she opened another home for ex-prisoners and other war victims. She died on her ninety-first birthday on April 15, 1983, after a lifetime of service.

Common Themes

Although there is no single road to meaning and purpose, many of the pathways contain common themes. Much of meaning and purpose is about developing our strengths and investing them in something larger than the self. Much of what is meaningful in life relates to using our strengths to elevate, serve, or love others—in short, helping to make others happier, which is the ultimate source of happiness (see helps for identifying strengths in the recommended resources). These efforts are uniquely personal and can be made consistent with our individual capacities.

Happiness tends to increase when we are absorbed in meaningful and satisfying activities—investing our best selves in ways that are challenging but not overwhelming. So seek meaningful pursuits. Do what you can, but don't overdo it.

Conclusion

I have repeatedly stressed how happiness and resilience are closely linked. Having a cause (or causes) that matters makes us happier and helps us persevere through difficult times. Please consider these reflections on meaning and purpose:

The primary motivational force in man is his striving for meaning.

It did not really matter what we expected from life, but rather what life expected from us.
—Viktor Frankl

Identify your regrets. This tells you something about what you still value, what matters to you, what is meaningful. —John Burt

Without a firm idea of himself and the purpose of his life, man cannot live, and would sooner destroy himself than remain on earth, even if he was surrounded with bread.
—Fyodor Dostoyevsky

At one time I used to say that all those guys died [in Vietnam] for nothing. Now I know better. Any man that lays down his life so others can be free is not only rich, I believe he sits at God's right hand. —Sergeant David A. Somerville

Chapter 18

Social Intelligence

Good relationships with other people generally make us happier, putting us in touch with our true loving nature—and our inner desires to love and be loved. The people with whom you have trusting, high-quality relationships can provide you with needed emotional support and other resources that can make you more resilient during difficult times. This chapter will explore what social scientists call *social intelligence*—skills that help us relate well to others. As you will see, genuine love is at the core of social intelligence.

What Is Social Intelligence?

Social intelligence is not simply having knowledge about relationships. It is also being able to quickly and effectively apply people skills in diverse situations. People skills allow us to love, lead, lift, motivate, persuade, get along with, respond to, work with, and ask for help of others. These skills can help us navigate everyday situations or survive crises. For instance, people skills might increase happiness at home; they might also help unify a community trying to survive a flood.

Socially intelligent people tend to be likable, respectful, believable, genuine, positive, approachable, appreciative, interested, and enthused. They tend to listen more than they speak and to attune to others' feelings in a caring way. Researchers (like Sanders 2005) have found that socially intelligent people tend to be happier, mentally and psychologically healthier, more successful professionally, and more ethical.

The sociability checkup (item 5 of the online resources that you can download at http://www.newharbinger.com/39409) will help you gauge your present skills at relating to others. The length of the checkup suggests the many complex aspects of social intelligence. However, at the heart of social intelligence is what in everyday language we call love, which will be the focus of this chapter. (For additional reading on social intelligence, see item 6 of the online resources.)

The Power of Love

After interviewing resilient WWII combat survivors, I concluded that mature, heartfelt love was at the heart of their resilience, and that "love" is perhaps the one word that best represents resilience. These remarkable individuals loved their families, country, buddies, God, and liberty more than comfort. They recounted moving stories of prisoners of war giving up food so that their friends might live, and acts of bravery inspired by love. Love is at the heart of courage, and in fact the word "courage" is derived from French and Latin roots for "heart."

I hesitated to share my conclusion about love because it sounded rather unscientific. However, scientific advances now support this conclusion. Although any positive emotion improves happiness, health, and performance, love has been called the supreme emotion because of its exceptional benefits (Fredrickson 2013).

Love affects body and soul. As we'll discuss in some detail, love can make us well, and lack of love can make us sick. Love positively impacts performance in the giver and receiver by increasing happiness. Love often gives us a reason to endure adversity (think of the grieving widow who might have quit but for the love of her children). Mature, heartfelt love, as opposed to giddiness or infatuation, is:

- **A feeling.** We naturally recognize and respond to genuine love. We don't need a book or a course to explain it. The capacity to love and be loved is part of who we are at the core.

- **An attitude.** Love is the attitude of wanting what's best for loved ones at each moment.

- **A decision and a commitment that we make every day.** We do so even when it is difficult or when we don't feel like it.

- **A skill that we cultivate through practice.** In other words, love is like the other skills of resilience. It is both innate and grown.

Positivity Resonance

The remarkable healer Dr. Karl Menninger is said to have observed that love cures both those who give it and those who receive it. Dr. Barbara Fredrickson (2013) studied a very simple form of love called *positivity resonance* (PR). PR refers to fleeting moments of warm, mutual connection with others in which we feel safe and good. PR might be a simple smile and nod as you walk by and silently wish someone a good day. It might be stopping to talk with someone, giving full presence in which eyes and hearts meet (no texting, wandering thoughts, or looking around). Perhaps it is sharing playful amusement or kind interest with another. The moments are unhurried. Bodies are relaxed and turned toward each other, with soft eyes and open hearts.

Fredrickson (2013) reported that PR changes biology in both parties. Oxytocin, the calm-and-connect hormone, increases. Oxytocin mutes the amygdala and calms fear, while helping people attune to others with greater trust and greater discernment. Less of the stress hormone cortisol is secreted, resulting in healthier brains, fewer colds, fewer instances of obesity, and fewer symptoms of the stress-related conditions. She notes that lack of PR is more damaging than smoking, being obese, or drinking excessively. Subjectively, people who experience PR say they feel more at home, at ease, whole, and like their true selves. Consistent with my observations of the WWII generation, Seligman (2011) concludes that the capacity to love and be loved is the single strength most clearly associated with happiness at age eighty.

Activity: Creating Positivity Resonance

Fredrickson (2013) concluded that fleeting moments of PR add up to greater happiness, more resilience, better health, and better relationships. Consider the countless exchanges that you have each day with others. Perhaps they occur with people that you pass by or offer only distracted attention. In the following table, identify five people, and consider how you might turn brief moments with them into moments of PR. Then, carry out your plan, making one PR connection per day. Notice how your actions impact you and the other people. You might write about this in your journal, if you keep one.

Day/Date	Person	What I'll Do to Create PR
Day 1		
Day 2		
Day 3		
Day 4		
Day 5		

Resilient Leadership: Leading from the Heart

We are all leaders, whether we lead ourselves, supervise others, or lead by example. Resilient people take care of themselves—body, mind, and spirit—while caring for those they live, work, and play with. Effective leaders lift those around them, whether or not those leaders are in positions of authority.

Love is at the heart of good leadership. If you think about it, would you follow another person wholeheartedly if that person didn't have your best interests at heart? I think of a publishing executive who said about her aunt, "I knew she loved me, so I let her lead me." A United States Military Academy study (Adamshick 2013) surveyed twelve thousand Army officers who ranked twenty-three strengths of effective leaders. The strengths ranked at the bottom were related to technical and tactical expertise. Among the top strengths were care and concern for others, which almost 90 percent of the officers viewed as necessary.

Good leadership is servant leadership. Good leaders create a supportive climate in which people feel secure enough to flourish. They build people up, helping them to be confident and to do their best work without fear of failing. Good leaders listen, believe in others, are approachable, and are concerned with those they lead. They empathize—that is, they sense or attune to others' emotions and thoughts in a caring way. Their people perceive them as "being in the trenches" with them and caring about them as individuals. They communicate expectations calmly and clearly and praise good work. One employee expressed his longing for caring leaders who connect with their people when he told me, "Leaders need to know how much they matter, how much they affect us. A simple 'good morning' or 'have a good evening,' or taking five minutes to ask 'How'd your weekend go?' or 'How's your family?'—things like that go a long way." The servant leader cares more about his or her people than personal advancement. Curiously, such leadership inspires loyalty and excellence in those who are led.

Positivity resonance is contagious. If a leader has a love-filled heart, it affects those nearby. Recall that the heart emits far more electromagnetic energy than the brain, and this energy can be measured ten feet away (Childre and Rozman 2005). A coherent heart syncs up the heart, brain, gut, and oxytocin levels of both the leader and those nearby.

Activity: Positivity Resonance with Those You Lead

Think about those you lead, whether directly or by example, at home or at work. How can you make time to be with them and show you care? How can you affect their lives for the good? How can you be involved with them and bring out their best? How can you listen? How can you discover their strengths and help them apply those strengths? (Workers who feel that leaders take the time to know them and help them to apply their strengths are happier and more engaged at work.) You may wish to journal about your answers to these questions and make a plan to connect more closely with those you lead.

Activity: Leading with a Coherent Heart

If your heart is coherent, the hearts of those around you will also tend to be coherent. As you may recall, experiencing mature love is the quickest way to heart coherence. Before you meet with people you lead, whether it be a group you work with or family members, practice the Quick Coherence® technique, as explained in chapter 3. This takes but a few moments but can have a positive effect on those with whom you associate.

In addition, if your team or group is about to begin a particularly challenging task, you might take a few moments to practice the Quick Coherence® technique together, as a team or group, to sync everyone's hearts and minds. See if this doesn't create a positive emotional tone that promotes effective functioning.

Conclusion

Bringing more love—genuine caring—to our interpersonal relationships can go a long way toward increasing happiness, health, and functioning in ourselves and those with whom we associate. Even small increases in love can reap large benefits. In this chapter we explored simple ways to increase love by bringing positivity resonance and heart coherence to everyday exchanges. In the next chapter, we will focus on applying social intelligence at home.

Chapter 19

Socially Intelligent Families

Happiness at home and happiness at work are linked. Socially intelligent people apply people skills to build happiness at home. Happiness at home, in turn, tends to influence happiness at work and resilience generally. This chapter will focus on strengthening couples and families.

Strong Couples

Satisfied couples balance shared enjoyment with handling conflict in ways that strengthen the relationship. They spend time together building respect, trust, and fond memories. They also solve problems constructively—calmly, and as equal members of a team. Most couples have differences that can't be resolved. Resilient couples learn to tolerate these differences. Considerable research has demonstrated the keys to strengthening couples.

Success in marriage usually takes time. It typically takes ten to fifteen years for a couple to reach high-quality intimacy: At first, partners in a relationship romantically think that their partner is perfect and able to fulfill all their needs. Over time, they recognize differences with their partner and struggle to work them out. Eventually, they choose to stay together, cooperate, and depend on each other because they enjoy being a team (Kovacs 2007). Note that the prospects of marital satisfaction are good. Among those who describe their marriages as very unhappy, 80 percent of those who stick it out for five years will say that their marriage is happy (Waite et al. 2002). The likelihood of success is better if partners learn good couples skills, such as how to disagree in ways that strengthen relationships (see "Resilient Couples and Family Skills" in the recommended resources).

Appreciate complementary gender differences. According to research by Tannen (2001), generally speaking men and women tend to process conflict differently, although both genders have the same goals of being treated with respect and equality. Much of the gender differences can be explained by brain differences. And while there are certainly exceptions to the general rules, understanding gender differences can help couples greatly. For example, women tend to pick up more emotional and intuitive cues and can discuss these more quickly and easily. Men tend to find it more difficult to put feelings into words, and they might need to say, "I'm taking time to process this." Men are more likely to say they prefer discussions to be calm and to follow predictable rules so they can think through issues logically—and they tend to withdraw when things get heated. Men prefer to solve or fix problems quickly, whereas women tend to want to explore complexities before deciding on a solution. Offering a quick fix might unintentionally communicate, "You're not smart enough to figure this out." Women might need to say, "I'm not asking you to solve the problem; I'm asking you to help me consider all the angles." Men might need to say, "Do you want my advice or shall I be a sounding board?"

Rather than getting defensive or trying to quickly fix a problem, first try to simply validate your partner's feelings and viewpoints. All couples have conflict. It is how conflict is handled that predicts marital satisfaction. If your partner is upset, sit down, face him or her, and calmly say, "Tell me about it." Try to acknowledge the other person's feelings, saying something like "I can see how that would be upsetting. Tell me more to help me understand." Check out your understanding by restating what you heard ("It sounds like you are feeling X because of Y. Is that right?"). Don't mind read or speak for your partner. Simply restate what your partner has said. When your partner feels *completely* heard and understood, only then express how you see the issue. It might take several hours of calm back-and-forth for both partners to feel understood. When you arrive at this point, then set a time in the future to brainstorm to try to solve the problem. End on a positive note (for example, "I'm sorry we had this disagreement, but I appreciate your talking about it. I love you"). This approach takes time and effort, but the effort is worthwhile, especially for hot issues.

Accentuate the positives. Appreciate at every opportunity. Don't criticize. Criticizing creates resentment and is a difficult habit to reverse. Focus on solving the problem, not attacking the person. Structure time for fun and friendship—time that is free of talking about problems. Brainstorm fun activities, and then alternate from each other's list. If you have a concern or criticism, make sure compliments and positive encounters outweigh these by at least five to one.

Have a weekly couples meetings to anticipate problems, to plan, and to value your partner. Emphasize what is going well. Thank your partner for what he or she is doing well. This can be as short as a half hour. Try to keep it fun.

Put your spouse first. Greet your spouse warmly before you greet others. Remember the courtesies that you used when courting, such as saying *please* and *thank you*. Secretly help your partner out without seeking credit, which can make the partner feel obligated. Call your partner or leave love notes just for fun.

Seek to value, not control, your partner. Both partners are happiest in relationships in which there is equality and mutual respect. Don't push too hard for something you desire. If a gentle invitation doesn't work, calm yourself, ease up, and try another approach.

Be 100 percent honest and faithful. Faithfully married couples are more sexually satisfied than all other sexually active groups (for example, Michael et al. 1994).

Activities: Building Strong Couples

Try these activities and see if they strengthen your relationship with your partner.

List things you most appreciate about your partner. Share one a week. Make it playful sometimes ("You know what I like about you?") but always sincere. Remember what first attracted you to your partner. Express appreciation when your partner shows these strengths. Remember your partner's potential.

Each day, notice something that your partner does. Does he or she take out the garbage, make the bed, spend time with the children? Express appreciation verbally or with a hug.

Ask your partner about hopes, dreams, or fears. Do this without judgment. If he says, "I'd love to travel to Tahiti," don't say, "You know we can't afford that." You might simply say, "That would be so nice to do someday."

Describe in writing what it would be like living with you if you were your partner. Explain why you do what you do, and ask your partner to do the same. Exchange what you've written. Then discuss and listen in a way that seeks understanding. This process often reveals fears and concerns that are not being understood, and it changes anger to empathy (Amatenstein 2010).

Share good news. When your partner shares good news, give your full presence. You might respond, "That's fantastic!"

Strong Families

Highly effective parents raise children who feel valued and respected. These parents communicate expectations ("I expect you to…"), set limits ("That's not acceptable"), and emphasize accomplishments and rewards rather than punishments and weaknesses. Consider the following habits of effective parents, and circle those you'd like to try.

Cultivate the family-as-team ethic. They repeat, "It's important to work as a team; we need to pull together." They explain the purpose of chores (it's more about building relationships than getting the work done) and work alongside their children.

Hold weekly family nights. Their purpose is to create family bonds and memories. Anything that is fun works: games, picnics, discussions, gardening, planning a vacation, or learning together.

Hold regular family councils. This is like a couples meeting that includes the whole family. Members come together to coordinate calendars, share goals, go over chores, plan, and encourage. The environment is open, safe, and positive. In one family, for example, all members shared their goals and progress from the previous month. One child said, "My goal was to run every day, and I was 50 percent successful." The whole family cheered. I thought to myself how much more motivating that was than focusing on the lapses. Try posting an agenda, to which each person can add an issue they'd like to address and a tentative solution. This trains children to be problem solvers. During the council, the whole family brainstorms, listing ideas without critiquing them at first. (All ideas are accepted as having merit; you never know what will emerge.) Then each alternative is weighed, and the best one to try is selected.

Follow up family councils with regular mom or dad interviews with each child. Plan a regular, anticipated time to encourage and listen to each child. Tell the child, "This is a time for you to talk about your interests and concerns, accomplishments, goals, and so forth. What would you like to talk about?" Make sure you keep the atmosphere positive—avoiding criticism and communicating your love and concern. Be sure you listen much more than you speak. As children learn that they can speak freely without censure, they will open up, and this practice can ward off problems.

I stayed with a young couple and their three daughters, aged three to eight. The three young girls immediately impressed me. They were so happy, secure, and engaging, even to me, a stranger. They also played together so nicely. In a quiet moment, I asked the father how the girls were turning out so well. He said, "First, we have no TV, so they've learned to entertain each other. We also have 'monthly chats,' where they talk with me about whatever interests them or is on their mind. It's a time they can ask questions. I want to know about their friends and what they are thinking. I hope that our trusting, open communication will continue through the difficult teenage years. I ask them how I can be a better dad. Often, they'll say, 'You're doing a great job.' At the end I just tell them I love them and I'm grateful to be their dad. They look forward to our chats and often say, 'We haven't had our monthly chat.' I'll say, 'Let's do it now,' or 'How about tonight?'"

Correct in private. All children need parents who love them enough to set limits. Correcting in private avoids resentment.

Tap the power of the family dinner. When families eat dinner together, the children perform better at school, are better nourished, and experience fewer mental health problems. When parents are able to eat dinner at home, they feel greater personal and family success and are more satisfied and productive at their jobs. Wise managers, then, will help their employees get home for dinner—perhaps offering flextime, encouraging workers to make it home for dinner, or encouraging them to go home and come back if necessary. Wise parents will plan a regular dinnertime and let children know that they are expected to be there. Turn off the phone and electronics, and ask the children to contribute to the preparation or cleanup. If you buy a meal out, pick it up and eat it at home (Jacob et al. 2008; Bergin 2009).

Make each child feel loved and appreciated. Remember to regularly express appreciation and affection. Have special parent–child date nights. (One family I know held VIP nights during which a child could stay up a little later with a parent. Years later, the child reminisced fondly of times spent folding laundry and talking with Mom.) Make scrapbooks with photographs, recorded memories and impressions, report cards, notes and art created by the children, and so on. It's more about the heart than techniques. One parent I met asked her child, "Why are you so good?" The child responded, "Because I know you love me."

Parent the child you have, not the child you wish you had. Children are all different and have different needs, capabilities, and strengths. If gentle requests are not working, be willing to set boundaries that hold children accountable, and then enforce consequences.

Conclusion

People consistently report that high-quality family relationships increase their happiness. As with the other determinants of happiness, generating happiness in family life takes time and commitment. It is rare, however, that people who invest the effort to strengthen their families regret doing so.

Chapter 20

Forgiveness

In life, nearly everyone will be emotionally wounded by serious offenses committed by others. When we forgive, we free ourselves from being victimized a second time. That is, we choose to release anger, resentment, and desires for revenge so that we can move on—freed of the heavy load that chains us to the past. Forgiveness is necessary in every relationship. It is also vital, and one of the last steps, to the healing process.

Forgiving was once considered only a theological concept. Today research has repeatedly demonstrated that choosing to forgive strengthens us psychologically, because forgiving changes our response to the past.

What Is Forgiveness?

Forgiveness means voluntarily canceling the debt owed by the offender. We choose to forgive not necessarily because the offender has asked for or deserves it, but because we no longer wish to be ruled by the past. Forgiveness does not mean forgetting the offense. It does not necessarily mean we again trust or reconcile with the offender. We might even choose to bring an offender to justice in order to protect the offender or others from harm. However, in forgiving we strive to replace negative feelings we have toward the offender (such as resentment or indifference) with compassion (someone who does that must himself be wounded) and wishes for his or her happiness. Thus, we can be wiser from our experience, but without carrying forward the strong distressing feelings that cripple us. As you can see, then, forgiving is a gift we give ourselves. It is also a gift to others: Sometimes our compassion can soften the offender's heart. Often, our loved ones benefit when we release the anger that we feel for offenders but unintentionally direct at our loved ones.

Popular and scientific literature is full of accounts of resilient survivors who have forgiven unspeakable crimes. For example, the appropriately titled "From Darkness to Light" recounts the story of Christopher (Hugh) Carrier (2000). As a trusting ten-year-old, he climbed off the school bus thinking of Christmas. He was approached by David McAllister, who said to him, in effect, "I'm a friend of your father; could you help me find him a gift?" Hugh got into McAllister's motor home and was driven to Florida's alligator-infested Everglades. There, McAllister repeatedly stabbed Hugh with an ice pick in revenge for the way Hugh's father had fired him for being drunk on the job. McAllister then shot the boy in the left temple, blinding him, and left him. After being unconscious for nearly a week, Hugh staggered to a road, where a motorist spotted him and took him to the hospital.

Hugh's life followed a downward spiral. He was afraid to sleep alone or go outside, deeply resentful, and self-conscious about his drooping, half-shut eye. Three years after the accident, Hugh opened up, telling his story to friends who encouraged him. For the first time, Hugh realized that he could release his anger and use his story to inspire others. He graduated from college, earned a master's degree, and married. He felt gratitude for having miraculously survived the Everglades. When he held his baby, he realized why God had kept him alive, and he saw that many youngsters opened up to him readily when they realized all he'd been through.

Twenty-two years after the crime, McAllister admitted his guilt in a nursing home. The police called Hugh, who had wondered what he'd do if he ever confronted his offender. Outside McAllister's room, Hugh took a deep breath, summoning all his courage to go in. Hugh introduced himself to a withered seventy-seven-year-old man who weighed seventy pounds. At first, McAllister said, "I don't know what you're talking about." Then he trembled and cried. Reaching out, he said, "I'm sorry. I'm so sorry" (Carrier 2000, 105).

Hugh told McAllister that what he had done to him had not been the end of meaning in his life. It was a beginning. McAllister squeezed Hugh's hand and whispered, "I'm very glad" (106). Hugh visited nearly every day for the next three weeks. McAllister shared his life story, one with no father, juvenile halls, heavy drinking by his teen years, no friends, anger and shame, and the belief that God was something only suckers believed in. With Hugh's help, McAllister began to pray. One night Hugh told McAllister, "I'm planning on going to heaven and I want you there too. I want our friendship to continue" (106). That night McAllister died in his sleep. Hugh reflected, "Strange as it seems, that old man did more for me than he ever could have known. In his darkness I found a light that guides me still. Forgiving David McAllister gave me a strength I will have forever" (106).

Notice that forgiving was difficult for Hugh. At first he was not sure he could do it, but he persisted. Forgiving was a process that began for him as a teen but was completed many years later. In this case, offender and offended met face to face and reconciled. This isn't always possible. But as Hugh released his bitterness, the positive aspects of his life became clearer.

Bitterness has costs. If forgiving releases distressing anger and helps people to bounce back from past wounds, then we would expect research to demonstrate the beneficial effects of forgiving. It does. Forgiveness researchers such as Robert Enright (2012) have found that the practice of forgiveness helps people be happier (the result of releasing negative feelings);

have higher self-esteem (forgiving connects us to our true, loving, higher self);

have greater hope (because our focus moves beyond the past and turns to the future again);

experience less stress, depression, anxiety, hostility, chronic pain, sleep problems, high blood pressure, and relapse from substance-use disorders (all of which reflect unresolved pain);

be more flexible (letting go of the past frees creative energy); and

have greater empathy and spirituality (forgiveness moves us to have compassion for ourselves and imperfect people who hurt others intentionally or unintentionally).

Forgiving is a skill that becomes easier with practice. In the following sections, I'll describe three aspects of forgiveness: receiving forgiveness, forgiving self, and forgiving others.

How to Receive Forgiveness

Louis Zamperini, whose life was depicted in the movie *Unbroken*, survived forty-seven days on a life raft after his WWII bomber went down in the Pacific. He made a promise that if his life was spared he would dedicate himself to serving God. The Japanese who captured him did not kill him because of his propaganda value (Zamperini was a former Olympic track star). He was, however, brutally tortured. One camp commandant put his head on a log and threatened daily to behead him. A particularly deranged guard repeatedly tried to break him psychologically and physically. Understandably, after the war Zamperini struggled with severe nightmares, heavy drinking, desires for revenge, and getting into fights. His marriage crumbled. Impulsive, greedy decisions bankrupted him. He realized that he had failed to keep his promise to seek and serve God. One night he committed his life to God and felt the sweet balm of forgiveness. He said that on that very night his nightmares stopped. He stopped drinking. Feeling forgiven gave him the peace and strength to return to Japan to forgive his tormentors. He spent the remainder of his life working with troubled youth, and he died peacefully and cheerfully in 2014. His anger had been replaced by love (Hillenbrand 2012).

Activity: Conversation with a Kind Moral Authority

Some erroneously think that their mistakes disqualify them from being forgiven or loved. Spiritual practices can be liberating, such as the one described in this activity (Litz et al. 2016).

1. Find a quiet place to relax, clear your mind, and focus your thoughts. Think of an experience—something that you did or failed to do—that has deeply troubled you.

2. Imagine yourself in the presence of a kind moral authority who cares deeply for you; is forgiving, and wants only what's best for you. This might be a kindly relative, best friend, spiritual guide, leader, coach, God, or other higher power. The kind moral authority does not want you to suffer anymore but only desires your happiness. Pause to sense in your body a growing sense of ease and safety in the presence of this kind moral authority.

3. Share your experience with this kind moral authority. Describe what you've done—how you've been harmed by the experience. You might recount the self-loathing, shame, sadness, and aggression you've experienced and the other ways that your life has changed due to the hurt you caused. Imagine the kind moral authority holding your pain with great compassion.

4. Sense the kindness and compassion emanating from the kind moral authority. Let your body feel this. On each out-breath, release the pain to the kind moral authority. On the in-breath, absorb the kindness and compassion and feel them filling your body.

5. Listen. What does the kind moral authority want to tell you? Might the kind moral authority introduce the possibility of forgiveness, perhaps shifting even fair blame to the hope of reparation, compassion, and wholeness? Perhaps you hear reassurances that you are worthwhile, loved, or have a purpose (Who better to help others going through a similar experience than you?).

6. You might conclude by imagining this loving figure embracing you or touching your shoulder with understanding and love.

Spiritual reminders, if consistent with your beliefs, might aid this process. For example, consider Ezekiel 18:21, from the Old Testament: "But if the wicked will turn from all his sins that he hath committed, and keep all my statutes, and do that which is lawful and right, he shall surely live."

How to Forgive Yourself

Which is harder: forgiving self or others? Many find it more difficult to forgive themselves, thinking, *But I knew better!* Perhaps they grew up in a critical home and erroneously believe that they can never change, that certain behaviors are beyond the reach of forgiveness, or that self-punishment is the only way to keep themselves on the straight and narrow.

Forgiving the self is a critical aspect of bouncing back from things you've done and is as important as forgiving others. Forgiving the self does not make light of past mistakes. It acknowledges them. Rather than staying mired in negative judgments and self-condemnation, self-forgiveness involves a turning toward a better, more fruitful, happier life. Self-forgiveness recognizes that imperfect people nevertheless are still worthwhile, and that many of the world's finest people changed course after making serious mistakes. Along with the steps found in the section "How to Grow Moral Strength" in chapter 16, you might try these steps:

1. **Drop the double standard.** If you are harder on yourself than you are on others, remind yourself that *all* people are imperfect—and infinitely perfectible! We all make mistakes, and we all can learn and commit to improving. If your child or best friend made a mistake and was trying to improve, wouldn't you let them off the hook? Why not give yourself the same gift? Who motivates you more: someone who believes in you, or someone who thinks you have no hope? Believe in yourself.

2. **Don't let your errors define you.** Each of us is so much more than our mistakes. Remember that getting turned around for a time does not negate what you still value, nor does it disqualify you from having a good life. Said Confucius, "Our greatest glory is not in never falling, but in rising every time we fall." After forgiving yourself, try to recall gratitude, remembering what you did well and what you have learned from your experience.

3. **Try writing yourself a letter of forgiveness.** Remind yourself of these points and your right to go on.

How to Forgive Others

Forgiving is replacing anger with love. Loving acts connect us to our true happy nature, which is why those who learn to forgive often say that they feel happier and whole. Although forgiving serious offenses is extremely difficult, it is possible. These steps might help:

1. **Heal.** Traumatic wounds might require that a skilled mental health professional guides you in the healing process. A skilled trauma therapist will help you process and settle those wounds, so that they don't fester and return with a vengeance. Some people try to forgive too early and are surprised when troubling symptoms remain. For lesser offenses, you might try the steps we've explored in this workbook, such as confiding your pain in writing (chapter 8) or describing the positives (chapter 17) that have resulted from your painful experience.

2. **Try to understand the offender.** Why might she have behaved that way? Without condoning the offense, acknowledge that the offense does not fully define the offender, just as your mistakes don't fully define you.

3. **Don't take it personally.** The offense reflects a wounded person and is not a statement of your worth. Many others have been hurt in the same way, and many have overcome the resulting bitterness.

4. **Let go of thoughts that keep you bound to the past.** Thoughts like *I can't believe someone I love could do that; I can't go on* can keep you stuck. In fact, imperfect people behave imperfectly, and you *can* go on when you liberate yourself from past offenses by detaching from the offender through forgiveness. No one, no matter how respected or beloved, was treated well by everyone.

5. **Begin the forgiveness process, and give it time.** You might start the process by writing a forgiveness letter describing the offense, its impact on you, the offender's challenges at the time, and your intent to forgive (Schiraldi 2016a; Schiraldi and Kerr 2002). Visit http://www.newharbinger.com/39409 to download a letter template (item 9). You can write a forgiveness letter to every person for every offense that still troubles you. Depending on the offender, you might choose to burn, rather than send, the letter. Don't be surprised or discouraged should negative feelings return. This result does not negate your progress. Your process might be two steps forward and one back. Take your time. Forgiveness might come unexpectedly once you form the intention.

6. **Take the offender to neutral.** Forgiving is easier when the offender acknowledges his hurtful action and his determination to improve. Often, however, the offender will not apologize or reform. Perhaps there are offenses that still seem unsettled, despite your best efforts to forgive. Perhaps the offender is unwilling or unable to offer solace. If so, you might try this approach, described by Baker, Greenberg, and Yalof (2007). Accept that the offender is not the person you wish he were. That person does not exist. If you can't feel positively toward the offender yet, let go and take him to neutral. Think, *He hasn't earned my love or trust. So I take him to neutral—nada, zip, zero. I don't even waste time thinking about him or remembering him.* Diagrammed, the approach looks like this:

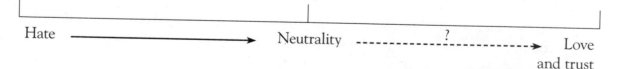

Notice how you feel after taking these steps. Did they help you accept the offender's limitations (perhaps she never learned the art of kindness and asking for forgiveness)? Does this acceptance feel like a permanent or temporary solution, or might you wish to attempt to more fully forgive at some future time, when you have more fully healed?

Conclusion

Although it can be very difficult, forgiving yourself and others is a skill well worth cultivating. Forgiveness can help us bounce back from difficult experiences and move ahead with greater happiness, healing, and resilience.

The skills that you've explored so far in this workbook have prepared you well for the final chapter in part 2, "Balance and Healthy Pleasures."

Chapter 21

Balance and Healthy Pleasures

Psychologists Philip Zimbardo and John Boyd (2008) have studied how our perspectives on time influence our lives. They found that happy people strike a healthy balance among the past, present, and future. Happy people tend to be at peace with their past and can recall memories with warmth and nostalgia. They've figured out how to settle and move beyond troubling memories. Perhaps therapy, writing about trauma (see chapter 8), and forgiving (see chapter 20) helped them. Keeping a scrapbook of mementos, expressing gratitude for positive memories, tracing one's family tree, or celebrating the culture of one's ancestors might also kindle fond connections to the past.

Happy people plan for a worthwhile future and are willing to work toward their goals (see Emmons 1986). They invest in their future but don't obsess about it. Excessive focus on the future can lead to worry or anger when plans are frustrated. So they have a plan that is driven by their values, but they are not so goal driven that they can't relax. Nor are they so rigid that they can't accept obstacles in the road.

Regarding the present, happy people find pleasure in everyday experiences—without being unrealistic or demanding. They make plans to enjoy themselves, carry out those plans, and find enjoyment in what they've planned.

Let's assume that you've made peace with the more troubling parts of your past and are making efforts to savor fond memories. Let's further assume that you've set specific, achievable short- and long-term goals for the future and that your goals are balanced among the important areas of family, friends, learning, profession, physical and emotional health, spirituality, leisure, and legacy (something you'll leave behind or do to better the world). Let's turn now to a skill area that is especially important in our time-urgent culture—the skill of enjoying wholesome pleasures in the present moment.

Balancing Work with Pleasure

Nearly all of the resilient WWII survivors I interviewed were actively engaged in a wide range of interesting and pleasant activities over the course of their lives. It was not unusual to find these octogenarians still enthusiastically traveling, enjoying the arts, playing bridge, reading, being docents at museums, dancing, and even playing sports (Schiraldi 2007). Pleasant activities help to keep the brain sharp and the mood upbeat. They are also among those factors outside of the workplace—along with sleep, exercise, diet, and social bonds—that appear to improve work performance.

Psychologists Peter Lewinsohn and colleagues (1986) observed an interesting downward spiral in depressed people. First, they became stressed, as typically happens with those who are "crazy busy." To save time, they stopped doing the pleasant things that had kept their mood up. As their mood became depressed, they pessimistically assumed that nothing could lift it again, so they stopped trying to engage in those mood-enhancing activities. Lewinsohn's team developed the pleasant events schedule to help depressed people again engage in pleasant pastimes. Doing so, they found, measurably improved mood. A modified version of the schedule follows.

Activity: Pleasant Events Schedule

This activity (adapted with permission from Lewinsohn et al. 1986) helps people check the balance in their lives and make needed adjustments in order to optimize mood. This very effective activity is well worth the time it takes to complete it. In a very structured way, you will identify activities you've enjoyed in the past and then make a plan to enjoy activities that will likely lift your mood—remembering that what makes us happier makes us more resilient.

Step 1: The pleasant events schedule (Lewinsohn, Munoz, Youngren, and Zeiss 1986) lists a wide range of activities organized beneath main topics. In the first column (ignore the second column for now), check those activities that you enjoyed in the past. Then rate how pleasant each checked item was on a scale from 1 to 10 (a score of 1 reflects little pleasure, and 10 reflects great pleasure.) For example, if you moderately enjoyed being with happy people but didn't enjoy being with friends or relatives, your first two items would look like this:

✓ 5 _____   1. Being with happy people

_____ _____   2. Being with friends/relatives

Social Interactions

These events occur with others. They tend to make us feel accepted, appreciated, liked, or understood. (Please note that you may feel that an activity belongs in another group. The grouping is not important.)

_____ _____ 1. Being with happy people

_____ _____ 2. Being with friends/relatives

_____ _____ 3. Thinking about people I like

_____ _____ 4. Planning an activity with people I care for

_____ _____ 5. Meeting someone new

_____ _____ 6. Going to a club, restaurant, or tavern

_____ _____ 7. Being at celebrations (for example, birthdays, weddings, baptisms, parties, family get-togethers)

_____ _____ 8. Meeting a friend for lunch or a drink

_____ _____ 9. Talking openly and honestly (for example, about hopes, fears, interests, what makes you laugh, what saddens you)

_____ _____ 10. Expressing true affection (verbal or physical)

_____ _____ 11. Showing interest in others

_____ _____ 12. Noticing successes and strengths in family and friends

_____ _____ 13. Dating, courting (this one is for married people, too)

_____ _____ 14. Having a lively conversation

_____ _____ 15. Inviting friends over

_____ _____ 16. Stopping in to visit friends

_____ _____ 17. Calling up someone I enjoy

_____ _____ 18. Apologizing

_____ _____ 19. Smiling at people

_____ _____ 20. Calmly talking over problems with people I live with

_____ _____ 21. Giving compliments, pats on the back, praise

_____ _____ 22. Teasing and bantering

_____ _____ 23. Amusing people or making them laugh

_____ _____ 24. Playing with children

_____ _____ 25. Other: _____

Activities

These activities make us feel capable, loving, useful, strong, or adequate.

_____ _____ 1. Starting a challenging job or doing it well

_____ _____ 2. Learning something new (for example, how to fix leaks, a new hobby, a new language)

_____ _____ 3. Helping someone (counseling, advising, listening)

_____ _____ 4. Contributing to religious, charitable, or other groups

_____ _____ 5. Driving skillfully

_____ _____ 6. Expressing myself clearly (out loud or in writing)

_____ _____ 7. Repairing something (for example, sewing, fixing a car or bike)

_____ _____ 8. Solving a problem or puzzle

_____ _____ 9. Exercising

_____ _____ 10. Thinking

_____ _____ 11. Going to a meeting (convention, business, civic)

_____ _____ 12. Visiting the ill, homebound, or troubled

_____ _____ 13. Telling a child a story

_____ _____ 14. Writing a card, note, or letter

_____ _____ 15. Improving my appearance (seeking medical or dental help, improving my diet, going to a barber or beautician)

_____ _____ 16. Planning for and budgeting time

_____ _____ 17. Discussing political issues

_____ _____ 18. Doing volunteer work or community service

_____ _____ 19. Planning a budget

_____ _____ 20. Protesting injustice, protecting someone, or stopping fraud or abuse

_____ _____ 21. Being honest or moral

_____ _____ 22. Correcting mistakes

_____ _____ 23. Organizing a party

_____ _____ 24. Other: _____

Intrinsically Pleasant Activities

These are activities that you simply enjoy.

_____ _____ 1. Laughing

_____ _____ 2. Relaxing, having peace and quiet

_____ _____ 3. Having a good meal

_____ _____ 4. Doing a hobby (cooking, fishing, woodworking, photography, acting, gardening, collecting things)

_____ _____ 5. Listening to good music

_____ _____ 6. Seeing beautiful scenery

_____ _____ 7. Going to bed early, sleeping soundly, and awakening early

_____ _____ 8. Wearing attractive clothes

_____ _____ 9. Wearing comfortable clothes

_____ _____ 10. Going to a concert, opera, ballet, or play

_____ _____ 11. Playing sports (tennis, softball, racquetball, golf, horseshoes, Frisbee)

_____ _____ 12. Going on trips or vacations

_____ _____ 13. Shopping for or buying something I like for myself

_____ _____ 14. Being outdoors (at the beach, in the country, in the mountains; kicking leaves; walking in the sand; floating in lakes)

_____ _____ 15. Doing artwork (painting, sculpting, drawing)

_____ _____ 16. Reading the scriptures or other sacred works

_____ _____ 17. Beautifying my home (redecorating, cleaning, yard work)

_____ _____ 18. Going to a sports event

_____ _____ 19. Reading (novels, poems, plays, newspapers, and so forth)

_____ _____ 20. Going to a lecture

_____ _____ 21. Going for a drive

_____ _____ 22. Sitting in the sun

_____ _____ 23. Visiting a museum

_____ _____ 24. Playing or singing music

_____ _____ 25. Boating

_____ _____ 26. Pleasing my family, friends, or employer

_____ _____ 27. Thinking about something good in the future

_____ _____ 28. Watching TV

_____ _____ 29. Camping or hunting

_____ _____ 30. Grooming myself (bathing, combing hair, shaving)

_____ _____ 31. Writing in my diary or journal

_____ _____ 32. Taking a bike ride, hiking, or walking

_____ _____ 33. Being with animals

_____ _____ 34. Watching people

_____ _____ 35. Taking a nap

_____ _____ 36. Listening to nature sounds

_____ _____ 37. Getting or giving a back rub

_____ _____ 38. Watching a storm, clouds, or the sky

_____ _____ 39. Having spare time

_____ _____ 40. Daydreaming

_____ _____ 41. Feeling the presence of the Lord in my life, praying, or worshipping

_____ _____ 42. Smelling a flower

_____ _____ 43. Talking about old times or special interests

_____ _____ 44. Going to auctions or garage sales

_____ _____ 45. Traveling

_____ _____ 46. Other: _____

Step 2: Check the second column if you've done the event in the past thirty days.

Step 3: Circle the number of the events that you'd probably enjoy (on a good day).

Step 4: Compare the first and second columns. Are there many items you've enjoyed in the past that you are not doing very often?

Step 5: Using the completed pleasant events schedule for ideas, make a list of the twenty-five activities that you feel you'd most enjoy doing.

Step 6: Make a plan to do more pleasant activities. Start with the simplest ones and those you are most likely to enjoy. Do as many pleasant events as you reasonably can. Try doing at least one each day, perhaps more on weekends. *Write* your plan on a calendar, and carry it out for at least two weeks. Each time you do an activity, rate it on a scale from 1 to 5 for pleasure (1 being not pleasurable, and 5 being highly enjoyable). This tests the stress-induced distortion that *nothing* is enjoyable. This rating may also help you later replace less enjoyable activities with others. Here are a few tips to help you make and keep a plan:

- Tune in to the physical world. Pay less attention to your thoughts; focus on your senses. Feel the wind, or the soapsuds as you wash the car. See and hear.

- Before doing an event, set yourself up to enjoy it. Identify three things you will enjoy about it. For example, say, "I will enjoy the sunshine, I will enjoy the breeze, and I will enjoy talking with my brother." Relax, and imagine yourself enjoying each aspect of the event as you repeat each statement.

- Ask yourself, "What can I do to make the activity enjoyable?"

- If you are concerned that you might not enjoy some activity that you'd like to try, break it into steps. Think small, so you can be satisfied in reaching your goal. For example, start by cleaning the house for only ten minutes, then stop. Reward yourself with a pat on the back.

- Check your schedule for balance. Can you spread out the "need tos" to make room for some "want tos"?

- Time is limited, so use it wisely. You needn't do activities you don't like just because they're convenient.

Balancing Technology with Tranquility

In his book on happiness, psychologist Nick Baylis (2009) considers how we can gain freedom from the crippling bonds of technology. He quotes the brilliant scientist Albert Einstein regarding time-saving technology. Einstein said, "Why does this magnificent applied science, which saves work and makes life easier, bring us little happiness? The simple answer runs: because we have not yet learned to make sensible use of it" (254). Ponder the electronic devices in your life, such as computers and cell phones, and ask yourself whether they connect you to or isolate you from things that matter to you. Check the appropriate boxes below.

My Electronic Devices...

Connect Me To	Isolate Me From	
☐	☐	Other people (Consider the terms *technoference* and *partner snub*, which refer to the way electronic devices can interfere with relationships.)
☐	☐	Nature
☐	☐	Myself (what I feel and need, who I am)
☐	☐	Reflection and relaxation time
☐	☐	Being fully present in the moment
☐	☐	Simple pleasures
☐	☐	Hobbies or other pleasurable recreational pursuits
☐	☐	My creative side
☐	☐	Sleep, exercise, and good eating

Activity: Technology and Happiness

Please write your reactions to this reflection:

Virtual reality isn't real. Spending hours using social media isn't the same as sitting face to face with a friend for hours. Would the world end if we turned off our smartphones during dinner or at a restaurant? Do we really need to spend hours sending e-mails, perusing social media, texting, *and* video chatting, or might we choose to do only one or none? Is your technology a boon or an addiction? Is it energizing or creating a frenzied exhaustion? Could we better limit our technology time and expand our tranquility time? What would happen if you turned your electronics off for a period of the day, during which you took a walk in nature or gave loved ones the gift of your full presence? What would happen if you turned off the news and went to bed earlier tonight?

_____

_____

_____

_____

_____

_____

_____

Conclusion

Zimbardo and Boyd (2008) noted that the time we save because of electronic devices is usually applied to working and accumulating wealth. The pursuit of wealth, however, can distract us from the deeper satisfactions that come from life's simple, inexpensive pleasures. This chapter aimed to broaden your approach to happiness by challenging you to expand your wholesome pleasures and limit overreliance on technology. The skills that you've learned in the workbook thus far lay a strong foundation for part 3—"Thriving: Peak Functioning and Adaptive Coping."

Part 3

THRIVING

Peak Functioning and Adaptive Coping

Chapter 22

Active Coping

So far we have explored resilience skills related to maximizing brain readiness, calming body and mind, managing negative emotions, and cultivating positive emotions and attitudes. In this part of the book we will build on these foundational skills, adding others that optimize performance and adaptive coping.

Adaptive coping is adjusting to changing circumstances and using whatever is available to your best advantage to solve problems, meet challenges, and move toward your goals. *Peak functioning* is giving your best possible effort in the service of meeting your goals. Your goals might relate to work, relationships, or play. Peak functioning revolves around three basic principles:

- Set a goal and want to achieve it.

- Believe you can achieve the goal, expecting success and feeling you can reach it.

- Commit to achieving the goal, working hard, persisting, and being disciplined. In the long run, commitment is more important than innate ability. Commitment includes focused mental preparation. Many people prepare sufficiently in a physical sense but buckle or choke under real-life pressure because they are not mentally prepared. So we must commit to mental practice at least as much as we do to physical practice.

All of the skills that you have learned so far promote peak functioning and adaptive coping. For example, practicing calming skills and managing negative emotions help us to stay composed and focused under pressure. Optimizing brain health enables the brain to function more quickly and effectively. Happiness skills help people to stay open to coping strategies and implement them more effectively.

In this part of the book we will explore three pillars of success: active coping, confidence, and flexibility and creativity. The final chapter, chapter 25, will prepare you for early treatment to get you back to optimal mood and functioning as soon as possible. We'll start with active coping. Considerable research suggests that having an active stance toward life is advantageous compared with a passive, avoidant stance. Let's consider the differences.

The Active Coper

Mindfulness training teaches us that the active coper turns *toward* problems, rather than away from them. This increases the likelihood of finding an appropriate response. People with an active stance toward life do the following. In order to raise your self-awareness, place a check next to those that describe you. Active copers:

_____ *Are proactive doers and problem solvers.* That is, they are engaged in life. They anticipate and prepare for difficulties, rather than waiting for crises to strike. They appraise situations and take reasonable action, applying (and in some cases learning) needed skills.

_____ *Are adventurous.* This means they are disposed to cope with the new and unknown.

_____ *Are curious.* Curious people don't get down when they feel stress but approach problems with pleasant and engaged interest.

_____ *Acknowledge that a problem exists.* They think about it, generate and weigh alternative solutions, make and follow a plan of action, and have a backup plan.

_____ *Are conscientious.* That is, they are determined to build a better life and improve. So they work hard, persist, and make use of needed resources (for example, they seek out confidants, uplifting relationships, or needed information and help).

_____ *Are disciplined.* They organize—creating structure, order, and routine. They follow through with their plans. They train themselves to forgo immediate pleasures and destructive shortcuts in the pursuit of a long-term goal. They act despite difficulties, fears, and risks.

_____ *Keep dreams and make goals.* These goals are guided by internal core values, not the dictates of others.

_____ *Make decisions without perfect knowledge (which we never have).* They allow themselves the freedom to take decisive action, take reasonable risks, make mistakes, and even fail. They realistically recognize personal and situational limitations (that is, what can and can't be done).

_____ *Recognize emotional needs and the need for emotional survival skills.* They may block out emotions in order to function during a crisis, but then they address them as soon as it is appropriate so that the emotions don't continue to trouble them.

_____ *Are not impulsive.* They think their actions through as much as possible before acting. They think about what they are doing and do not take unreasonable risks.

_____ *Maintain focus.* They continuously ask, "What's the most important thing to do right now to get me closer to my goal?"

In *I Love a Fire Fighter*, Dr. Ellen Kirschman (2004) describes an active stance toward troubling emotions, as well as a model for dealing with them: act during the crisis, then acknowledge and process distressing feelings. She describes a water rescue training in a storm, during which a boat capsized. Afterward, one emotionally courageous firefighter said to his assembled comrades, "I don't know about you guys but I thought I was going to die out there today and I doubt I'm the only one who felt that way" (180). One by one crewmembers opened up, expressing their fears of never seeing family again and of going out on the water again, anger at dying so young, and sadness for an incomplete life. Acknowledging these feelings brought this team together. The next day everyone went out again on the water to train. Until they had talked, each person felt isolated. Realizing that they were all in the same boat emotionally actually helped them move past their feelings and prepare for their training. Conversely, many highly trained and capable emergency service providers are engaged at work in their physical tasks, but then disengage from their feelings when they come home, shutting down or burying their emotions.

In Vietnam's prisoner-of-war camps, many outward freedoms were taken away. When prisoners could not actively escape, they exercised their freedom to be as active as possible. For example, Larry Chesley (1973) noted that many of his comrades in the "Hanoi Hilton" exercised to keep in good physical condition, despite the hunger it caused. They walked back and forth in their cell, three paces one way and then back, thinking and planning as they exercised. Others made competitions for sit-ups, push-ups (several reached several hundred), and deep-knee bends. The prisoners also used covert communications to keep morale high. On the cell walls, they tapped a code learned in Boy Scouts. Because speaking was forbidden, they hummed or whistled a prisoner's favorite tune to let his comrades know that he was still alive. In arguably the worst conditions humans can find themselves in, these men actively coped with their situation.

The Passive Coper

Passive copers take an avoidant stance toward life. They find ways to leave the problem, leaving it unsolved. Check any of the following that seem to describe your present coping style. Passive copers:

_____ *Don't think about troubling thoughts, emotions, or situations.* Thus, they do little to modify them.

_____ *Try to escape or block out negative emotions.* Tactics include excessive humor, drugs, workaholism, whining, worrying, suicide, risky recreation, gambling, and overconfidence. Notice that some of these might appear to be active attempts at coping, but each is a maladaptive way to avoid emotions. For example, one can worry obsessively—intellectually trying to understand the problem—without acknowledging the emotions or acting to resolve them.

_____ *Deny something is wrong or minimize problems.* For example, they might think, *Nothing is wrong* or *It doesn't bother me* or *It used to bother me but now it doesn't.*

_____ *Get stuck or freeze.* For example, they might:

- Assume they are helpless and then give up (There is always *something* to try.)

- Blame self or others

- Dwell on "Why is this happening?" rather than "What does this situation require of me?" or "How will I grow from this?"

- Think, *I don't believe this is happening.*

- Wish things were better

- Try to forget something that happened

- Become bewildered, deliberate excessively, or wait for instructions when action is called for

- Give in to discouragement

_____ *Use cynicism or an uncaring, indifferent attitude to protect themselves from pain.*

_____ *Might tackle problems at work but come home and try to ignore or drown out negative feelings.* They might do this with television, computer games, and so forth.

_____ *Withdraw.* They avoid people, places, or situations that are distressing; isolate themselves and don't tell others what is going on inside.

Author Ben Sherwood has observed (2009) that only 10 percent of people facing a crisis take decisive, constructive action; 80 percent freeze and wait for instructions; and 10 percent do the wrong thing, acting in self-destructive ways. For example, during the attack on the World Trade Center on 9/11, most of its occupants were lethargic, not panicked (Ripley 2008). They waited an average of six minutes before descending the stairs. Some waited for as long as forty-five minutes, calling relatives and friends or checking e-mail. Many milled around, as if in a trance, perhaps fearing that overreacting might lead to embarrassment, or perhaps denying the reality of the situation. (A similar response was observed in the 1977 Beverly Hills Supper Club fire, during which many who passively awaited instructions died.) Others died on 9/11 because they wasted time ascending stairs, trying to exit through doors on the roof that were locked. Ripley asserts that we must acknowledge a threat and thoroughly, repeatedly, and realistically rehearse for it so that everyone knows what to do quickly and decisively during the crisis.

The Consequences of Avoidance

Those with avoidant coping styles don't solve problems. They don't become stronger or more confident through wrestling with and overcoming problems. In the long run, avoidance leads to more stress, which has been linked to many negative outcomes:

- Weakened immunity (for example, more sickness because cortisol, a stress hormone, weakens the immune system)

- Impaired relationships (problems that are not acknowledged and confronted tend to persist)

- Poorer cognitive, job, and athletic functioning (problem solving, preparation, and functioning require full focus)

- Mental disorders (those who are unwilling to stay in contact with distressing thoughts, memories, emotions, and bodily sensations long enough to process them are more likely to suffer from PTSD, anxiety, depression, and general distress)

Active coping is generally associated with the opposite outcomes. (We'll explore some exceptions in chapter 24.)

How to Cultivate Active Coping

We can choose our response to adversity, whether that's to relax into a given situation and act to the best of our ability (which is all anyone can ever do), or to try to escape it. We can:

- **Acknowledge a problem.** Whether it is family disharmony or the threat of terrorism, develop an action plan and rehearse it, despite resistance from other people. Recall that Rick Rescorla anticipated the terrorist attack on the World Trade Center, developed an action plan of escape, and drilled his people repeatedly until they were able to successfully execute the plan under pressure—despite the complaints of those who lacked his vision.

- **Drop the battle with distressing thoughts, memories, emotions, images, and sensations.** Instead of fighting them, avoiding them, or giving into them in passive resignation, we can *actively accept* them—turning toward them and inviting them in with compassionate acceptance, as mindfulness training directs (see chapter 6). At first we do this in quiet and calm moments. Eventually, we can kindly accept the full range of emotions even in crises and respond to them calmly so that we can perform optimally. For example, we might acknowledge fear calmly and without judgment, and then act effectively. Otherwise, fear can immobilize us or lead to frenzied reactions. Also remember to use the skills from chapters 4 through 9 to manage distressing emotions.

- **Reframe problems as challenges.** Approach challenges with optimism (see chapter 13), which is the attitude that leads to active coping. Likewise, think about our purposes in life—our reasons to survive—as these motivate us to act productively.

- **Use calming skills to help us see options clearly, and then act.** Rehearse calming skills repeatedly under both calm and real-life training conditions.

Activity: Increase Motivation to Successfully Act

Motivation and drive predict performance. Being clear about your motivations can help you to persevere during periods of excessive stress, fatigue, nutritional or sleep deprivation, noise, and overseriousness. This activity, suggested by sports psychologist Spencer G. Wood (2003), will clarify your motivations and help you develop a motivating dialogue.

1. Determine what motivates you to act. Place a check beside those that apply to your life:

_____ Competitive excellence

_____ Courage

_____ Enjoyment

_____ Excellence

_____ Friendship

_____ Healthy pride in knowing you've done your best

_____ Helping others heal

_____ Helping the underserved

_____ Love

_____ Mastery

_____ Meaning and purpose

_____ Novelty and stimulation

_____ Personal growth

_____ Saving lives

_____ Security

_____ Service

_____ Teamwork

_____ A worthy cause

_____ Other motivations: _____

2. Write down three or four reasonable goals that are consistent with the motivations that you checked above. For example:

- Improve the bonds of friendship by creating trust and sharing enjoyable experiences

- Improve concentration—focusing on my tasks despite noise, confusion, and so on

- Stay composed and poised under pressure

- Gain the satisfaction of knowing I've done my best in a given situation

As you do this, focus more on the process, not the outcome. We can't always control the outcome. As arguably the most successful athlete-coach in sports history, John Wooden taught his players that success is not defined by the scoreboard (sometimes the other team is simply better) but by the satisfaction in knowing you did your best. Doing your best at any given moment is something you can control.

3. Remembering that mental rehearsal is as important as physical preparation, create a mental rehearsal dialogue that includes several affirmations for each goal. For example, an athlete in training might create this dialogue, which could easily be adapted to meet a challenge at home or work:

I am composed, even more so in the most important games. I feel alert, poised, relaxed, capable, prepared, and focused. I see what is needed and respond calmly and effectively. I concentrate well despite fatigue and distractions. I enjoy working alongside and supporting my friends. I love using my skills with those I care about, doing something I love. I'm looking forward to doing my best. My movements are fluid and nearly effortless. I'm confident in my abilities. I'm committed to doing my personal best, not worrying about the outcome or what others think. I do my best and let the outcome take care of itself. I am in the flow, fully engaged and concentrating, and enjoying the feeling of my best performance. I make decisions quickly and act decisively, without hurrying. I am comfortable with all the emotions that arise, and I respond to all in the same calm, nonjudgmental way. Afterward, I look back on my performance with quiet satisfaction, knowing that I did my best.

4. Mentally rehearse. Relax. Visualize yourself in practice or real life as you repeat this dialogue until this active stance becomes ingrained.

Activity: Writing for Problem Solving

Writing can help you effectively problem solve. This activity, developed by Pennebaker and Smyth (2016, 73), will help you through the process.

1. Write down a problem or challenge you are facing. Write freely, without regard for spelling or grammar, for about ten minutes.

2. Review your writing and identify the key impediments or barriers. Now write about these, again for about ten minutes.

3. Put it all together. Reread both writing samples and write a final time, again for ten minutes, synthesizing your thoughts and insights about the problem, barriers to overcoming it, and potential solutions or ways to solve the problem.

Sometimes, this exercise may give rise to immediate insights (or even a solution), but often it facilitates a process that yields a solution in time.

Conclusion

The basic theme of active coping is to turn toward problems in a calm, nonjudgmental way, trusting that you will make progress—either solving a problem or figuring out a better way to cope. Drop the expectation of performing perfectly. Rather, strive for a very good job. Remember self-acceptance and self-compassion as you strive imperfectly to do your best.

Chapter 23

Self-Confidence

Confidence and an active coping stance go hand in hand. An active stance says, "I *will* do my best to succeed—I will do what is needed and persist." Confidence says, "I *can* do that—I have the skills and resources that I need and know how to apply them effectively."

Confidence, called self-efficacy in the scientific literature, is closely tied to resilience. Confidence correlates with:

- *Less avoidance.* We find it easier to face challenges when we believe we can do something about them.

- *Better performance in various domains of life.* Confidence lifts one's mood, which changes the brain and improves performance. Confidence also counters distracting fears and self-doubts, which interfere with us doing our best.

- *Greater self-esteem.* Although confidence is not the same as self-esteem, when people develop confidence they are reminded of their worth.

- *Fewer anxiety, depression, pain, and post-traumatic stress symptoms.* Self-doubt is stressful, and stress exacerbates the symptoms of the stress-related conditions.

Confidence Principles

Confidence must be based on experience. Confidence improves with experiences of success—real or imagined. Both physical practice and mental rehearsal work about equally well. The combination of both kinds of practice is ideal.

Confidence must be realistic. Overconfidence is a form of avoidance and self-deceit. It can take us by surprise and make failure more likely. One must know what he or she can and cannot do. Without this awareness, we won't make the effort to gain mastery and might make foolish decisions under pressure.

Training must be so rigorous that the real-life challenge is easier. Legendary coach John Wooden so rigorously trained his basketball players that the games seemed much easier than practice.

To perform confidently, one must know how to regulate arousal and distractions. Excessive stress degrades performance and can be regulated with mindfulness practice, abdominal breathing, relaxation training, and other skills described earlier in this book. Through training we can learn to maintain concentration and composure despite noise, visual distractions, some fatigue, and the like.

Regular participation in exercise (especially aerobic exercise) and sports is firmly linked to greater self-confidence. At the gym at West Point there is displayed a famous quote by General Douglas MacArthur: "On the fields of friendly strife are sown the seeds that on other days and other fields will bear the fruits of victory." Physical fitness instills confidence. Athletic competition teaches focus and perseverance.

Nearly everyone with average learning ability can achieve professional competence in nearly any field with lots of practice. Dr. Nick Baylis (2009) explains that it takes about three thousand hours of determined practice to go from novice to a remarkable amateur in music (or nearly any other field)—about two hours per day, six days a week, for five years. It takes about ten thousand hours of concentrated effort to reach a professional standard in virtually any field, and at least ten years of full-time, dedicated practice to reach world-class level. About half of America's leading concert pianists had parents who played no instruments. What they did have, typically, were warm, encouraging parents (or teachers). Those who excel also tend to have highly relaxed minds (which absorb more) and the determination to concentrate (multitasking degrades concentration and the ability to learn).

Perfectionism degrades confidence. Focus on doing a good job, even an excellent job, but not a perfect job. Baylis notes that only about a quarter of Shakespeare's works are celebrated today. Not everything we produce will be a masterpiece, so we can relax, do our best, and enjoy the "occasional gem" (2009, 212).

The confident person is poised. John Wooden (2003) defined "poise" as just being yourself, not acting or pretending, but performing at your personal best level without undue pressure or concern for others' judgments or expectations. Confident people watch, learn from, and are inspired by successful individuals, but they are secure in their uniqueness.

Confident people enjoy being tested because they are prepared. Because they are prepared, they feel that challenges will bring out their best and that they will likely succeed.

Confidence usually grows best when it is cultivated gradually, patiently, and with warmt There are two basic training models for instilling confidence. One tries to overwhelm and eliminate the weak. We find this model used in many elite special-operations training programs, such as that of the Army Rangers and Navy SEALS. These programs start with the cream of the crop and weed out many candidates through exposure to grueling conditions. Those who remain standing know that they can trust both themselves and their teammates in virtually any situation.

The second model aims to strengthen and build—challenging but not overwhelming individuals. For example, British commando training adapts a mentoring approach wherein trainers train alongside trainees, offering encouragement and support. They make the training increasingly challenging but never exceed the readiness and capabilities of individuals. Trainers view each trainee as a valuable asset that they don't want to lose. Rather than leading by fear and criticism, leaders try to inspire, and they allow trainees to learn from their mistakes through natural consequences. The Outward Bound program employs a similar training model. Participants are gently encouraged to perform at their best, say by pushing past their fears to complete a challenging ropes course. Then participants gather around the supportive leader, who praises their effort and asks them how they were able to perform as well as they did. The leader might also ask what they learned from their experience. This model tends to draw out and build upon existing strengths. People who are so trained tend to have less fear and tend to persevere and perform better under pressure, compared with those trained by harsh, domineering leaders. This model usually works best for most workplaces, families, and schools. This approach says, "I care about you and your growth."

To be confident is to have the confidence to "fail." Mortals will always be fallible, meaning we are imperfect and make mistakes. When we reframe failure as efforts toward success or as falling short of our goals, then "failure" becomes less intimidating. Without judging or condemning ourselves, we simply examine our efforts and aim to improve performance—erring less and less with time and experience.

How to Build Confidence

The principles outlined suggest a number of approaches to build confidence. If you are not doing so already, you might engage in an exercise or sports program. You might regulate arousal by practicing abdominal breathing or other skills introduced in part 1. Look for every opportunity to gain expertise and experience by reading, taking classes, training, and gaining real-life experience. The rest of this chapter will explore mental preparation for everyday life challenges.

Activity: Bringing Confidence Forward

Negative feelings such anxiety and lack of confidence can interfere with doing your best. This technique actively counters such feelings by weaving confidence into your mental preparation for a daunting challenge, such as one you might be facing at work, at home, or in sports.

1. **Identify your daunting challenge.** Examples include taking an important promotion test, tackling a difficult assignment, or having a potentially difficult discussion with a family member or boss.

2. **Break your daunting challenge into a staircase of items.** Each step should represent one chronological step of about one or two dozen steps total. Thus, for an important promotion test, the staircase might look like this:

   a. Studying three months before

   b. Studying two weeks before

   c. Discussing the test with a coworker a week before

   d. Studying the night before

   e. Reviewing the morning before

   f. Driving to the test site

   g. Walking into the testing room

   h. Taking a seat

   i. Receiving a copy of the test

   j. Reading the first question

   k. Reading a question I can't answer

   l. Finishing the test

   m. Leaving the testing room

3. **Create a list of past successes and achievements.** Write down four or five events from your life when you behaved capably and felt good about your performance. Perhaps it was an event where you were challenged to perform well and felt anxiety, but you persisted and performed competently. For each event, describe the circumstances in detail, noting your surroundings (weather, distractions, and so forth), what you did (for example, see yourself persisting and performing well), and how you felt during and afterward (for example, determined, satisfied, energized). Just remembering positive events lifts mood and increases confidence. Perhaps you can think of a past

achievement that relates to your present challenge. For example, having success riding a bicycle might transfer to learning to ride a motorcycle. However, it is not critical that the past achievement be related to the present challenge. Any experience of success will work. Select one that is especially pleasant to remember.

4. **Start with the first item on your staircase.** Visualize and experience it fully and in detail for about a minute. Then recall the selected success or achievement experience fully and in as much detail as possible. Immerse yourself fully in the recall. Then superimpose this image over the image of your daunting challenge. Sit with this experience until you feel confidence associated with this step on the staircase.

5. **Repeat this process for each step on the staircase.** Perhaps each day you'll link two or three steps to your success or achievement experience.

The power of this strategy rests on the fact that the image of success or achievement comes from your real experience and uses your genuine feelings of confidence to counter any negative feelings associated with your challenge. Note that you can also use this staircase in other ways. You can experience and then pair each step with relaxation, mindfulness, rational self-statements, humor, or success or rebounding imagery (both described below).

Activity: Success (Mastery) Imagery

With success imagery, you use mental rehearsal to strengthen neural pathways in the brain associated with successful performance. It is best to combine this strategy with real-life practice. You can apply this strategy to any situation at home or work or on the playing field. The key to success is to keep imagery vivid, imagining and experiencing all the details—what you see, hear, smell, touch, and taste. Most of your awareness will be from the perspective of what you are seeing and sensing from the inside. Perhaps only 25 percent of your awareness will focus on what you would see from the outside, as if you were watching yourself through a video camera.

1. **Lie down or sit comfortably.** Spend about five minutes relaxing and composing yourself. Use abdominal breathing, progressive muscle relaxation, meditation, or any other skill from part 1.

2. **Imagine yourself succeeding—coping and performing effectively—for about fifteen minutes.**

   a. Start by seeing yourself in a pressure-packed situation. You notice that your breathing is calm and regular. Though you are perspiring, your thinking is clear and your body is relaxed and fluid. Your body is moving with confidence and poise. Sense that inside your body.

b. You see yourself executing your task effectively—smoothly, almost effortlessly, with great concentration. You notice with great clarity what you are focusing on. You sense all parts of your body moving extremely effectively. You enjoy the fun of being in the flow—fully absorbed and meeting each challenge with relaxed efficiency and power.

3. **Practice your imagined success frequently so that the mentally rehearsed execution comes naturally when it matters the most.** It is usually best to rehearse one movement or aspect of successful performance frequently before moving on to another aspect. Eventually, you might put the pieces together, as Dr. Spencer Wood (2003) has done in this success imagery for golf (modified slightly and used with permission).

> You are at one of the biggest golf tournaments of the year. The time is near for you to tee off and you are looking forward to your opening drive even more so than usual. You are at your very best and you are really enjoying your great form. Take some time to really enjoy your surroundings. Take a deep breath. Relax. See the green fairways, the carefully sculptured hills and bunkers. You can hear the distinctive swish of the clubs being swung as they cut an elegant path through the air. You hear the solid connection of the golf ball and club head. As you address the ball of your opening drive you feel an incredible sense of power, and energy, and joy for the game you love. You love competition and you love competing in golf, one of your favorite things to do in the world. You are so composed, relaxed, and poised. Your concentration and focus are at their very best, and you feel supremely confident. You are committed to doing your best, and you are performing at your very best. You have a great swing. You are accurate and powerful. Your strokes are smooth, fluid, effortless, and accurate. You feel confident and energized, and your positive body language shows it. Your concentration is amazing. You are in a relaxed, comfortable shell of concentration. External distractions such as weather conditions, opponents, or crowd noise do not affect your great composure, concentration, and confidence. You are putting with incredible form and accuracy. You love sharing your putting skills with the crowd. Your short game is just as accurate as your long game. You are at your very best.
>
> Take a deep breath. Relax. Feel free to stay in this warm and comfortable state of relaxation for as long as you wish. You are relaxed and fully refreshed.

Activity: Rebounding (Coping) Imagery

Rebounding (or coping) imagery is mental rehearsal that adds the skill of recovering from common states that interfere with performance, such as excessive anxiety, tension, negative thinking, or faulty execution. It begins, as success imagery does, with five minutes of relaxation. Then you vividly imagine the pressure-packed situation. However, this time you notice yourself experiencing one or more of these common negative states. With calm awareness and without judgment, you simply see yourself correcting these states, as shown in the following table. Many people prefer this type of imagery over success imagery because slipping and then recovering is more typical of real life. Once you've performed the steps of this imagery, then complete those of success imagery as described previously.

For This State...	You See Yourself...
Anxiety	Pausing to mindfully accept the feeling without judgment. Next, you let awareness of the anxiety dissolve, and then return your concentration to proper execution.
Tension	Stopping to calm your breathing and relax your muscles.
Negative thoughts, such as... • *Oh, no, what if I fail?* • *I can't.* • *I'm too anxious to function.* • *I must do this perfectly.*	Calmly thinking... • *I love doing my best.* • *I can.* • *I enjoy concentrating and doing well.* • *I keep my focus on the moment-to-moment process.*
Fatigue, perspiration, elevated heart rate	Thinking, *I feel so relaxed.*
Making a mistake	Regaining composure and concentration quickly, and executing the next movement successfully.

Follow-Up Self-Talk

After working through a daunting challenge in real life, remember to pay attention to your follow-up self-talk, which affects confidence in the future. If you did reasonably well, reinforce your success. You might think *Good job* or *All in all, not bad* or *It felt good to prepare and succeed.* Take a moment to savor the feeling of satisfaction for what you did to succeed. This will motivate you to do well in the future. If things didn't go well, you might think, *That was a tough situation; next time I'll prepare differently,* or *It's water under the bridge, and now I'll move on.*

Conclusion

It is possible to function well when you're distraught. However, you'll typically perform better when you're calm and confident but not overconfident. Would you prefer to live with confidence or self-doubt? The choice is yours. It's encouraging to learn that you can develop confidence, just like the other strengths in this workbook.

Chapter 24

Flexibility and Creativity

People who function at their peak cleverly apply the two closely intertwined strengths of flexibility and creativity. These strengths open the mind. Both are built upon a foundation of discipline, so we'll start our exploration there, followed by discussions of flexibility and creativity.

Discipline

To build on chapter 22, peak performers are situationally aware. This means that they look deeply and with curiosity at the challenges before them, while tapping resources within and outside of themselves. They prepare for challenges by filling their minds with information, seeking input from many others, learning needed skills, and gaining real-life experience. They make intelligent plans and persist when the going gets tough.

Renowned psychologist Mihaly Csikszentmihalyi (1996) has noted that peak performers have efficient habits that help them focus, reduce distractions, preserve energy, and minimize time wasting. These habits include working during their most productive times of the day and dressing simply or in the same way each day. They get plenty of sleep, which pays off in more productivity the next day. They use an efficient retrieval system, such as filing cabinets, to reduce time wasted in searching for what they need. They turn off passive, mentally fatiguing entertainment, such as TV and computer games. They create a workplace that is free of unwanted distractions, and they tend not to divide their focus by multitasking.

Flexibility

Peak performance requires mental flexibility, or the ability to adapt to changing situations. Peak performers can shift gears when standard procedures aren't working. Let's suppose you have made a good plan. You are mindfully aware of how things are going, and you realize that your plan isn't working. What do you do? Will you be flexible? Take the flexibility checkup below to gauge your present level of flexibility.

The Flexibility Checkup

The following scale shows the degree to which you have cultivated flexibility. Rate each statement from 1 to 10 (0 means you are never flexible in the slightest, and 10 means you are exceptionally flexible, as flexible as humanly possible).

_____ I usually have a plan, but I don't "fall in love with" my plan (that is, I'm not rigidly attached to a plan that isn't working).

_____ I constantly think of alternative routes to success.

_____ I always have a backup plan, a plan B.

_____ I willingly and rapidly adapt to changing situations.

_____ I know when to change course and devise a new strategy.

_____ When a goal is unachievable, I can accept defeat—to live to fight another day. I know when to cut my losses.

_____ I am willing to take action based on my best judgment, but I accept what I can't control.

_____ I have a nimble mind; I think well on my feet.

_____ I see when change is needed and welcome it.

_____ I will consider and take risks that are appropriate.

_____ When under stress, I'm willing to try something new.

_____ I don't let my mental maps (seeing things as I want or expect them to be) stop me from seeing things as they really are. I am open to all new evidence.

_____ I accept what can't realistically be changed or controlled, but I think of many ways to cope with such situations.

_____ I roll with the punches when things don't go as planned; I don't get bent out of shape.

_____ I quickly adapt, but I don't hurry into things about which I'm not reasonably certain.

_____ I don't always have to be right.

Effective copers are usually securely rooted in self, values, and methods that work. But they can bend when bending is called for. The opposite of flexibility is inflexibility or rigidity.

Those who are always the same might lose their advantage in changing circumstances. For example, a pitcher who always throws a fastball, no matter how fast, will eventually get hit against if he doesn't switch speeds or the location of the ball relative to home plate. And companies that produce a great product will be overtaken by the competition if they don't adapt to changing demands.

Additional Flexibility Principles

The idea that winners never quit and quitters never win is inaccurate. Evidence suggests that people who repeatedly fail in their quest for an implausible goal experience a range of health problems. It is thought that frustration increases levels of the stress hormone cortisol, which leads to inflammation and symptoms of various medical and psychological conditions. Sometimes the wisest course is to disengage from an impossible goal and switch to a new one. As W. C. Fields said, "If at first you don't succeed, try, try again. Then quit [or seek a new goal]. There's no point in being a damn fool about it" (Nixon 2008, 7).

Don't rely overmuch on past training and experience. And don't assume that training has totally prepared you. It takes years to become an expert, and experts usually outperform novices. But if something happens to change the rules, the differences shrink. For example, many overconfident, complacent experts rely on old habits and miss new developments. Pay attention. Continue to learn. Don't be imprisoned by your old paradigm (the old way of looking at things).

Reflections on Flexibility

Please consider these reflections before reading on.

There is no sin punished more implacably by nature than the sin of resistance to change.
—Anne Morrow Lindbergh

Blessed are the flexible, for they shall not be bent out of shape. —Anonymous

When you discover you're riding a dead horse, dismount. —Bill O'Hanlon

But change will come, and if you acknowledge this simple but indisputable fact of life, and understand that you must adjust to all change, then you will have a head start.
—Arthur Ashe

In the beginner's mind there are many possibilities. In the expert's mind there are few.
—Zen saying

Creativity

Flexibility readies us for change. Creativity reveals possibilities. History is full of instances when people used creativity to solve problems and improve conditions.

During World War II, the Allied invasion stalled at Normandy. Over the centuries, the farmers of Normandy had created small rectangular fields surrounded by steep banks of earth, stone, and thick vegetation. The mounds, called hedgerows, were up to ten feet wide and eight feet high. Between the hedgerows were narrow roads. If American tanks moved down these roads, they were blasted by German fire, blocking tanks behind them. If the tank drivers tried to climb the steep banks, they exposed the tank's unarmored underbelly to antitank fire. While officers debated what to do, Sergeant Curtis G. Culin took scrap metal from German roadblocks and welded teeth onto the front of American Sherman tanks. These so-called Rhino tanks could then punch through the hedgerows and allow other tanks to pass through and fan out. This simple invention saved countless lives.

Creativity means coming up with something new and useful. Often creativity is merely seeing what is already there, rearranging it or giving it a new twist, and making something wholly or partly new. What we come up with might be an idea, strategy, or product that improves our lives—our health, performance, mood, or leisure. Consider, for example, that the bicycle was around for seventy years before someone thought in 1861 to add a chain and gears to the pedals, resulting in a more useful recreational vehicle and mode of travel. Or consider how many hours have been saved by the invention of the zipper around 1900.

Today, creativity is a basic survival tool that is vital to optimizing functioning and coping in a complex, rapidly changing world. Creativity can increase our resilience and reduce our stress when we are under adversity by revealing more options when old ways are not working.

Most people erroneously assume that

creativity is only found in the arts,

you must be genetically favored with creative brilliance (either you have it or you don't),

creativity always comes in sudden bursts without hard work, or

you must come up with an astounding finished product in order to be considered creative.

In truth, creativity, like resilience, is standard issue. Everyone has creative potential that can be grown with time, discipline, and effort. The generally accepted rule is that it takes at least ten years of immersion in a field before one can make a distinctive mark in that field. For example, Einstein labored for ten years on relativity before the theory came together. Many people who haven't developed school intelligence are creatively intelligent. Even if you don't get complete results, you can still enjoy the creative process. You can find satisfaction in partial successes, knowing you are drawing closer to your final goal while strengthening your creative skills.

Creativity can be demonstrated and nurtured in many ways. Because of brain plasticity, neural pathways that are strengthened in one creative endeavor can be used in other creative areas of life. The following inventory helps to reveal how you might already be exercising creativity in your life and helps to dispel the myth that only artists are creative.

The Creativity Checkup

The following are ways that people express creativity. Rate each from 0 to 10, where 0 means you are never creative in the slightest, and 10 means that you are exceptionally creative, as much as humanly possible.

_____ Acquiring money (to meet basic needs, to buy things that are needed to create, and so forth)

_____ Amusing others (such as children or friends)

_____ Amusing yourself

_____ Applying your strengths in a unique way

_____ Bargaining with a salesperson

_____ Beautifying a space; making it attractive or orderly

_____ Bringing joy or friendliness to others

_____ Cleaning

_____ Cooking (tweaking recipes or making something from scratch without a recipe)

_____ Creating an environment that encourages people to innovate

_____ Dancing

_____ Entertaining or planning leisure activities

_____ Explaining or teaching things simply or clearly

_____ Expressing feelings

_____ Finding enjoyment in difficult situations

_____ Finding meaning during difficult times

_____ Finding shortcuts; saving time

_____ Finding ways to calm yourself and maintain focus in crisis

_____ Gardening

_____ Getting ahead of problems (anticipating problems and devising solutions before they occur)

_____ Getting others to work together constructively; building teamwork

_____ Inventing games (or giving old games a new twist)

_____ Looking at situations in ways that encourage solutions (for instance, "My boss isn't a tyrant; he's frustrated.")

_____ Making family memories

_____ Making good decisions after considering different options

_____ Making new designs, processes, ideas, or programs

_____ Making others smile or feel good

_____ Making a satisfying, meaningful life

_____ Making tasks easier or simpler

_____ Motivating or encouraging people

_____ Organizing (for example, a room, an event, a mission); bringing order to chaos or confusion

_____ Playing sports

_____ Putting ideas together in a new way

_____ Putting others at ease

_____ Questioning conventional methods and imagining new ones

_____ Raising children (motivating, encouraging, disciplining, providing, or loving)

_____ Resolving conflict

_____ Seeing several options before deciding

_____ Solving problems; overcoming obstacles

_____ Spotting personal weaknesses and finding ways to improve

_____ Strengthening your relationships

_____ Talking your way out of a jam

_____ Telling stories

_____ Turning complex ideas into simple ones

_____ Turning life's negatives into positives

_____ Turning mistakes or guilt into growth

_____ Writing (such as letters, stories, reports, or books)

You'll probably notice that creativity is already being expressed in numerous ways in your life. While few people realistically record 10s, it is also likely that there are few if any 0s—suggesting that your creative potential is already being tapped and is ready for further development. For areas with low ratings, you might simply think, *That's just an area that hasn't been developed* yet.

The Creative Process

Creative people pay attention. They are aware of what is going on outside of themselves. They see the entire situation—problems and opportunities, available resources, barriers to success, and what is needed. They also pay attention to what is going on inside of themselves— inner resources, hunches or intuitive promptings of the mind, and ideas that bubble up. Then they go to work. In reality, it is usually more accurate to say that they go to *play*, because creative people typically immerse themselves in what they love to do and enjoy the process.

When under stress, most people narrow their focus, operating in old ways and missing new possibilities. Creative people, however, step back and open their minds to new possibilities, breaking through presumed limits to do something new, perhaps something that had been thought impossible. The following principles nurture creativity.

Relax and trust the creative process. The creative process usually takes time and patience. Over time, the brain acquires isolated pieces of needed information until it is able to put the pieces together in a new way. Intense pressure to meet unreasonable deadlines stifles the creative process. Conversely, a reasonable time line can keep us on task. Trust that solutions will usually bubble up with sufficient time and effort.

Reframe a problem as a challenge and an interesting opportunity for growth. Approach challenges with a welcoming attitude of curiosity, rather than negativity. Curiosity fans the creative fires, whereas negativity dampens them.

Observe. Be mindful. Without judging or attaching to any particular outcome, simply notice the situation (What is going on? In what context is this happening? What might help? What resources are available? What is lacking?). Notice your inner feelings about the situation. Pay attention to your hunches. Watch with interest and curiosity.

Get started early. Early activity permits time for ideas to incubate. Procrastination doesn't. Although many people share the illusion that pressure promotes creativity, the pressure caused by procrastination usually constricts creative thinking and results in a poorer outcome. The exception to the rule occurs when a prepared person is fully engaged in a flow state—in which one gives full attention to a meaningful task and capabilities are not overwhelmed.

Have the courage to persevere. In studying scores of the most creative contributors in various domains, Csikszentmihalyi concludes, "A genuinely creative accomplishment is almost never the result of a sudden insight, a lightbulb flashing on in the dark, but comes after years of hard work" (1996, 1). Creative contributors don't necessarily have higher IQs, but they do persist. Be willing to work long and hard. Expect to make a meaningful contribution. Stay motivated by writing down why your efforts matter to you. Remember, a cause such as bettering the world or helping others is usually more motivating than causes that are primarily materialistic.

Fill your mind from many sources. Keep your mind open to new ideas. Pick the brains of the best thinkers you can find—experts, friends, family, children, cabbies. Most people like to share ideas and opinions. Attend conferences in the field, and sometimes in unrelated fields, to get different perspectives to draw from. Study other disciplines and cultures, and past contributions. Visit museums. Study how people around the world solve problems. Such efforts might pay off for you later, as you integrate ideas or adapt them to your particular challenge. Gain experience through training and experimentation. As the Navy SEALs creed says, "My training is never complete." In other words, creativity is a lifelong process.

Give your mind time to spin free. After focused effort, give your mind a break. This allows you to step back, see things afresh, and give the right brain time to connect disparate thoughts. Long walks, bike rides, swimming, or other forms of exercise have been used by the likes of Benjamin Franklin, Thomas Jefferson, Albert Einstein, and other highly creative people. Try meditation. Paradoxically, emptying your mind of cares promotes creativity.

Do something daily to lift your mood. Growing evidence indicates that positive emotions promote creative, flexible thinking and problem solving—and adaptive coping generally (Lyubomirsky 2007). Remember to apply the happiness skills of part 2, especially when under stress—when the needs and benefits of emotional uplifts are greatest. Downplay mistakes. Everyone makes them as they attempt new strategies. After mistakes, calmly ask yourself, "Next time, what could I do differently?"

Replace destroyer thoughts. Certain negative thoughts stifle creativity. Table 24.1 lists common limiting thoughts and constructive replacements. The limiting thoughts are like the expert's mind, which forecloses possibilities. The beginner's mind is open to possibilities.

Table 24.1: Limiting and empowering thoughts

Limiting Thoughts (Expert's Mind)	Empowering Thoughts (Beginner's Mind)
I'm not creative.	Everyone is creative. Perhaps I'm not very creative in this area yet.
That can't be done. It won't work.	That's what scoffers said about flight, breaking the sound barrier, breaking the four-minute mile, walking on the moon, regulating the immune system, and inventing the telephone, laptops, and countless other innovations.
I can't.	Maybe I can. Maybe a way will appear.
I must find the right way and follow the rules.	There are often several useful ways to solve a problem. I'm willing to take some risks—even risking "failure"—in order to learn and grow. Some solutions might toss out old ways and replace them with new ways. Others preserve and refine old ways.
Past failure means I won't succeed.	The past isn't prologue. Dr. Seuss failed art in high school. Each of his children's books took about a year to complete, yet he did succeed. Charles Schulz's drawings were rejected from his high school yearbook, and yet he went on to create *Peanuts*.
My ego is on the line. I must not fail.	My productivity doesn't equal my worth. I'll approach this with a more playful attitude.
We've never done it that way.	Perhaps there's a better way. I'm open to new possibilities. I'll give it a try.
I must be certain before risking.	Many, if not most decisions in life, are made without complete information.
We tried it that way before.	What exactly was *that way*? Perhaps there's a way to improve that approach.

Limiting Thoughts (Expert's Mind)	Empowering Thoughts (Beginner's Mind)
I can't leave my comfort zone. I won't change.	My survival may require my willingness to change. Is it worth it to resist this change? I have a range of options, ranging from no change, to some change, to radical change.
We must do it my way.	Perhaps there's a better way I'm not seeing yet. What have I got to lose by being open-minded?

Ask questions to stimulate the creativity process. Creative people frequently ask questions such as: "What would happen if…?" "What if we tried it this way?" "Why not try it this way?" "What would it take to do this?" "Why didn't that past attempt work?" "What would I (or others) like to see happen?"

Go back and forth between extremes. Csikszentmihalyi (1996) notes that creative people flexibly alternate between extremes as the occasion requires. For example, the creative person, knowing that recreation *re-creates*, alternates between disciplined work and play. Here are some other extremes that creative people alternate between (Csikszentmihalyi 1996).

- *Great energy and concentration* and *rest and idleness* (Appropriate rest and idleness recharge the batteries.)

- *Extroversion* and *introversion* (Allow yourself time to be alone to integrate the ideas of others.)

- *Wholesome humility* and *wholesome pride* (Wholesome humility says, "I don't know everything." Wholesome pride says, "I'm confident.")

- *Realism* (practicality) and *being imaginative* (seeing possibilities)

- *Convergent thinking* (homing in, focusing in the present) and *divergent thinking* (stepping back, seeing the big picture, generating ideas)

- *Ambition and aggressiveness* (including the willingness to sacrifice one's own comfort to get the job done) and *selflessness and cooperation*

- *Appreciation* (understanding and respect) *for culture and old rules* and *willingness to break with tradition and take risks* (If you're only conservative, there will be no change; if you're only rebellious, your work will rarely be constructive or appreciated.)

- *Passion for work* and *objectivity* (Passion keeps interest alive during adversity; objectivity keeps judgment alive and controls emotions.)

- *Pain* and *enjoyment* (Pain springs from criticism—people don't always appreciate novelty—and the sacrifices needed to produce. Enjoyment comes from flow—the wholehearted involvement in valuable work, which is enjoyable for its own sake.)

- *Tolerance of ambiguity* ("I acknowledge what is") and *intolerance of ambiguity* ("I seek a better way")

Make a creative environment. If you are a leader, create a culture in which people feel safe to experiment and take risks without fear of excessive criticism or competition. Encourage people often with comments, such as "Good work," "Tell me about your idea," or "Why don't you try that out?" Then step back and let your people create.

Seek a team that is supportive, respectful of new ideas, and unified in its goals. Structure the physical environment so that it is most conducive to creativity. You might prefer a quiet, more Spartan environment free of distractions. Others like music and soft furniture. Finally, enrich your marriage. The most creative contributors tend to have stable and satisfying marriages, according to Csikszentmihalyi (1996).

Write down ideas as they come or you'll forget them. File them so you can easily access them when you have additional ideas.

Activity: Creative Problem Solving

When old practices are working well and efficiently, creativity might not be needed or desirable. However, when difficult real-life situations call for change, creative problem solving can often uncover better practices. People who are skilled in creative problem solving generally have better mental health (for example, suffering from less depression, substance abuse, anxiety, hopelessness, and hostility) because they can devise a greater number of coping options. This strategy teaches one to actively solve problems rather than give in to passive worrying.

1. **Identify a problem you would like to solve, or an area of life you'd like to improve.** It could be conflict with a boss, coworker, or family member. It might be excess weight, poor sleep, or disliking your job. Naming the problem creates an opportunity to improve your life. We can't solve what we are not aware of, and the more we run from problems, the worse we feel. If you can't identify a specific irritant, identify cues of discomfort, such as feelings of sadness or anxiety, or troubling behaviors, such as drinking.

2. **Describe the problem from many different perspectives.** The more ways we can view the problem, the more likely we are to find new solutions. So spend considerable time describing the problem in writing. For example, see if you can come up with a range of explanations: Why is this happening? (Think of as many causes as possible.) What's really going on? See it from different angles. And try the reverse formulation strategy (Csikszentmihalyi 1996). Let's say you feel you've been denied a raise because the boss dislikes you. Reversing the explanation might yield, "I dislike the boss." Other possible explanations: "I've been distracted by problems at home." "Maybe I was more concerned with prestige than doing a good job." "Maybe I didn't give the boss what she wanted." The next section lists other ways to view the problem differently.

Creative Ways to View a Problem Differently

In order to see a problem from different angles, you might try the following strategies.

Describe the problem from multiple perspectives. With this strategy (Michalko 2001), you first describe the problem from your own point of view, then from at least two others (such as someone who is close to the problem, a government leader, an entrepreneur, a wise counselor, a spouse, or a reporter). Then synthesize the descriptions. If you are working with others, ask each participant to come up with a personal perspective on the problem and the ideal solution.

Journal about the problem and describe your entry with one word. For example, Don, a cop, was feeling overwhelmed by the strain of having two jobs to support his family, getting too little sleep, and having problems at work. He watched too much television, exercised too little, and ate poorly. Lacking social skills, he had few friends in law enforcement and even fewer outside of the force. He felt tempted to overuse alcohol to calm his nerves. He doubted his abilities. The word that he selected, "inadequate," suggested a number of possible solutions. Michalko (2001) suggests that further defining the word using a dictionary or thesaurus, or by providing your own meaning, might also help to trigger more solutions.

To jolt your usual thinking, create a metaphor, analogy, or symbol and describe how the problem is like that. For example, negotiating a contract with that client is like talking to a brick wall. Eventually, a solution will suggest itself, for a brick wall can be dismantled gently, one brick at a time (Biech 1996).

Use wordplay to change your focus. Change, delete, or add words to your problem description. For example, the original explanation of "My boss is Satan, an immoral, judgmental underachiever with no leadership ability who must be stopped!" shifts to "He is unhappy and in need of help."

Formulate a question that captures the problem, and then change the question. For example, Toyota employees were asked how they could become more productive. The question got little response. After rewording the question to "How can you make your job easier?" the executives were inundated with ideas (Michalko 2001, 33). Try switching out the verb in your questions to see what that triggers. For example, "How can I increase sales?" might become "How can I attract sales?" Or *repeat* sales? Or *extend* sales?

Ask and respond to questions.

- Is the obvious irritant part of a larger problem that needs addressing (such as low self-esteem or poor social skills)?

- How bad is it? How bad will it be years from now? Is it possible that it's not a big problem in the grand scheme of things?

- What would happen if I did nothing? What is the cost of doing nothing?

- How might I be a cause of the problem?

- What barriers are blocking progress?

- Is there something beautiful or interesting I can find about this problem? (Michalko 2001, 48)

Try describing the problem through artistic expression. Painting, drawing, and sculpting, among other art forms, can yield insight that verbal expression doesn't. Don't worry about the quality of the art.

Gather information from as many sources as possible. Seek understanding, advice, and possible solutions from books, the Internet, people you know, experts, and so forth.

Conceive of the outcome. Can you imagine what you'd like to see happen? What would be an acceptable outcome? What would be the ideal? Clarifying the outcome can suggest pathways to reaching it. The following strategies can facilitate this:

- *State the intention.* Solution-focused psychotherapists suggest contemplating this statement: I would be happy to understand how to _____ [state the desired outcome, such as work well with the boss or increase friendships]. This encouraging, upbeat statement invites a positive approach to the problem-solving process and increases the likelihood of a solution unfolding.

- *Visualize the problem solved.* Suppose you went to bed and when you woke up some sort of change had happened. You've gotten over or around the barrier. What would be the first thing you'd notice? What other pleasant physical and emotional reactions would you notice? How would life be better for you and others? Imagining the problem solved and attaching pleasant emotions to the problem-solving process facilitate the process (Echterling, Presbury, and McKee 2005). Sometimes simply changing the way we look at the problem, or our feelings toward the problem, is the most workable strategy, since some situations can't be "fixed."

- *Draw, paint, or sculpt what the desired outcome feels and looks like.* Again, artistic expression can generate insights that verbal expression may not.

Generate a range of possible solutions. Insanity is doing the same thing repeatedly and expecting different results. When the old way isn't working, come up with as many new possibilities as you can. The more problem-solving strategies you can conceive, the more likely you'll be to find the best possible option. Here are some strategies for generating solutions:

- *Brainstorm.* This is a process for generating as many solutions as possible. Although individuals can do this alone, this process works best in a team where the ideas and support of many can be tapped. Each person is considered an equal colleague who holds a key to solving the problem, or a piece of the puzzle. All contributions are respected, and the atmosphere is friendly. A week or two before the brainstorming session, ask each team member to think about and bring ideas for solving the problem. This allows time for ideas to percolate. At the brainstorming session, all ideas are listed, say on a whiteboard. To this list everyone adds the solutions that bubble up spontaneously. This is a freewheeling process in which anything goes. All ideas are recorded without evaluation, discussion, judgment, or criticism, all of which stifle the creative process. One idea might piggyback on another—even unlikely ideas can suggest more ideas. Try to keep the session light and moving. When ideas stall, try saying something like "The stock market will crash if we don't come up with five more solutions." Be on the lookout for ways to blend suggestions. Thus, one might learn to like the boss, pay more attention to his needs, focus more on intrinsic motivations for working, retool for a new job, accept the way things are, or find more satisfaction outside of work.

- *Play with the opposite.* Suppose you want to improve your relationship with the boss. Now, think of ways you could estrange yourself from her (for example, ignore her or be aloof, forget assignments, look disdainful). The list will paradoxically suggest solutions to the original problem.

- *Use the scaling technique.* This technique (Walter and Peller 1992) can sometimes help identify solutions. To start, identify where the situation is on a scale of 1 to 10, where 10 is the ideal solution. As you get to a higher number, what would be happening differently? At what number would you feel you're in control? What would your next step be, to get to a higher number?

- *Take another's view.* Ask, "What would [someone who is skilled or respected] do?"

Evaluate the options. After generating possible solutions, evaluate each one. Weigh the pros and cons of each. Ask questions: How would that help? Why? How might this be a bad idea? (Thinking like your adversary might help you tweak the solution.) You might allow for incubation time to allow team members to further evaluate the options and how they might be implemented.

Select the "best" plan (or combinations of plans), implement it, and evaluate progress. In making an action plan, consider questions such as who, what, where, when, and how. Write down the specifics. Calendar a time to check on your progress, being open to the need for adjustments in your plan.

Creativity in the North Vietnam Prison Camps

In the Hanoi Hilton, the creativity exercised by American prisoners of war helped many to survive. Larry Chesley (1973) relates that he and his fellow prisoners set up an educational program, with each of forty-eight prisoners teaching a subject area: American history, psychology, sociology, physiology, religion, languages, trigonometry, and dance, among others. They even had music lessons on an imaginary piano keyboard, drawn on the floor with a piece of brick. Each man was given a key and a pitch. The prisoners played simple tunes by hopping on and off keys. They learned chords by having three or four stand on their respective keys simultaneously. In the evenings they discussed hobbies, special interests, and how to be better husbands and fathers. Chesley memorized poems that lifted his soul, such as Henley's "Invictus" and Kipling's "If," along with Psalm 23, which made him conscious that God had not forgotten them.

Conclusion

Flexibility and creativity are extremely useful skills that can be cultivated. Flexibility and creativity assert that there are always different possibilities for addressing life's problems. Some possibilities present solutions. When solutions are not forthcoming, perhaps change your perspective or your response. The idea is to keep your mind open, as the beginner or child does. We'll conclude this chapter with the following reflections on creativity.

Creativity is not optional equipment. It's a built-in potential, a seedling planted deep in the human personality. And like any other human possibility, creativity can be helped to grow and flourish. —Thomas Kinkade

We are either victims or creators of reality. —Anonymous

We are all artists by birth, realists by training. —Anonymous

Chapter 25

Early Treatment Readiness

Following overwhelming experiences, a substantial minority of people understandably develop mental conditions that are serious enough to require professional help. Resilient individuals are masters at rebounding from stress. They are also wise enough to know that no one is immune to PTSD and other stress-related mental disorders and to know when they need help to rebound. Rather than worrying about *appearing* strong, they are concerned with *healing* (becoming whole again) so that they can be 100 percent there again for themselves, their friends, and their families. Resilient people actively seek needed help, rather than waiting and hoping that time will heal emotional wounds.

Why Is Early Treatment Important?

Recall that PTSD is the most complex of the stress-related mental disorders, and that understanding it helps us better understand the other stress-related mental conditions. So in this chapter we'll focus on the early treatment of PTSD. It is critical to understand that:

- **Many people do not spontaneously recover with time and needlessly suffer decades after the crisis has passed.** For some, symptoms might appear months or years after the traumatic event.

- **PTSD is a highly comorbid disorder.** Most of the time, a range of medical and psychological conditions co-occur with PTSD, such as depression, anxiety, substance abuse, anger, hostility, cardiovascular disease, cancer, diabetes, gastrointestinal problems, headaches, chronic pain, skin problems, autoimmune diseases, suicidal ideation, accidents, poorer lipid profiles, greater unhappiness, and greater overall mortality, to name a few. Those with PTSD typically use more medical care. They also tend to cause strain on family members, who feel like they are walking on eggshells and who may exhibit similar symptoms.

- **PTSD treatments are highly effective.** Early treatment can often prevent post-traumatic stress symptoms from becoming PTSD. However, even skillfully combined treatments provided decades after exposure to traumatic events have been shown to be highly effective (Creamer et al. 2006). There is no need to suffer needlessly for decades when there are scores of effective treatment strategies. A skilled trauma therapist can help survivors find the right treatment or combination of treatment modalities.

- **When you are healed, you are better prepared for the next crisis.** Treatment can bring you back to full capacity. Conversely, unresolved trauma can make you more prone to problems when future crises occur. The treatment process will likely teach you new coping skills that will benefit you in the future. When you have confidence in the healing process, you can urge others who need help to get it.

  Regarding treatment, be flexible. You might have survived a crisis by thinking things like *Press on, Suck it up, Don't quit,* or *Deny pain.* Once the crisis has passed, be ready to shift to the healing mode. Stop and admit needs; unburden and heal emotional wounds; replace the water in the well so you can carry on better. Effective treatment will help you function at your best again. Some people will respect the fact that you sought help. There is no shame in this.

The treatment of PTSD usually involves helping the survivor to stabilize and manage symptoms; confront, neutralize, and properly store traumatic memories; and restore balance in life. It is helpful to think of the trauma specialist with whom you might choose to work as a coach. He or she will help you improve your coping skills, much like a golf coach would help you improve your game. Become an expert by reading about PTSD—its nature and treatment options. This will help you gain more from the treatment process and will help you be a more effective resource to others who also experience PTSD.

How Will I Know When I Have Recovered?

There are a number of indications of recovery. These are adapted from Dr. Mary Harvey (1992):

- You'll be able to recall or dismiss the traumatic memory consciously (with minimal intrusions, nightmares, or flashbacks).

- You can name and tolerate the feelings associated with the memory.

- You tolerate other symptoms (such as depression, anxiety, grief, or sexual dysfunction) well, or they diminish.

- A sense of self-worth, enjoyment, and meaning in life is restored.

- You are comfortable with all feelings—positive, negative, and neutral.

- You are committed to your future.

The Myths and Distortions that Complicate Recovery

If you are suffering from PTSD, you might feel shattered, and that nothing will ever put you back together again. This is normal and quite common. Fortunately, healing and recovery are quite likely when you find the right treatment. Sadly, most people with PTSD do not get proper treatment and thus suffer needlessly for years. Many others whose symptoms do not rise to the level of a formal PTSD diagnosis nevertheless suffer from troubling PTSD symptoms. They, too, could benefit from treatment.

So many people don't obtain critically needed treatment for several reasons. Some don't know where to find it. Others fear that treatment might jeopardize their career or reputation. And others are blocked from seeking help by common myths and distortions, which are listed here—along with counterarguments:

- **Those who seek treatment are weak and dependent.** It is strength to recognize areas in which help would benefit us. An intelligent treatment plan encourages greater self-reliance, and healing helps us reach this. Healing PTSD also helps to improve the comorbid psychological conditions that block progress and enjoyment.

- **I should be able to "soldier on" alone.** Why? Is it written somewhere that one must never get assistance from others? If help ultimately strengthens us, is it weakness to ask for it, or is it strength and wisdom?

- **If I show that I have feelings, I will lose control.** Actually, people are more likely to lose control by bottling up feelings in an unhealthy way. It is liberating to realize that we can show human emotions such as grief, fear, and pain, and even shed tears—as we might at a funeral—and then return to full functioning. With emotional flexibility, we are less likely to snap. It is only by acknowledging vulnerability in certain areas that we can strengthen those areas. As the saying goes, we have to feel it to heal it.

- **I should only be tough and mean.** Many strong people are also tenderhearted. Most people would prefer to serve beside and be around strong individuals who also have a heart. It is okay to show and ask for warmth and affection.

- **I must always be on guard and never relax.** A rubber band that is constantly stretched will break. Be vigilant when needed, then take a breather when it's safe so that you can function better.

- **These symptoms will go away with time.** They might, but if they are severe they likely won't.

- **I'll lose it and never recover if I start talking about the trauma. I couldn't stand the pain of talking about the trauma.** Verbalizing helps to integrate and neutralize traumatic memories. Talking about trauma might be uncomfortable initially, but usually it becomes easier with repetition—especially when we choose the proper setting. A skilled trauma specialist will help you do this only when you are ready, and then at a pace that is acceptable to you.

- **Talking about the trauma makes it worse.** See the comments above.

- **Denying my feelings will make the pain go away. Distancing or drinking will get me through.** Ignored pain tends to accumulate until it erupts, often destructively.

- **I shouldn't have to suffer. I shouldn't have to work at healing.** Why would that be the case when everyone suffers? Perhaps you could adopt a softer, more accepting response to suffering as you work to solve your problems. Consider reading item 13 of the online resources (available at http://www.newharbinger.com/39409); it's about resilient suffering.

- **I should not request time to recover.** When time is needed to recover, have the courage to ask for it.

- **I must appear strong so that no one thinks I'm weak. I should be ashamed for having symptoms.** This keeps many from getting help and causes many to self-medicate to disguise symptoms. Would you rather *look* strong, or invest the effort to *be and feel* strong inside?

- **I should be over this by now.** Recovery takes time—as long as it takes. Often, the slower you go in treatment, the faster the recovery.

- **All problems can be resolved with willpower and getting back to work.** Obviously this doesn't work well in many cases of PTSD, since many symptoms can persist for decades until new approaches are tried.

- **Mental health professionals are useless, touchy-feely incompetents who can't relate to what I've been through.** As with any profession, some trauma specialists are effective and some are not (Artwohl and Christensen 1997). Some have experienced what you have, and some who have not have tried hard to understand experiences like yours. Some have a capacity to care and help even though they have not experienced what you have. Nevertheless, shop around until you find one you can respect, relate to, and work with.

- **I'm irrevocably bad for what I did. I'll never get over it.** Would a truly bad person feel the remorse that you do? Humans are able to listen to guilt, make needed changes, and then release it. Eventually, the guilt subsides.

Finding Needed Help

Fortunately there are many useful resources available for those with PTSD (see the recommended resources). The Sidran Institute, for example, helps people locate a trauma specialist in their geographic area. (Because the complexities of treating PTSD require an exceptional degree of expertise in PTSD, when looking for a mental health professional, it is best to find a trauma specialist.) The *Post-Traumatic Stress Disorder Sourcebook* (Schiraldi 2016a) explores the nature of PTSD and its treatment options in a clear and comprehensive way. This book also contains an extensive list of additional resources.

If symptoms have persisted or are disrupting any area of your life, and self-management strategies are insufficient, consider finding a trauma specialist. Be a good consumer. Prepare for your search by reading as much as you can about PTSD. Know beforehand which treatment modalities seem right for you. Discuss with a potential provider which treatment (or treatments) she or he uses, and be reasonably certain that you will be comfortable working with the provider.

Conclusion

Most people would not choose to suffer from the effects of trauma or other stress-related conditions. However, you can minimize suffering when you take the steps needed to recover and heal. In the recovery process, you'll likely learn new coping skills that will help you throughout your life. Through this process, suffering can ultimately make you more resilient.

Putting It All Together

Congratulations for completing this workbook! I sincerely hope that it has been a rewarding experience.

Please consider for a moment the many important skills you've explored. In part 1 we started with ways to strengthen the brain that lift your mood and help you implement the other skills of resilience. Then you learned tools to manage your physical stress levels and troubling emotions so that you can feel and function at your best.

Happiness is its own reward. However, positive psychology has shown that a happy person is also a more resilient person. So in part 2, we explored proven ways to increase happiness. All of these skills prepared you for the thriving skills in the last part of the workbook, part 3.

Please consider a few points in summary and conclusion:

- You already have within you the seeds of remarkable resilience—strengths in embryo, which can be cultivated.

- Skills practice, more than knowledge, is the key to growing your resilience strengths.

- Growing strengths is a lifelong process.

- If you patiently pursue the pathways to growing resilience, growth will happen—perhaps gradually and almost imperceptibly, but it will happen.

The more you practice resilience skills, the more developed the brain's neural pathways related to resilience become (and the more you can access these skills under pressure). Conversely, with disuse, these pathways can fade. That's why it's important to remember and practice your resilience skills.

Perhaps you will remember some skills with little effort. Perhaps life will throw you a curveball that sends you back to this book to review needed skills. Or perhaps, like an elite athlete, you understand that skills take time to acquire and practice to maintain.

This final activity will help to reinforce your learning. It will help you remember the principles and skills that matter the most to you.

Activity: Remembering What Works

What would you most like to take away from this workbook? Please start by thumbing through the entire workbook. In the spaces that follow, write the ideas (or principles) and skills that you'd most like to remember. You might also note the page numbers for handy reference in difficult times. Once you've completed this, please consider making a written year's plan for the weekly practice of your favorite skills. The only rule is that the plan works for you.

Ideas I Most Want to Remember

_____

_____

_____

_____

_____

_____

_____

_____

_____

_____

_____

Skills I Most Want to Remember

_____

_____

_____

_____

_____

_____

_____

_____

_____

_____

_____

_____

_____

Conclusion

When we teach, we learn. One way to keep resilience skills fresh is to form a group (such as family, neighbors, or a work team) in which members teach each other, one that meets frequently. A group member (usually a different one each meeting) might walk members through a different skill at each meeting. Alternatively, a group member might devise a challenging scenario and ask members to identify and apply a combination of useful skills for before, during, and after. And please consider lifelong learning to strengthen your resilience (see the recommended resources for ideas). The free online resources are important additions to this workbook that can help with lifelong learning. Visit http://www.newharbinger.com/39409 to access and download them.

Going forward, please remember the many strengths, skills, and resources you have to draw on in challenging times. May you be confident, ever learning, and ever becoming more resilient.

Acknowledgments

This guide to growing resilience has been my most challenging and satisfying writing endeavor—challenging because resilience is such a broad and deep topic, and satisfying because the gains of growing resilience are so enormous. I realize that this undertaking would still be a dream without the aid of many important people.

I first wish to thank the students at the University of Maryland who, through their patience and determination in the resilience courses I developed and facilitated, have helped me to better understand how people actually cultivate resilience. Similarly, I thank the many individuals—leaders, employees, family members, emergency responders, peer counselors, and mental health professionals—who have taken my resilience training workshops. You have inspired and taught me more than you know, and you have greatly deepened my appreciation for the courage and resilience of the human spirit.

I express sincere appreciation to the tireless researchers who have clarified the complexities of resilience. The pioneers in resilience research include Drs. Emmy E. Werner, Emory L. Cowen, George E. Vaillant, Norman Garmezy, Michael Rutter, William R. Beardslee, and Ann S. Masten. Others whose research I have especially appreciated include positive psychology researchers Drs. Martin Seligman, Christopher Petersen, Ed Diener, Sonja Lyubomirsky, and Barbara L. Fredrickson.

Body-oriented approaches to regulating arousal were pioneered by master clinicians Patricia Ogden, Peter Levine, Bessel van der Kolk, and Elaine Miller-Karas. I'm grateful to them for providing the missing piece of the puzzle to understanding trauma and resilience.

I am most grateful to the many people who gave so generously of their time to review this book, provide feedback, and suggest helpful improvements: Drs. Greg Baer, Alan D. Boss, George S. Everly Jr., Charles R. Figley, Edward Tick, Mary Neal Vieten, and Spencer Wood; Chaplain Glenn Calkins, Captain William J. Donaldson, Detective Robert B. Dwyer, Sergeant Sergio Falzi, Major General Thomas W. Garrett, Mrs. Janet Harkness, Major Colby Jenkins, Director Peter Jonsson, Captain Monica Kleinman, Chief of Police Peter Volkmann, and members of my dear family.

Finally, I acknowledge the many resilient people who by their examples show us that it is possible to face adversity with determination and a triumphant will. Some are famous, such as Mother Teresa, Arthur Ashe, Christopher Reeve, and Viktor Frankl. Most are ordinary people—family members, neighbors, and friends. I dedicate this work to all who have weathered and bounced back from the storms of life with honor and courage, and in so doing inspire us all. Thank you one and all.

Portions of this book are adapted from my previous works, including *World War II Survivors: Lessons in Resilience*; *The Post-Traumatic Stress Disorder Sourcebook*; *The Self-Esteem Workbook*; *10 Simple Solutions for Building Self-Esteem*; *The Resilient Warrior Before, During, and After War*; *The Anger Management Sourcebook*; and *The Complete Guide to Resilience*.

Free Online Resources

Lifelong learning increases resilience. The recommended resource section includes many additional aids. The free online resources (visit http://www.newharbinger.com/39409) that accompany this workbook are also important and useful tools.

Resilience Basics

1. **The MIND Diet** is a promising Mediterranean-style diet that appears to strengthen the brain.

2. The **Log Sheet for Resilience Strategies** can be reproduced to record your progress.

3. The **Blank Daily Thought Record** can be reproduced and used for practice of cognitive restructuring.

Happiness

4. The **Optimism Questionnaire** raises awareness of your thinking style and suggests a range of optimistic thoughts to choose.

5. The **Sociability Checkup** identifies the many dimensions of social intelligence.

6. **Social Intelligence** presents many principles and skills for improving interpersonal relationships.

7. **Money Attitudes and Management** usually affect happiness more than wealth.

8. **Religion and Spirituality** are strongly related in the research to resilience and happiness.

9. **The Forgiveness Letter** is a blank template related to chapter 20 of this book.

10. **Meditation** is linked to many benefits, including happiness. This section covers additional methods.

Looking Ahead: Preparing Emotionally for Difficult Times

11. **Preparing Emotionally for Crisis** introduces the powerful principle of emotional inoculation.

12. **Preparing for Post-Crisis Stress Symptoms** keeps us from being caught by surprise following distressing situations.

13. **Resilient Suffering** explores perspectives that help us navigate painful times.

14. **Emotional Inoculation for Emergency Responders** covers considerations that are especially useful for high-risk groups (such as military, police, and firefighters) and those who support them.

Additional Resilience Reflections

Online Bibliography

Brain Health Planning Form

On the next page, write down what you plan to eat and drink each day, including the amounts of both food and liquid. Try to align your plan with the nutrition guidelines in chapter 1 to ensure you are getting the nutrients your brain needs.

	Mon.	Tue.	Wed.	Thurs.	Fri.	Sat.	Sun.
Breakfast							
Snack							
Lunch							
Snack							
Dinner							
Snack							

An Initial Fourteen-Day Commitment

On the next page, keep a record to see how well you stick to your health plan for fourteen days. Throughout the fourteen days make whatever adjustments you need, and then continue the plan as you read the rest of the book.

Day	Date	Exercise (in minutes)	Number of Meals Eaten (Rate 1–10 how closely your eating for the day matches the nutritional guidelines in chapter 1.)	Sleep		
				Number of Hours	Time to Bed	Time Out of Bed
1						
2						
3						
4						
5						
6						
7						

Day	Date	Exercise (in minutes)	Number of Meals Eaten (Rate 1–10 how closely your eating for the day matches the nutritional guidelines in chapter 1.)	Sleep		
				Number of Hours	Time to Bed	Time Out of Bed
8						
9						
10						
11						
12						
13						
14						

Log Sheet for Resilience Strategies

Keeping a log and recording progress can be motivating. A log can also remind you of what has worked for you or show how the effectiveness of different strategies compare. You can make copies of the blank log sheet on the next page, or download copies of the log from the website for this book and use it to gauge the effectiveness of the various strategies in this workbook, rating them on a scale of 1 to 10 (1 being not effective and 10 highly effective).

Strategy practiced: _____

Date	Time of Day	Situation	Effectiveness	
			Physical	Emotional

Date	Time of Day	Situation	Effectiveness	
			Physical	Emotional

Recommended Resources

Anticholinergic Drugs

Aging Brain Care Program of the Indiana University Center for Aging Research. 2012. *Anticholinergic Cognitive Burden Scale*. Regenstrief Institute. http://www.agingbraincare .org/uploads/products/ACB_scale_-_legal_size.pdf. This scale identifies anticholinergic medications.

General Resilience

Ashe, A., and A. Rampersad. 1993. *Days of Grace: A Memoir*. New York: Ballantine. About retaining inner peace and optimism, despite tragedy. By the dignified tennis champion who contracted AIDS from open-heart surgery.

Frankl, V. 2014. *Man's Search for Meaning*. Boston: Beacon Press. The classic work on discovering meaning in one's life out of suffering. Written by the Holocaust survivor who founded logotherapy.

Geisel, T. S. 1990. *Oh, the Places You'll Go!* New York: Random House. Part of the Dr. Seuss series; a clever, humorous treatise on human growth and fallibility.

Gonzales, L. 2004. *Deep Survival: Who Lives, Who Dies, and Why*. New York: W. W. Norton. Survival skills that transfer to everyday life, including surrendering to the situation, reasoned action, calmly taking responsibility, and persistence.

Kushner, H. S. 2004. *When Bad Things Happen to Good People*. New York: Anchor Books. A rabbi's profound insights on suffering.

Lewis. C. S. 2015. *A Grief Observed*. New York: HarperCollins. Insights on enduring and recovering from the crushing loss of a loved one.

Marx, J. 2004. *Season of Life: A Football Star, a Boy, a Journey to Manhood*. New York: Simon and Schuster. Inspired by Viktor Frankl, former NFL star Joe Ehrmann teaches highly successful young athletes that manhood is not found in athletic prowess, sexual exploitation, or materialism, but in love and meaning.

Nhat Hanh, T. 2013. *Peace Is Every Step: The Path of Mindfulness in Everyday Life*. New York: Bantam. A peaceful monk's practical ways to cultivate inner peace, joy, serenity, and balance.

Opdyke, I. G., and J. Armstrong. 2001. *In My Hands: Memories of a Holocaust Rescuer*. New York: Anchor Books. A stirring story of the courageous Holocaust rescuer who remained tender inside, despite incalculable suffering.

Petrie, A., and J. Petrie. 1986. *Mother Teresa*. DVD documentary directed by Ann and Jeanette Petrie. New York: Petrie Productions. Powerful modeling and universal messages of unconditional love, forgiveness, and faith.

Schiraldi, G. R. 2007. *10 Simple Solutions for Building Self-Esteem: How to End Self-Doubt, Gain Confidence, and Create a Positive Self-Image*. Oakland, CA: New Harbinger Publications. Combines cognitive behavioral, mindfulness, and ACT strategies. Based on the effective "Beyond 9/11: Stress, Survival, and Coping" course I taught at the University of Maryland.

Schiraldi, G. R. 2007. *World War II Survivors: Lessons in Resilience*. Ellicott City, MD: Chevron Publishing. Forty-one combat survivors explain how they preserved their sanity and the ability to function under many forms of extreme duress. Their lessons are applicable to all of us today.

Schiraldi, G. R. 2016. *The Self-Esteem Workbook*. 2nd ed. Oakland, CA: New Harbinger Publications. Based on the successful "Stress and the Healthy Mind" course I taught at the University of Maryland. Detailed instructions for many effective skills.

ten Boom, C., E. Sherrill, and J. Sherrill. 2006. *The Hiding Place*. 35th anniversary ed. Grand Rapids, MI: Chosen Books. Imprisoned in the German concentration camps for rescuing Jews, Corrie ten Boom tells of living with compassion and courage in a world of hatred.

Vaillant, G. E. 2003. *Aging Well: Surprising Guideposts to a Happier Life from the Landmark Harvard Study of Adult Development*. New York: Little, Brown. Warm and powerful insights for adults of all ages on thriving mentally, physically, and socially, from what is generally considered the finest longitudinal study of lifetime development. Also by Dr. Vaillant are *Adaptation to Life* (1998) and *Spiritual Evolution: A Scientific Defense of Faith* (2008).

Wooden, J., and J Carty. 2005. *Coach Wooden's Pyramid of Success: Building Blocks for a Better Life*. Ventura, CA: Regal Books. Wooden, who died at ninety-nine, was an extraordinarily successful and beloved athlete and coach who masterfully applied the principles of positive psychology. See also N. L. Johnson's *The John Wooden Pyramid of Success* (2003), which includes more moving principles and wisdom.

Happiness Books

Brooks, A. C. 2008. *Gross National Happiness: Why Happiness Matters for America—and How We Can Get More of It*. New York: Basic Books. An accomplished researcher draws from large and reputable databases, mostly from recent studies, to draw conclusions on topics ranging from politics to family and religious values as they relate to happiness.

Dalai Lama, and H. C. Cutler. 2009. *The Art of Happiness: A Handbook for Living*. 10th anniversary, updated ed. New York: Riverhead Books. Profound insights on self-esteem and compassion.

Emmons, R. 2007. *Thanks! How the New Science of Gratitude Can Make You Happier*. New York: Houghton Mifflin. Provides scientific and religious underpinnings, plus practical guidelines for counting blessings in all circumstances.

Lyubomirsky, S. 2007. *The How of Happiness: A Scientific Approach to Getting the Life You Want*. New York: Penguin Books. A masterful combination of solid research and practical, tested methods to enhance happiness.

Heart Coherence

HeartMath® Institute (800–711–6221; info@heartmath.com; http://www.heartmath.org/; http://www.heartmathstore.com). Located in Boulder Creek, CA. Provides books, videos, music, and other products related to heart coherence, as well as emWave products that enable you to monitor heart rhythms in real time as you practice HeartMath skills.

Mindfulness-Based Stress Reduction (MBSR)

Do an Internet search using the terms "mindfulness" or "mindfulness-based stress reduction" to locate local resources.

There are also good mindfulness meditation CDs and tapes by Jon Kabat-Zinn, PhD (http://www.stressreductiontapes.com).

University of Massachusetts Medical School, Center for Mindfulness (https://www.cfmhome.org) hosts trainings and identifies places where MBSR classes are available.

Mindfulness Books

Brach, T. 2003. *Radical Acceptance: Embracing Your Life with the Heart of a Buddha*. New York: Bantam Books. A comforting guide.

Kabat-Zinn, J. 1990. *Full Catastrophe Living: Using the Wisdom of Your Body and Mind to Face Stress, Pain, and Illness*. New York: Bantam Dell. Still the classic work.

Schiraldi, G. R. 2007. *10 Simple Solutions for Building Self-Esteem: How to End Self-Doubt, Gain Confidence, and Create a Positive Self-Image*. Oakland, CA: New Harbinger Publications. Includes instructions for mindfulness meditation within the context of self-esteem enhancement.

Moral Strength

O'Malley, W. J. 2010. *Building Your Own Conscience (Batteries Not Included)*. Allen, TX: Tabor Publishing. Principles, activities, and quotations that skillfully stimulate one to be aware of and grow a peaceful conscience.

Nutrition

The Nutrition Data website (http://nutritiondata.com) offers a user-friendly way to count calories in everyday foods and those found at restaurants and fast-food chains.

The USDA's user-friendly https://www.ChooseMyPlate.gov, based on solid research, offers a wealth of useful information to help you tailor an eating plan to your needs.

Physical Fitness

Christensen, A. 1999. *The American Yoga Association's Easy Does It Yoga: The Safe and Gentle Way to Health and Well-Being*. New York: Touchstone. Instructions for gentle postures for the aged, injured, or inactive. Many can be done at your desk and are thus useful for all to relax and increase energy and flexibility.

Ross, D. D., and C. J. McPhee. 2008. *Flow Motion: The Simplified T'ai Chi Workout*. DVD. Directed by D. D. Ross and C. J. McPhee. Los Angeles: Lightworks Audio and Video. Gentle beginner's workouts in tai chi, which has been found to lower blood pressure and improve fitness.

To find lists of certified fitness instructors, go to the American Council on Exercise (http://www.acefitness.org) and the American College of Sports Medicine (http://www.acsm.org).

Positive Psychology

Fredrickson, B. 2009. "Positivity." http://www.positivityratio.com. The twenty-question self-test by Dr. Fredrickson shows if your daily positivity ratio exceeds the target of three positive emotions to one negative one. Most don't, but we can increase that ratio.

Siegel, R. D., and S. M. Allison. EDs. 2009. *Positive Psychology: Harnessing the Power of Happiness, Mindfulness, and Personal Strength*. Boston: Harvard Health Publications. Very effectively and succinctly traces the evolution of positive psychology, outlines major findings, and presents many practical skills.

University of Pennsylvania. n.d. "Authentic Happiness." http://www.authentichappiness.sas.upenn.edu. Contains various happiness questionnaires, including the VIA survey of character strengths, which identifies your top five of twenty-four character strengths. (Also visit http://www.viacharacter.org to rank all twenty-four strengths.)

Protectors

Gilmartin, K. M. 2002. *Emotional Survival for Law Enforcement: A Guide for Officers and Their Families*. Tucson, AZ: E-S Press. Down to earth, often humorous.

Grossman, D., and L. W. Christensen. 2008. *On Combat: The Psychology and Physiology of Deadly Conflict in War and in Peace*. 3rd ed. Millstadt, IL: Warrior Science Publications. A very thoughtful treatise on knowing what to expect and how to prepare to kill, when that is required. Lieutenant Colonel Grossman's *On Killing* (2009) is also recommended.

Kirschman, E. 2006. *I Love a Cop: What Police Families Need to Know*. Rev. ed. New York: Guilford Press. A balanced treatment of the stresses no one talks about, as well as many practical tips. Useful for both cops and their families. The author also wrote *I Love a Fire Fighter* (2004), which is very useful for firefighters and their families.

Schiraldi, G. R. 2012. *The Resilient Warrior: Before, During, and After War*. Ashburn, VA: Resilience Training International. The essential guide for anyone who is preparing to go to, is serving in, or has returned from a war zone—and their families.

Tick, E. 2005. *War and the Soul: Healing Our Nation's Veterans from Post-Traumatic Stress Disorder*. Wheaton, IL: Quest Books. Tick argues that PTSD is best understood as an identity disorder and soul wound, and moral pain is a root cause. This book is about how the honorable warrior soul is healed and reclaimed.

PTSD

Schiraldi, G. R. 2016. *The Post-Traumatic Stress Disorder Sourcebook: A Guide to Healing, Recovery and Growth*. 2nd ed. revised. New York: McGraw-Hill. Clearly explains and normalizes the symptoms of PTSD, explains the range of treatment options (for example, groups, professional, or self-managed) and how to find them, and provides a comprehensive listing of resources. Dr. George Everly, founding executive editor of the *International Journal of Emergency Mental Health*, calls it "The most valuable, user-friendly manual on PTSD I have ever seen. Must reading for victims, their families, and their therapists."

Finding a Trauma Specialist

Anxiety and Depression Association of America (240-485-1001; http://www.adaa.org). In Silver Spring, MD. Provides members with a list of professionals who specialize in the treatment of stress-related conditions. Also provides information about self-help and support groups in your area. Has a catalog of available brochures, books, and audiocassettes; puts out a newsletter; and puts on an annual national conference.

Intensive Trauma Therapy, Inc. (304-291-2912; http://www.traumatherapy.us). In Morgantown, WV. Skillfully combines hypnosis, video technology, and art therapy into one- to two-week intensive programs with excellent results. Also trains providers.

Mental Health America (formerly the National Mental Health Association) (703-684-7722; 800-969-NMHA; crisis line 800-273-TALK; http://www.NMHA.org). In Alexandria, VA. Provides a list of affiliate mental health organizations in your area that can provide resources and information about self-help groups, treatment professionals, and community clinics.

Seeking Safety (http://www.seekingsafety.org). A source for this method of treating the dual diagnosis of PTSD and substance abuse.

SIDRAN Institute (410-825-8888; help@sidran.org; http://www.sidran.org). In Baltimore, MD. Can help you locate psychotherapists specializing in PTSD and offer readings and other resources.

Resilient Couples and Family Skills

Garcia-Prats, C. M., J. A. Garcia-Prats. 1997. *Good Families Don't Just Happen: What We Learned from Raising Our 10 Sons and How It Can Work for You*. Holbrook, MA: Adams Media Corporation. Principle-based skills, starting with respect between spouses.

Lundberg, G. B., and J. S. Lundberg. 2000. *I Don't Have to Make Everything All Better: Six Practical Principles that Empower Others to Solve Their Own Problems While Enriching Your Relationships*. New York: Viking. A treasure chest of methods for relating to people. Learn how to walk alongside people emotionally (validating), rather than arguing or criticizing.

Lundberg, G. B., and J. S. Lundberg. 2002. *Married for Better, Not Worse: The Fourteen Secrets to a Happy Marriage*. New York: Penguin Books. Another down-to-earth treasure for creating a satisfying marriage.

Markman, H., S. Stanley, and S. L. Blumberg. 2001. *Fighting for Your Marriage: Positive Steps for Preventing Divorce and Preserving a Lasting Love*. San Francisco: Jossey-Bass. From conflict resolution to increasing fun. Practical. Based on solid research.

Prevention and Relationship Enhancement Program (PREP), Greenwood Village, CO (800-366-0166; https://www.prepinc.com). Offers resources for a loving marriage, such as *Fighting for Your Marriage* and other books as well as excellent, practical DVDs to help you develop communication skills, solve problems, and promote intimacy. The PREP program is well researched and respected.

Sleep

The American Academy of Sleep Medicine (http://www.aasmnet.org; http://www.sleepeducation.com) lists hundreds of accredited centers and board-certified sleep specialists.

Thought Field Therapy

Thought field therapy founder Dr. Roger Callahan's website: http://www.tfttapping.com/.

Trauma Relief Organizations

Outward Bound (866-467-7651; http://www.outwardbound.org). In Golden, CO. Since 1941 has offered courses in a range of challenging wilderness environments coupled with emotional support to inspire self-respect and care for others, community, and environment. Courses can be customized for survivors of violence, war, sexual assault, incest, cancer, substance-use disorders, mild traumatic brain injury, and grief.

Serve and Protect (615-373-8000, a 24/7 confidential hotline; http://www.serveprotect.org). In Brentwood, TN. Connects public service personnel (police, other emergency service personnel, and veterans) to trauma therapists, residential treatments, or other treatments (equine, canine, and so forth) as needed.

References

Adamshick, M. 2013. *Chief of Staff of the Army Leader Development Task Force Final Report.* Washington, DC: Department of the Army. Retrieved from cape.army.mil/repository/CSA%20LDTF%20Final%20Report%20062113.pdf.

Amatenstein, S. 2010. *The Complete Marriage Counselor: Relationship-Saving Advice from America's Top 50+ Couples Therapists.* Avon, MA: Adams Media.

American Psychological Association. 2001. "Helping a Nation Heal: The Pentagon." *Monitor on Psychology* 32: 16. Retrieved from http://www.apa.org/monitor/nov01/pentagon.aspx.

Artwohl, A., and L. W. Christensen. 1997. *Deadly Force Encounters: What Cops Need to Know to Mentally and Physically Prepare for and Survive a Gunfight.* Boulder, CO: Paladin Press.

Ashe, A., and A. Rampersad. 1993. *Days of Grace: A Memoir.* New York: Ballantine Books.

Austenfeld, J. L., A. M. Paolo, and A. L. Stanton. 2006. "Effects of Writing About Emotions Versus Goals on Psychological and Physical Health Among Third-Year Medical Students." *Journal of Personality* 74: 267–286.

Baker, D., C. Greenberg, and I. L. Yalof. 2007. *What Happy Women Know: How New Findings in Positive Psychology Can Change Women's Lives for the Better.* New York: Rodale.

Barker, D. B. 2007. "Antecedents of Stressful Experiences: Depressive Symptoms, Self-Esteem, Gender, and Coping." *International Journal of Stress Management* 14: 333–349.

Barrett, D., ed. 1996. *Trauma and Dreams.* Cambridge, MA: Harvard University Press.

Baylis, N. 2009. *The Rough Guide to Happiness.* London: Rough Guides.

Bergin, M. S. 2009. "Making Dinner Together Time." *BYU Magazine,* Winter, 24–25.

Biech, E. 1996. *Creativity and Innovation: The ASTD Trainer's Sourcebook.* New York: McGraw-Hill.

Boscarino, J. A., and R. E. Adams. 2008. "Overview of Findings from the World Trade Center Disaster Outcome Study: Recommendations for Future Research After Exposure to Psychological Trauma." *International Journal of Emergency Mental Health* 10: 275–290.

Boscarino, J. A., R. E. Adams, and C. R. Figley. 2005. "A Prospective Cohort Study of the Effectiveness of Employer-Sponsored Crisis Interventions After a Major Disaster." *International Journal of Emergency Mental Health* 7: 9–22.

Bray, R. L. 2017. "Thought Field Therapy of San Diego." Retrieved from http://www.rlbray.com.

Brooks, A. C. 2008. *Gross National Happiness: Why Happiness Matters for America—and How We Can Get More of It*. New York: Basic Books.

Carrier, C. 2000. "From Darkness to Light." *Reader's Digest*, May, 100–106.

Chaffee, J. 1998. *The Thinker's Way: 8 Steps to a Richer Life*. New York: Little, Brown.

Chesley, L. 1973. *Seven Years in Hanoi: A POW Tells His Story*. Salt Lake City, UT: Bookcraft.

Childre, D. L., and D. Rozman. 2003. *Transforming Anger: The HeartMath Solution for Letting Go of Rage, Frustration, and Irritation*. Oakland, CA: New Harbinger Publications.

Childre, D. L., and D. Rozman. 2005. *Transforming Stress: The HeartMath Solution for Relieving Worry, Fatigue, and Tension*. Oakland, CA: New Harbinger Publications.

Cicchetti, D., F. A. Rogosch, M. Lynch, and K. D. Holt. 1993. "Resilience in Maltreated Children: Processes Leading to Adaptive Outcome." *Development and Psychopathology* 5: 629–647.

Creamer, M., P. Elliott, D. Forbes, D. Biddle, and G. Hawthorne. 2006. "Treatment for Combat-Related Posttraumatic Stress Disorder: Two-Year Follow-Up." *Journal of Traumatic Stress* 19: 675–685.

Csikszentmihalyi, M. 1996. *Creativity: Flow and the Psychology of Discovery and Invention*. New York: HarperCollins.

Diener, E., and R. Biswas-Diener. 2008. *Happiness: Unlocking the Mysteries of Psychological Wealth*. Malden, MA: Blackwell Publishing.

Diener, E., and M. Diener. 1995. "Cross-Cultural Correlates of Life Satisfaction and Self-Esteem." *Journal of Personality and Social Psychology* 68: 653–663.

Doidge, N., 2007. *The Brain That Changes Itself: Stories of Personal Triumph from the Frontiers of Brain Science*. New York: Penguin.

Dumont, M., and M. A. Provost. 1999. "Resilience in Adolescents: Protective Role of Social Support, Coping Strategies, Self-Esteem, and Social Activities on Experience of Stress and Depression." *Journal of Youth and Adolescence* 28: 343–363.

Echterling, L. G., J. H. Presbury, and J. E. McKee. 2005. *Crisis Intervention: Promoting Resilience and Resolution in Troubled Times*. Upper Saddle River, NJ: Pearson.

Emmons, R. A. 1986. "Personal Strivings: An Approach to Personality and Subjective Well-Being." *Journal of Personality and Social Psychology* 51: 1058–1068.

Emmons, R. A. and M. E. McCullough. 2003. "Counting Blessings Versus Burdens: An Experimental Investigation of Gratitude and Subjective Well-Being in Daily Life." *Journal of Personality and Social Psychology* 84: 377–389.

Enright, R. 2012. *The Forgiving Life: A Pathway to Overcoming Resentment and Creating a Legacy of Love.* Washington, DC: American Psychological Association.

Eyre, L., and R. Eyre. 1980. *Teaching Children Joy.* Salt Lake City, UT: Deseret Books.

Felitti, V. J. 2002. "The Relation Between Adverse Childhood Experiences and Adult Health: Turning Gold into Lead." *Permanente Journal* 6: 44–47.

Follette, V. M., and J. Pistorello. 2007. *Finding Life Beyond Trauma: Using Acceptance and Commitment Therapy to Heal from Post-Traumatic Stress and Trauma-Related Problems.* Oakland, CA: New Harbinger Publications.

Frankl, V. 1963. *Man's Search for Meaning.* New York: Pocket Books.

Franzini, L. R. 2002. *Kids Who Laugh: How to Develop Your Child's Sense of Humor.* Garden City Park, NY: Square One Publishers.

Fredrickson, B. L. 2009. *Positivity: Top-Notch Research Reveals the 3 to 1 Ratio That Will Change Your Life.* New York: Three Rivers Press.

Fredrickson, B. L. 2013. *Love 2.0: How Our Supreme Emotion Affects Everything We Feel, Think, Do, and Become.* New York: Hudson Street Press.

Fredrickson, B. L., M. M. Tugade, C. E. Waugh, and G. R. Larkin. 2003. "What Good Are Positive Emotions in Crises? A Prospective Study of Resilience and Emotions Following the Terrorist Attacks on the United States on September 11th, 2001." *Journal of Personality and Social Psychology* 84: 365–376.

Gardener, H., C. B. Wright, C. Dong, K. Cheung, J. DeRosa, M. Nannery, Y. Stern, M. S. V. Elkind, and R. L. Sacco. 2016. "Ideal Cardiovascular Health and Cognitive Aging in the Northern Manhattan Study." *Journal of the American Heart Association* 5: e002731.

Gauthier, J., D. Pellerin, and P. Renaud. 1983. "The Enhancement of Self-Esteem: A Comparison of Two Cognitive Strategies." *Cognitive Therapy and Research* 7: 389–398.

Goldman, L. 2005. "Building Resiliency in Traumatized Kids: Coping with 21st Century Realities." *Healing Magazine*, Fall/Winter, 19–20.

Grossman, D., and L. W. Christensen. 2004. *On Combat.* Millstadt, IL: PPCT Research Publications.

Harter, S. 1986. "Cognitive-Developmental Processes in the Integration of Concepts About Emotions and the Self." *Social Cognition* 4: 119–151.

Harter, S. 1999. *The Construction of the Self*. New York: Guilford Press.

Harvey, M. 1992. "Cambridge Hospital Victims of Violence Program Resolution Criteria." In "Date Rape," ed. M. P. Koss, *Harvard Mental Health Letter* 9, September 6.

Hillenbrand, L. 2012. *Unbroken: A World War II Story of Survival, Resilience, and Redemption*. New York: Random House.

Hobfoll, S. E., and P. London. 1986. "The Relationship of Self-Concept and Social Support to Emotional Distress Among Women During War." *Journal of Social and Clinical Psychology* 4: 189–203.

Hobfoll, S. E., and S. Walfisch. 1984. "Coping with a Threat to Life: A Longitudinal Study of Self-Concept, Social Support, and Psychological Distress." *American Journal of Community Psychology* 12: 87–100.

Jacob, J. I., S. Allen, E. J. Hill, N. L. Mead, and M. Ferris. 2008. "Work Interference with Dinnertime as a Mediator and Moderator Between Work Hours and Work and Family Outcomes." *Family and Consumer Sciences Research Journal* 36: 310–327.

Johnson, C., M. Shala, X. Sejdijaj, R. Odell, and K. Dabishevci. 2001. "Thought Field Therapy: Soothing the Bad Moments of Kosovo." *Journal of Clinical Psychology* 57: 1237–1240.

Kessler, R. C., P. Berglund, O. Demler, R. Jin, K. R. Merikangas, and E. E. Walters. 2005. "Lifetime Prevalence and Age-of-Onset Distributions of *DSM-IV* Disorders in the National Comorbidity Survey Replication." *Archives of General Psychiatry* 62: 593–602.

Kessler, R. C., K. A. McGonagle, S. Zhao, C. B. Nelson, M. Hughes, S. Eshleman, H. U. Wittchen, and K. S. Kender. 1994. "Lifetime and 12-Month Prevalence of *DSM-III-R* Psychiatric Disorders in the United States." *Archives of General Psychiatry* 51: 8–19.

King, L. A. 2001. "The Health Benefits of Writing About Life Goals." *Personality and Social Psychology Bulletin* 27: 798–807.

Kirschman, E. 2004. *I Love a Fire Fighter: What the Family Needs to Know*. New York: Guilford Press.

Klein, A. 1989. *The Healing Power of Humor: Techniques for Getting Through Loss, Setbacks, Upsets, Disappointments, Difficulties, Trials, Tribulations, and All That Not-So-Funny Stuff*. New York: Jeremy P. Tarcher/Putnam.

Kovacs, L. 2007. *Building a Reality-Based Relationship: The Six Stages of Modern Marriage*. Lincoln, NE: iUniverse.

Levine, P. A. 2010. *In an Unspoken Voice: How the Body Releases Trauma and Restores Goodness*. Berkeley, CA: North Atlantic Books.

Lewinsohn, P., R. Muñoz, M. A. Youngren, and A. M. Zeiss. 1986. *Control Your Depression*. New York: Prentice Hall.

Litz, B. T., L. Lebowitz, M. J. Gray, and W. P Nash. 2016. *Adaptive Disclosure: A New Treatment for Military Trauma, Loss, and Moral Injury*. New York: Guilford Press.

Lyubomirsky, S. 2007. *The How of Happiness: A Scientific Approach to Getting the Life You Want*. New York: Penguin Books.

Lyubomirsky, S., and M. D. Della Porta. 2010. "Boosting Happiness, Buttressing Resilience: Results from Cognitive and Behavioral Interventions." In *Handbook of Adult Resilience: Concepts, Methods, and Applications*, edited by J. W. Reich, A. J. Zautra, and J. S. Hall, 450–464. New York: Guilford Press.

Martin, R. A. 2007. *The Psychology of Humor: An Integrative Approach*. Boston: Elsevier Academic Press.

McCraty, R. and D. Childre. 2004. "The Grateful Heart: The Psychophysiology of Appreciation." In *The Psychology of Gratitude* (Series in Affective Science), Edited by R. A. Emmons and M. E. McCullough. Eds. New York, Oxford University Press, 230–256.

McCraty, R. and D. Tomasino. 2004. "Heart Rhythm Coherence Feedback: A New Tool for Stress Reduction, Rehabilitation, and Performance Enhancement." Proceedings of the First Baltic Forum on Neuronal Regulation and Biofeedback, Riga, Latvia. November 2–5. https://www.heartmath.org/assets/uploads/2015/01/hrv-biofeedback.pdf.

McGhee, P. E. 1999. *Health, Healing and the Amuse System: Humor as Survival Training*. 3rd ed. Dubuque, IA: Kendall Hunt.

Medoff, M. 1986. "In Praise of Teachers." *New York Times Magazine*, November 9. http://www.nytimes.com/2+9+/11/09/magazine/in-praise-of-teachers.html.

Michael, R. T., J. H. Gagnon, E. O. Laumann, and G. Kolata. 1994. *Sex in America: A Definitive Survey*. Boston: Little, Brown.

Michalko, M. 2001. *Cracking Creativity: The Secrets of Creative Genius*. Berkeley, CA: Ten Speed Press.

Miller-Karas, E. 2015. *Building Resilience to Trauma: The Trauma and Community Resiliency Models*. New York: Routledge.

Monson, T. S. 2005. "The Profound Power of Gratitude." *Ensign*, September 4. https://www.lds.org/ensign/2005/09/the-profound-power-of-gratitude?lang=eng.

Nakamura, J., and M. Csikszentmihalyi. 2003. "The Construction of Meaning Through Vital Engagement." In *Flourishing: Positive Psychology and the Life Well-Lived*, edited by C. L. M. Keyes and J. Haidt, 83–104. Washington, DC: American Psychological Association.

National Institute on Aging. n. d. "About Alzheimer's." https://www.nia.nih.gov/alzheimers.

Neff. K. 2011. *Self-Compassion: The Proven Power of Being Kind to Yourself*. New York: William Morrow.

Nelson, A. P., ed. 2008. *Improving Memory: Understanding Age-Related Memory Loss*. Boston, MA: Harvard Health Publications.

Nixon, R. 2008. "Mind Your Body: Quit While You're Behind; Persistence Doesn't Always Pay: The Benefits of Plan B." *Psychology Today*, May/June, 57. https:www.psychologytoday.com/articles/200805/mind-your-body-quit-while-youre-behind.

Ogden, P., and J. Fischer. 2015. *Sensorimotor Psychotherapy: Interventions for Trauma and Attachment*. New York: W. W. Norton.

Ogden, P., K. Minton, and C. Pain. 2006. *Trauma and the Body: A Sensorimotor Approach to Psychotherapy*. New York: W. W. Norton.

Pennebaker, J. W. 1997. *Opening Up: The Healing Power of Expressing Emotions*. New York: Guilford Press.

Pennebaker, J. W. and J. F. Evans. 2014. *Expressive Writing: Words That Heal*. Enumclaw, WA: Idyll Arbor.

Pennebaker, J. W., and J. M. Smyth. 2016. *Opening Up by Writing It Down: How Expressive Writing Improves Health and Eases Emotional Pain*. 3rd ed. New York: Guilford Press.

Peterson, C. and L. M. Bossio. 1991. *Health and Optimism: New Research on the Relationship Between Positive Thinking and Physical Well-Being*. New York: Free Press.

Petrie, A., and J. Petrie. 1986. *Mother Teresa*. DVD documentary directed by Ann and Jeanette Petrie. New York: Petrie Productions.

Porges, S. W. 2011. *The Polyvagal Theory: Neurophysiological Foundations of Emotions, Attachment, Communication, and Self-Regulation*. New York: W. W. Norton.

Prigerson, H. G., A. J. Bierhals, S. V. Kasl, C. F. Reynolds 3rd, M. K. Shear, N. Day, L. C. Beery, J. T. Newsom, and S. Jacobs. 1997. "Traumatic Grief as a Risk Factor for Mental and Physical Morbidity." *American Journal of Psychiatry*, 154: 616–623.

Ripley, A. 2008. *The Unthinkable: Who Survives When Disaster Strikes—and Why*. New York: Crown.

Sakai, C. E., S. M. Connolly, and P. Oas. 2010. "Treatment of PTSD in Rwandan Child Genocide Survivors Using Thought Field Therapy." *International Journal of Emergency Mental Health* 12: 41–50. http://:www.tftcenter.com/articles_treatment_of_ptsd_rwanda.html.

Sanders, T. 2005. *The Likeability Factor: How to Boost Your L-Factor and Achieve Your Life's Dreams*. New York: Crown.

Schiraldi, G. R. 2007a. *10 Simple Solutions for Building Self-Esteem: How to End Self-Doubt, Gain Confidence, and Create Positive Self-Image*. Oakland, CA: New Harbinger Publications.

Schiraldi, G. R. 2007b. *World War II Survivors: Lessons in Resilience*. Ellicott City, MD: Chevron Publishing.

Schiraldi, G. R. 2016a. *The Post-Traumatic Stress Disorder Sourcebook: A Guide to Healing, Recovery, and Growth*. 2nd ed. New York: McGraw-Hill.

Schiraldi, G. R. 2016b. *The Self-Esteem Workbook*. 2nd ed. Oakland, CA: New Harbinger Publications.

Schiraldi, G. R., and M. H. Kerr. 2002. *The Anger Management Sourcebook*. New York: McGraw-Hill.

Schiraldi, G. R., T. K. Jackson, S. L. Brown, and J. B. Jordan. 2010. "Resilience Training for Functioning Adults: Program Description and Preliminary Findings from a Pilot Investigation." *International Journal of Emergency Mental Health* 12: 117–129.

Seligman, M. E. P. 2002. *Authentic Happiness: Using the New Positive Psychology to Realize Your Potential for Lasting Fulfillment*. New York: Free Press.

Seligman, M. E. P. 2006. *Learned Optimism: How to Change Your Mind and Your Life*. New York: Vintage Books.

Seligman, M. E. P. 2011. *Flourish: A Visionary New Understanding of Happiness and Well-Being*. New York: Free Press.

Shay, J. 2002. *Odysseus in America: Combat Trauma and the Trials of Homecoming*. New York: Scribner.

Sherwood, B. 2009. "Ben Sherwood: 'The Survivor's Club' (Grand Central)" [Interview]. By Diane Rehm. January 29. http://dianerehm.org/shows/2009–01–29/ben-sherwood-survivors-club-grand-central.

Siebert, A. 1996. *The Survivor Personality: Why Some People Are Stronger, Smarter, and More Skillful at Handling Life's Difficulties…and How You Can Be, Too*. New York: Perigee.

Sin, N. L. and S. Lyubomirsky. 2009. "Enhancing Well-Being and Alleviating Depressive Symptoms with Positive Psychology Interventions: A Practice-Friendly Meta-Analysis." *Journal of Clinical Psychology: In Session* 65: 467–487.

Smith, T. W. 2007. *Job Satisfaction in America: Trends and Socio-demographic Correlates*. Chicago: National Opinion Research Center Report, University of Chicago. http://www.news.uchicago.edu/releases/07/pdf/070827.jobs.pdf.

Smyth, L. D. 1996. *Treating Anxiety Disorders with a Cognitive-Behavioral Exposure Based Approach and the Eye-Movement Technique: Video and Viewer's Guide*. Havre de Grace, MD: Red Toad Road Publishing.

Sprott, J. B., and A. N. Doob. 2000. "Bad, Sad, and Rejected: The Lives of Aggressive Children." *Canadian Journal of Criminology* 42: 123–133.

Stewart, J. B. 2002. *Heart of a Soldier: A Story of Love, Heroism, and September 11th*. New York: Simon and Schuster.

Stoltz, P. G. 2014. *Grit: The New Science of What It Takes to Persevere, Flourish, Succeed*. San Luis Obispo, CA: ClimbStrong Press.

Sullivan, M. R., S. L. Brown, and G. R. Schiraldi. 2011. "Comprehensive Resilience Training: A Comparison of Three Approaches." Poster, International Critical Incident Stress Foundation 12th World Congress on Stress, Trauma, and Coping, Baltimore, MD, February 22–23. Armed Forces Public Health Conference, Hampton, VA, March 18–25.

Tannen, D. 2001. *I Only Say This Because I Love You: How the Way We Talk Can Make or Break Family Relationships Throughout Our Lives*. New York: Random House.

ten Boom, C., J. Sherrill, and E. Sherrill. 1971. *The Hiding Place*. New York: Bantam Books.

Tick, E. 2005. *War and the Soul: Healing Our Nation's Veterans from Post-Traumatic Stress Disorder*. Wheaton, IL: Quest Books.

Twain, M. 1971. *Mark Twain's Notebook*. Prepared for publication with comments by Albert Bigelow Paine. [2nd ed.] New York, Harper, 1935. Reprinted St. Clair Shore, MI: Scholarly Press.

U.S. Department of Health and Human Services and U.S. Department of Agriculture. *2015-2020 Dietary Guidelines for Americans*. http://health.gov/dietaryguidelines/2015/guidelines/.

Vaillant, G. E. 1977. *Adaptation to Life*. Boston: Little, Brown.

Van der Kolk, B. A. 2014. *The Body Keeps the Score: Brain, Mind, and Body in the Healing of Trauma*. New York: Viking.

Verdelle, C. L. 1960. "Effect of Mental Practice on the Development of a Certain Motor Skill." *Research Quarterly of the American Association for Health, Physical Education and Recreation* 31: 560–569.

Waite, L. J., D. Browning, W. J. Doherty, M. Gallagher, Y. Luo, S. M. Stanley. 2002. *Does Divorce Make People Happy? Findings from a Study of Unhappy Marriages*. New York: Institute for American Values.

Walter, J. L., and J. E. Peller. 1992. *Becoming Solution-Focused in Brief Therapy*. New York: Brunner/Mazel.

Watkins, P. C., L. Cruz, H. Holben, and R. L. Kolts. 2008. "Taking Care of Business? Grateful Processing of Unpleasant Memories." *Journal of Positive Psychology* 3: 87–99.

Werner, E. E. 1992. "The Children of Kauai: Resiliency and Recovery in Adolescence and Adulthood." *Journal of Adolescent Health* 13: 262–268.

Wolin, S. J., and S. Wolin. 1993. *The Resilient Self: How Survivors of Troubled Families Rise Above Adversity*. New York: Villard Books.

Wood, S. G. 2003. *Icebox™: The Ultimate Mental Skills and Toughness Training System for Athletes*. CD. Peachtree City, GA: Icebox Athlete.

Wooden, J. R. 2003. *John Wooden: Values, Victory, and Peace of Mind*. DVD. Steve Jamison, Executive Producer. Albuquerqu, NM: Santa Fe Productions.

Wrzesniewski, A., C. R. McCauley, P. Rozin, and B. Schwartz. 1997. "Jobs, Careers, and Callings: People's Relations to Their Work." *Journal of Research in Personality* 31: 21–33.

Yalom, I. D. 1980. *Existential Psychotherapy*. New York: Basic Books.

Zhang, L. 2005. "Prediction of Chinese Life Satisfaction: Contribution of Collective Self-Esteem." *International Journal of Psychology* 40: 189–200.

Zimbardo, P. G., and J. Boyd. 2008. *The Time Paradox: The New Psychology of Time That Will Change Your Life*. New York: Free Press.

Glenn R. Schiraldi, PhD, has served on the stress management faculties at the Pentagon, the International Critical Incident Stress Foundation, and the University of Maryland, where he received the Outstanding Teaching Award and other teaching and service awards. His books on stress-related topics have been translated into sixteen languages, and include: *The Resilience Workbook*; *The Self-Esteem Workbook*; *Ten Simple Solutions for Building Self-Esteem*; *The Post-Traumatic Stress Disorder Sourcebook*; and *The Anger Management Sourcebook*. Glenn's writing has been recognized by various scholarly and popular sources, including *The Washington Post*, *American Journal of Health Promotion*, *Mind/Body Health Review*, and the *International Stress and Tension Control Society Newsletter*. He has trained laypersons and clinicians around the world on various aspects of resilience and trauma, with the goal of optimizing mental health and performance while preventing and promoting recovery from stress-related conditions. His skills-based mind/body courses at the University of Maryland have been found to improve self-esteem, resilience, happiness, optimism, and curiosity, while reducing symptoms of depression, anxiety, and anger. He has served on the editorial board of the *International Journal of Emergency Mental Health and Human Resilience*, and the board of directors of the Depression and Related Affective Disorders Association. A graduate of the United States Military Academy, West Point, he holds graduate degrees from Brigham Young University and the University of Maryland.